TOWAR
DIVERSIF
PSYCHOLOG
AND T

1990
Published and distributed by the American Psychological Association
Washington, DC

TOWARD ETHNIC DIVERSIFICATION IN PSYCHOLOGY EDUCATION AND TRAINING

Edited by: George Stricker
Elizabeth Davis-Russell
Edward Bourg
Eduardo Duran
W. Rodney Hammond
James McHolland
Kenneth Polite
Billy E. Vaughn

Library of Congress Cataloging-in-Publication Data

Toward ethnic diversification in psychology education and training /
   [editors, George Stricker . . . et al.].
      p.   cm.
   Papers of a National Council of Schools of Professional Psychology
(NCSPP) conference held in Puerto Rico during the winter of 1988–1989.
   Includes bibliographical references.
   1. Psychology—Study and teaching—Congresses.   2. Minorities in
psychology—Congresses.   I. Stricker, George.   II. National Council
of Schools of Professional Psychology (U.S.)
BF77.T68   1990
150′.71′173—dc20   90-39496

Published by
American Psychological Association
1200 Seventeenth Street, N.W.
Washington, DC 20036

Copies may be ordered from
APA Order Department
P.O. Box 2710
Hyattsville, MD 20784

Typeset by Harper Graphics, Waldorf, MD
Printed by Capital City Press, Inc., Montpelier, VT

First printing, July 1990
Second printing, December 1991

There is very little difference between one man and another;
but what little there is, is very important.

William James

This book is dedicated to the differences among us
and their inherent promise to enrich us all.

TABLE OF CONTENTS

PREFACE

George Stricker

Derner Institute, Adelphi University
Garden City, New York

Between February 1987 and February 1989, the National Council of Schools of Professional Psychology (NCSPP) has been on a journey. On a path neither straight, nor without obstacles, NCSPP has moved forward in its efforts to achieve ethnic diversification in psychology education and training. The process of moving from ethnocentrism to multiculturalism is not easy. It requires a change in mind-set that must precede a change in action. Embracing only the similar and the familiar must give way to perceiving, appreciating, and honoring differences. And, once having developed this new perception, it must be made integral to psychology education and training and to service delivery.

NCSPP is an organization of professional programs in psychology whose mission is the mutual enrichment and enhancement of professional psychology training. Founded in 1974, the organization currently consists of 35 member schools. In order to fulfill its objectives, NCSPP identifies specific areas of interest and concern that have relevance to the membership and to the profession. Designated committees undertake the study and organization of pertinent information. Committee work is assimilated and formally presented to the membership for its consideration and determination at the organization's annual conferences.

At the Mission Bay conference, NCSPP's midwinter 1986–1987 annual meeting, some members expressed concern about the lack of ethnic diversity in professional psychology training and service. The Committee on Minority Participation and Service to Underserved Populations (CMPSUP) was established to find ways to increase ethnic diversification in professional psychology training programs and to develop methods to monitor service delivery to ethnically diverse populations. In the following year, at the midwinter 1987–1988 Scottsdale conference, CMPSUP presented its findings to the membership. It was clear that the issues involved in ethnic diversification were vast, complex, and eminently important. In order to facilitate further study, CMPSUP was divided into four subcommittees covering these topics: faculty/administration recruitment and retention, student recruitment and retention, curriculum, and service to underserved populations. In addition, NCSPP resolved to devote its forthcoming 1988–1989 annual agenda and midwinter Puerto Rico conference to ethnic diversification in psychology education and training as its affirmation of the significance of this issue.

From the outset, the planning committee envisioned the attainment of ethnic diversification as a multiphasic, continuous process. After a year-long coordinated study by individuals and committees, the issues were presented to the membership at the Puerto Rico conference. The conference papers were designed to encourage the development of resolutions with behavioral objectives, as well as methods for evaluation of implementation. After the conference, member school representatives would be responsible for facilitating implementation at home campuses. NCSPP would assess each institution's progress in meeting stated objectives and, if appropriate, make suggestions for reworking. Implementation, evaluation, and reworking were considered to be continuous, never-ending stages of the process.

The chapters in this book originally were the Puerto Rico conference papers; the book's organization is patterned after the conference schedule. Part I (Introduction) includes the keynote address, the report of an experiential workshop, and the invitational address. Part II (Institutional Change) is the compilation of the work of a special committee, organized during the conference planning process. It focuses on an important area that was not specifically within the province of any subcommittee. Part III (Faculty/Administration Recruitment and Retention), Part IV (Student Recruitment and Retention), Part V (Curriculum), and Part VI (Serving Underserved Populations) are the results of the work of the four subcommittees. The Epilogue, written after the conference, is a summary of the conference process and content.

Twenty-four of the 27 chapters were written by members of NCSPP. Three chapters were written by invited presenters: chapter 2, by Valerie A. Batts, Executive Director and Director of Training and Consultation Services of VISIONS, Inc., of Cambridge, MA; chapter 3, by James M. Jones, Executive Director for Public Interest of the American Psychological Association (APA); and chapter 16, co-authored by Jessica Kohout, Research Officer of the APA Office of Demographic, Employment, and Educational Research, and Georgine Pion, Research Associate at Vanderbilt Institute for Public Policy Studies, Vanderbilt University. A list of all conference participants can be found at the conclusion of the book.

Although this book is a compendium of NCSPP's Puerto Rico conference, its contents represent a part of a continuum rather than a singular, unconnected event. The work begun in the winter of 1986–1987 was synthesized in the winter of 1988–1989 but not finished, nor was it intended to be finished. In fact, the word *toward* in the book's title, *Toward Ethnic Diversification In Psychology Education And Training*, was chosen to underscore NCSPP's conceptualization of ethnic diversification as a continuous process. Just as a photograph captures one moment in time and, yet, connotes a story with a past and a future, so this book recounts the proceedings of one conference and, yet, reflects all that preceded it and, I hope, predicts all that will follow.

PART I
INTRODUCTION

1

KEYNOTE ADDRESS: MINORITY ISSUES IN PROFESSIONAL TRAINING

George Stricker

Derner Institute, Adelphi University
Garden City, New York

This address is somewhat different from one that I might have delivered last year because some of my values and attitudes have changed. I have been enlightened and affected by my participation in the preparation for this conference and the consciousness raising that has occurred, as recently as last evening. I wish to express my gratitude to my colleagues on the executive committee and the Committee on Minority Participation and Service to Underserved Populations for helping me to understand more clearly the facts and the feelings of multiculturalism. I acknowledge my inadequacy in those areas in which I remain dense. I hope that I, and all of us, will continue to learn, and that this conference will be instrumental in furthering such learning.

This midwinter 1988–1989 Puerto Rico conference is a part of the continuing effort by the National Council of Schools of Professional Psychology (NCSPP) to attain ethnic diversity in clinical psychology training programs. Within our member schools, we are striving to achieve ethnically diversified faculties, student bodies, curricula, and services that reflect the diversity of the community-at-large. Within NCSPP itself, we are striving to achieve this same diversity in member school representation.

The issue for this conference is not whether we should establish ethnic diversity, but how. Our goal is to produce specific and viable resolutions, not mere declarations. Our intention is to conclude with specific resolutions and plans for implementation that lend themselves to being evaluated in terms of whether and when we have reached them. This is a joint task; each committee will be responsible for contributing to the final product, and the executive committee will be accountable for ensuring that the efforts of this week do not end on Saturday afternoon, when the conference ends. I wish us all luck and eagerly look forward to the products of our collective effort.

The most important question that each school of professional psychology (SPP) must ask itself is, "Why ethnic diversity?" If the institutional reply is simply a thoughtless, knee-jerk liberal response to a social issue, or an attempt to comply with an external requirement viewed as onerous, the degree and intensity of ethnic diversification will be very limited. Ethnic diversification is not easily accomplished. It requires commitment, energy, resources, and the willingness to unlearn old attitudes, perceptions, and values and to embrace new ones. If diversification is viewed as an assignment rather than a moral imperative, it will undoubtedly fail.

Even at the outset, difficult questions arise. If we want to respect, honor, and appreciate differences among people, how do we identify the different? Who are they? How do we train them? How do we serve them? Are women, who are traditionally underrepresented, a minority? Or are men, who are currently outnumbered, a minority? Blacks are usually designated as minorities. But, are Black minorities restricted to American-born and American-educated Blacks? Do we also include native Africans and West Indians? Hispanics are usually identified as minorities. But, are Hispanic minorities limited to Hispanic Americans (Mexican Americans, Puerto Ricans, Cuban Americans, etc.)? Do we also include South Americans, Central Americans, and European Hispanics?

Increasingly, Asian Americans are being considered as minorities. Does specific training and treatment need to be developed for Asian Americans? If so, what kind of training? How do we implement it? Native Americans are designated as minorities. SPPs notoriously have had little success in recruiting them. How do we change this? How do we train international students? And, are the issues involved in training international students different from the issues involved in training multicultural students?

As a rule, minorities are delineated by ethnicity, race, sex, social class, age, religion, sexual orientation, and so forth. However, these categorical definitions per se may become invalid if viewed in social and historical isolation. Concerns about minorities represent a response to sociocultural phenomena and are defined by current environmental considerations. For example, some decades back, Jews and Catholics were considered minorities. Now, although they remain a quantitative minority, Jews and Catholics ordinarily are not designated as such. In another illustration, until the 1970s, the relatively few Asian Americans generally were ignored by ethnic diversification efforts. Now, members of this growing group usually are specified as minorities and included in the sphere of minority interests. Each group moving out of the realm of minority concerns represents a step forward for society if barriers to equal opportunity have been removed without demands for divestiture of group uniqueness.

Regardless of the difficulties inherent in an incisive definition of *minority*, it is axiomatic that the establishment of ethnic diversification demands the creation of a critical mass of people of color. In SPPs, part of the complex process of attaining ethnic diversification necessitates increasing the number of minority faculty and students to achieve this critical mass. Expanding the size of minority faculties must, by necessity, precede increasing the number of minority students. Programs that attempt to create ethnic diversification by beginning with vigorous minority student recruitment, before the presence of a minority faculty is established, generally do not succeed.

It has been demonstrated that potential minority students measure institutional sensitivity to minority concerns by the presence or absence of minority faculty members, and they select programs accordingly. Most programs require the specific abilities of ethnic minority faculty members to teach courses and supervise students in a manner that relates ethnicity to clinical procedure. Obviously, ethnic minority faculty members are needed to serve as role models and mentors for the students.

At its worst, one of the reasons for the recruitment of minority faculty is the need to be "covered." The American Psychological Association (APA) regularly asks for a census of minority faculty members. Perhaps, the commitment of some SPPs to ethnic diversity is limited to their need to comply with the APA requirement. The request on the part of the APA Committee on Accreditation is an appropriate and helpful method for ensuring attention to the issue of ethnic diversification. However, if the recruitment of minority faculty is no more than compliance, it perpetuates tokenism and diminishes, if not abrogates, the opportunity to enrich the quality of training for all.

There is a tension that often occurs on faculties when minority faculty members are hired. The nonminority faculty may feel resentful about what they perceive as special treatment for the minority faculty. At the same time, minority faculty members may feel exploited and resent the assumption that they will supervise minority students, teach minority-oriented courses, serve on minority committees, and generally be identified by ethnicity rather than by talent. Minority faculty often feel as though they have to be twice as good as anyone else in order to be accepted as capable in their own right. At the same time, they often are treated as if they are only half as good because ethnicity, not competence, was deemed the most critical qualification for appointment.

With both actual and potential contributions lost behind ethnic identities, ethnic minority faculty members may feel underappreciated, devalued, and, if they identify with the aggressor, inadequate. Ironically, although concerned about what they perceive as inferior status, minority faculty are often viewed by nonminorities as being in a superior position, and they are resented for it. Is it any wonder that tension exists?

There is a critical need to empower minority faculty members who are in danger of isolation and neglect. When faculty members of color arrive at most campuses, they quickly note that most of their colleagues do not look like them. Role models or mentors are strikingly absent. This perception of isolation is closely related to a sense of powerlessness, to say nothing of loneliness. The difference between the token minority and a critical mass may be the difference between compliance with regulations and a meaningful and effective minority presence on a faculty.

Minority student recruitment is valued for some wrong reasons and many good reasons. Self-indulgently, an ethnically diverse student body helps to meet quotas, facilitates accreditation, and allows the White majority to feel good about itself. More important, the number of minorities in psychology training programs is disproportionate to their representation in the United States population and disproportionate to the numbers of ethnic minority individuals who may need psychological services. The present shortage of ethnic minority psychologists is more disturbing when one considers the demographic prediction that minorities will constitute one-third of the United States population after the turn of the 21st century (American Council on Education, 1988). Furthermore, in the training environment minority students add a point of view and set of experiences that can be instructive to all students and faculty, including a special perspective relevant to the rendering of services to disadvantaged patients.

The question of criteria for admission is critical. Often, the traditional criterion of standardized tests disallows the selection of minority students whose test scores are lower, perhaps because of strikingly disadvantaged earlier educational opportunities. If accepted, many ethnically diverse students have performed as well as more educationally advantaged students with higher Graduate Record Examination scores. Therefore, should special criteria or population-specific approaches to admission be adopted? Are quotas that ensure a target number of minority students acceptable? Will special criteria and quotas incur the resentment of students accepted through traditional channels, and the anger of those with better academic records who have been rejected?

Student admission, like faculty recruitment, is a zero-sum game. Most programs have a fixed number of students that they can accept. Every student accepted represents another student rejected. This creates a tension similar to the tension existing in faculties that are in the process of ethnic diversification. Students of color often feel that they have to be twice as good, although they may be regarded as being only half as good. Minority students often feel that they were admitted because of their ethnicity, not for their talents and potential contributions. Nonminority students feel jealous of what they perceive as privileged status for students of color.

SPPs are responsible for providing quality education and training for those students who will make the best use of it. Among the many factors that contribute to excellence of education are the nature and the diversity of the student body. Choosing students who represent a breadth of experiences and backgrounds enriches an entire program and is an educationally sound undertaking. It is important to determine that all students—White students and students of color—who are admitted into the programs are able to profit from the training experience. In order to decide which students will benefit, SPPs must use whatever criteria are suitable to help in the attainment of the stated goal. This requires flexibility in admissions protocols because a diverse student body requires diverse selection procedures.

Accountability, however, must underlie all admission criteria. All students who are accepted into a program must be held accountable for meeting the articulated requirements for acceptance into the profession. Otherwise, SPPs might be in the untenable position of seeming to support the fabrication that minority students do not need to know as much or be as well trained as Whites because minority professionals are going to treat minority patients who do not need as highly developed a set of services.

The importance of each SPP examining its rationale for creating ethnic diversification cannot be overemphasized. The integrity of commitment often predicts the success of the endeavor. When people of color are deciding whether or not to come to a particular program, they want to know why the program wants to have them. Available candidates will not be interested in programs whose efforts to recruit minority faculty and students are no more than attempts to fulfill self-serving exigencies. Most likely, minority candidates will be attracted to the programs that have created the kind of environment in which minority faculty and students feel comfortable, respected, supported, and able to be productive.

There is a continuing conflict between the generic and the specific approach to relationships with minority colleagues. The generic approach holds that people of color are just like everybody else. The specific approach says that people of color are unique and should be appreciated as such. I believe that the orthodoxy of each approach is invalid and that reality lies somewhere between the two. People are more alike than they are different, but they are certainly not the same. If we do not respect and honor differences, there are real questions about the purpose of minority recruitment and whose needs it satisfies. If we do not understand similarities, there is the danger of treating minority students and faculty members as trophies or curiosities rather than as colleagues.

Recruitment is the first step in the continuous process of multicultural diversification. Recruitment efforts must be followed by retention concerns and attention to professional advancement. When ethnically diverse people are welcomed into an institution, they need to function within the kind of supportive climate that will ensure that they remain and thrive. A supportive climate is essential for people who may be vulnerable to loneliness, isolation, and exploitation. For example, if a program made use of diverse admissions criteria to accept minority students whose prior educational experiences were different from those of White students, it must be prepared to provide appropriate support services, in a manner that is sustaining and encouraging rather than condescending and demeaning. In another illustration, if a program has placed value on the involvement of a new minority faculty member in a variety of minority-related activities, it must also provide the time, support, and acknowledgment of contribution to ensure that these activities do not undermine the path toward tenure. The barriers to advancement for many minority faculty members rest within rigid university policies. More attention to the special problems of minority academic status, including promotion and tenure, is warranted.

The delivery of professional services and the preparation of students for careers in service delivery are among the majors areas of concern for SPPs. Ethnic diversification in faculty, student bodies, and curricula is particularly important to service delivery because many of the patients to be served have multicultural backgrounds. Although some psychologists believe that minority professionals may be more capable of rendering services to minority patients, the point is debatable because it has been demonstrated that White psychologists who have incorporated the minority perspective are able to render quality service to ethnically diverse populations. Nonetheless, the *presence* of minority professionals makes service more credible and attractive to potential minority patients. SPPs need to focus on ethnically diverse patients who might benefit from services and do not avail themselves of them, as well as on the outcome of services actually delivered to minority patients.

The most critical effect of ethnically diverse students in service settings may be to promote the cultural competence of all members of the professional staff. Cultural competence requires that professionals recognize, accept, and honor cultural differences. Psychologists must be aware of their own cultural values, be knowledgeable about patients' cultures, be aware of how cultural differences are related to the helping process, and be able to adapt their skills to these cultural needs. The interaction between White students and students from diverse cultures provides the opportunity for all students to develop sensitivity to ethnically diverse people and issues and to be better able to deliver quality service as a result of this interaction. The bottom line is that an ethnically diverse student body creates an environment that encourages better provision of services by a broader group of professionals to a broader group of patients, and that is the mission of the professional school.

Before closing, I would like to take a flight of fancy. My clinical orientation leads me to be attuned to matters of parallel process, and I suspect that just such a process is in effect. For many years, SPPs have experienced minority group status in the community of psychology training programs. As a result, we have done many things that minorities have done. Some of us have been defiant, ignoring the self-destructiveness inherent in such a stance. Others among us have attempted to be absorbed by the larger culture, denying the differences that are the essence of our being. Still others have identified with the aggressor, experiencing unwarranted self-hate and loathing, and fueling the opposition to all SPPs by undermining each other in exchange for a kind word from the traditional structure.

For the past two years, NCSPP has been fulfilling its ongoing commitment to study and develop strategies for creating multicultural training environments. From this parallel process, we have been given the opportunity to learn that SPPs can grow as a professional movement if we appreciate the differences that make us distinct and the common mission that brings us together. And, we can learn from this parallel process and extend this understanding to our appreciation of ethnic diversity in our programs and among our patients.

By expanding ethnic diversity in our student bodies, faculties, curricula, and service centers, we are reflecting the values that should underlie all helping professions. But, make no mistake! We are not merely increasing a census, a quantitative gain that is relatively easy to achieve. We will not be satisfied with simply more dark skins or unfamiliar languages in our midst. Rather, we are adding to the depth of our offerings and the strength of our training programs, qualitative goals that require thought and planning. As Rollo May (cited in Wirt & Beckstrom, 1974) said, "Nature does not require that we be perfect; it requires only that we grow" (p. 100). By honoring diversity, we are creating growth opportunities for all.

2

AN EXPERIENTIAL WORKSHOP: INTRODUCTION TO MULTICULTURALISM

Valerie A. Batts
VISIONS, Inc.
Cambridge, Massachusetts

It is exciting to have the opportunity to describe the work that occurred at the midwinter 1988–1989 Puerto Rico conference of the National Council of Schools of Professional Psychology (NCSPP) from my perspective as a consultant and trainer in the area of multiculturalism. Although I work with many institutions in the public and private sectors, it seems that much too often the field of psychology has attempted to overlook the importance of a directed, active focus on increasing the role of diversity within the discipline (S. Sue, 1988; S. Sue & Zane, 1987). Thus it was an important and meaningful experience to be invited to consult with an organization that is proactively expediting its explicitly stated commitments regarding the creation and maintenance of culturally inclusive structures and processes (Bourg, Bent, McHolland, & Stricker, 1989). Furthermore, finding such a commitment within my own discipline, psychology, was even more exciting.

The NCSPP Puerto Rico conference focused on the role of cultural diversity in the education and training of professional psychologists. My responsibility was to conduct the opening experiential workshop for the conference. I also had the opportunity to share in conference activities, through listening to speakers, reading papers and reports of presentations, and conversing formally and informally with conference organizers and psychologists in attendance.

Fifty-nine psychologists, representing 27 schools of professional psychology (SPPs) and the American Psychological Association, attended the conference. The conference process included inviting people of color from member schools throughout the association to share their expertise in a variety of arenas in which change is needed in order to ensure a successful multicultural presence. In total, there were 21 people of color and 38 White ethnic conferees. In this chapter, I summarize the workshop that I conducted. Then, I offer an assessment of the conference process and some implications for future organizational efforts in this area.

The Workshop

VISIONS, Inc. (Vigorous InterventionS In On-going Natural Settings) has developed workshops to help organizations enhance their ability to use cultural diversity effectively. The process makes use of many assumptions, theories, and methods that are familiar to professional psychologists. Conference participants were told that the workshop they were about to experience was part of a VISIONS, Inc., process.

The VISIONS Process

The workshop began with certain assumptions. For example, it is assumed that individuals can and do make choices in their personal and professional lives. Some choices support the creation and maintenance of effective multicultural environments. Others collude with the perpetuation of predominantly White, monocultural environments in which White, Anglo-Saxon, heterosexual, young to middle-aged, middle-class, and male-oriented norms and values are deemed most acceptable. Participants were encouraged to "try on" this assumption and several others in order to enhance their ability to perceive the choices that they are most likely to make in their professional and personal lives.

The VISIONS process was summarized as including the following steps:

1. Creating a safe environment in which individuals are free to explore their attitudes, feelings, and behaviors with respect to people who are different, without fear of being blamed or attacked. Individuals are encouraged to take responsibility for the legacy of oppression that we have inherited, not willed, in this country.
2. Facilitating participants' ability to recognize, understand, and appreciate differences. Attitudes about differences and similarities occur progressively over time. It is often difficult to see or to identify how people are different because, within the context of our training as United States citizens, we have spent most of our energy noticing similarities (Batts, 1988). For many of us, taking differences into account involves attending to people in new ways. Such new ways of seeing help us come to understand how variables such as race, ethnicity, class, sex, age, sexual orientation, physical ability, and religious affiliation affect individual and group functioning. It is through this understanding that we are likely to become able to value and appreciate fully such differences, over time, assuming sufficient contact with different others.
3. Helping people understand both the systemic and the personal impact of the "isms." Racism, sexism, classism, agism, and monoculturalism, as well as oppression of religious groups, gay men and lesbians, and people with physical disabilities are all examples. It is crucial to explicate how cultural norms, institutional practices, interpersonal attitudes and behaviors, and beliefs and feelings all contribute to the perpetuation of these "isms."
4. Helping individuals build working cross-cultural alliances. Such relationships enhance the likelihood that personal and systemic change will be optimally desirable and will be maintained over time.
5. Practicing and monitoring changes over time at the cultural, institutional, in-

terpersonal, and individual levels. This final step is ongoing and is used to help identify when reworking of other steps in the process is needed.

Targeting

Participants were introduced to the concept of systemic oppression, that is, the targeting of certain groups within the society as less than, or different in an inferior way from, the majority (Sherover-Marcuse, 1980). The target group, relative to its numbers, is less likely statistically to succeed than is the nontarget group. Targeting leads to the perpetuation of cognitive and affective misinformation (Batts, 1982). For example, within the field of psychology, historically there were few Blacks or other people of color admitted into the discipline, thereby supporting the accepted, legally sanctioned view that Blacks are inferior.

This view was upheld by research and theories promulgated by the discipline (Guthrie, 1976). Within this historical tradition, Black culture was considered deficient (J. White, 1984). Participants were reminded that, as recently as 24 years ago (prior to 1965), this historical tradition was considered acceptable, even legal. As psychologists, conferees understood that it would take longer than 24 years to change socialization practices, affect, and behaviors accompanying a view of people that was part and parcel of the fabric of American life for over 300 years.

Modern Racism and Internalized Oppression

Participants were introduced to the concepts of modern racism and internalized oppression. Modern racism is the attribution of non–race-related reasons for behaviors and practices that continue to deny Blacks and other target group members equal access to opportunity (McConahay, Hardee, & Batts, 1981). Internalized oppression is the target group's response to modern racism. Illustrations were provided to show how these processes—often operative in post-1960s institutional, cultural, and personal practices—keep cultural diversity from being realized within American institutions.

Modern racism helps to explain how most Americans are able to believe that racism is all but gone in the United States and, yet, equal access to opportunity continues to be withheld from Blacks and other target groups. Racism has become a major way to handle racial discomfort or discomfort with other differences. In the late 1960s, for example, several poverty programs were set up in an attempt to solve the problems of the ghetto efficiently and to ease the discomfort caused by violent unrest. These programs, in many instances, set people up to fail (Ryan, 1976). Welfare mothers were given financial assistance from the government, under the condition that they did not work or did not receive financial assistance from a male partner. Women who accepted their welfare status and discontinued their attempts to survive independently demonstrated internalized oppression in response to modern racism.

Participants were invited to do an exercise, described in Table 1, that encouraged them to begin to explore how they might have practiced modern racism or internalized oppression in their own lives. The exercise was introduced at this point in the workshop to facilitate the participants' affective as well as cognitive understanding of the two concepts. After they completed the "Most Recent Encounter Exercise," the con-

Table 1
The "Most Recent Encounter" Exercise, Conducted for Workshop
Participants of the 1989 NCSPP Conference, Puerto Rico

1. Participants are invited to relax, get in a comfortable position, closing their eyes if it helps them to focus.

2. Recall your most recent dysfunctional or uncomfortable work-related encounter with a person of another race or with someone of the opposite sex.

3. Be there, as if it were happening now.

4. What is happening? What is the theme of the encounter?

5. What are you liking about the encounter?

6. What is uncomfortable or problematic?

7. Now imagine that your mother or mother figure came in the room. What might she think, what might she feel, and what might she say?

8. Imagine now that your father or father figure came in the room. What might he think, what might he feel, what might he say?

9. After participants have completed the recall, do a round, having them share. Ask them and the group to identify the kind of modern racism/sexism or internalized oppression that might be going on.

ferees were asked to think of their experiences as being illustrative of five behavioral manifestations of modern racism. Five corresponding types of internalized oppression were described. The manifestations of modern racism and types of internalized oppression are listed and defined in Table 2.

Afterward, several participants shared their experiences. A person of color recounted an incident in which she and her young child were shopping in a department store. The child ran up to a White infant who was in a stroller, next to her mom. The older child was smiling, appeared delighted to see the infant, and wanted to get a closer view. When the Black child reached out to touch the baby, the White mother pulled the stroller away, saying in an angry tone, "Don't you dare touch my baby." The child of color appeared stunned and hurt by the intensity of the rejection.

This episode was discussed, and different interpretations were offered. The incident actually might reflect old fashioned racism (McConahay et al., 1981), that is, overt affirmation that a Black person's touch is unacceptable. It might also reflect a more subtle need to avoid contact with Blacks, explained as, and actually believed to be, merely the White mother's effort to protect her baby. Regardless of the motivation, the perception by the Black mother and her child was that the Black child's touch was, in some way, bad.

A White participant disclosed his tendency to be overly nice to students of color, fearing that if he acted otherwise, they would think he was racist. Recently, he had bent over backwards to help a Black student, reordering his schedule in order to be of assistance. The feedback that he then gave to the student proved to be inadequate because of the limitations of his available time. He was aware that he resented the student for asking for time and that he felt guilty about the entire situation. He felt that he would have handled the situation differently with a White student and would not have worried about the reaction.

Table 2
Manifestations of Modern Racism and Internalized Oppression Listed by
Workshop Participants at the 1989 NCSPP Conference, Puerto Rico

Modern Racism	Internalized Oppression
1. *Dysfunctional rescuing* • Helping people of color based on the assumption that they cannot help themselves. • Helping people of color in such a way that it limits their ability to help themselves.	*System beating* • "Getting around" the system, manipulating others or the system through guilt, games, illicit activities, acting out anger, playing dumb, clowning, or being invisible.
2. *Blaming the victim* • Ignoring the impact of racism on the lives of Blacks, thus blaming Blacks for creating their current social and economic situation. Attributing the result of systemic oppression to its victims.	*Blaming the system* • Blaming the system or another for one's problems and failing to acknowledge mental, emotional, and stress-related issues.
3. *Avoidance of contact* • Avoiding an effort to learn about conditions in the Black community, avoiding social or professional contact with Blacks, and not being concerned about anyone but Whites.	*Anti-White, avoidance of contact* • Avoiding contact with Whites, distrusting all Whites, rejecting other Blacks, and exhibiting escapist behavior.
4. *Denial of cultural differences* • Minimizing obvious physical or behavioral differences between people, and discounting the influence of African culture and Black American experience.	*Denial of Blackness* • Distrusting Blacks, deferring to Whites, devaluing African heritage, and accepting Whites as superior.
5. *Denial of political significance* • Denying the significance of racial differences and their impact on social, political, and economic dimensions in the lives of Blacks and Whites, thus minimizing the influence of these variables.	*Denial of political significance* • Acting passively, feeling or acting powerless, internalizing anger, sexist behavior, copious buying, etc.

Table 3

Target and Nontarget Groups Present at the 1989 NCSPP Conference Multicultural Workshop, Puerto Rico

Target Groups	Nontarget Groups
People of color	Whites
Women	Men
Jews	Christians
Gay men and lesbians	Heterosexuals
Working-class people	Middle- and upper-class people
Elderly people	Young to middle-aged people
Blacks	
Asians	
Hispanics	

The willingness of participants to acknowledge the ways in which they sometimes buy into modern racism or internalized oppression enabled group members to function more authentically with each other. It also allowed for seeing a glimmer of possible new behaviors. Unfortunately, there was not enough time to develop the richness of learning that occurs when all participants in such an experience are allowed to discuss their situations, to identify the types of modern racism or internalized oppression that might be operative, and to explore alternative strategies. The participants, however, were able to see the wealth of possibilities inherent in such an activity.

Building Intragroup Cohesiveness

The final part of the workshop provided an opportunity for the participants to identify all of the target and nontarget groups within NCSPP. Table 3 indicates the groups that were identified. In order to build intragroup cohesiveness, the conferees were invited to spend time together in either one of the target groups or one of the nontarget groups. They were encouraged to consider how intragroup understanding is a prerequisite to building effective cross-cultural alliances. Within these groups, members focused on validation, self-definition, and what they needed from, and were willing to bring to, a coalition. They recorded all of their responses on a worksheet. The workshop ended with all the participants reviewing the worksheets of each group.

Assessment of the Conference Process

The conference steering committee was structured to ensure that the perspectives of people of color and Whites would be heard. The committee was explicit in its handling of several process issues that had arisen during the evolution of the organization. The first issue, the "loss" for White members of the old organization as they knew it, was confronted directly. The steering committee's excitement about the gains they were experiencing from the intragroup process became crucial in helping the organization realize the potential benefits of engaging in similar activities.

The use of people of color from member schools as resource people was an important validation of the skills and expertise available within NCSPP. The diverse mix of conferees was significant because it reflected an explicit commitment toward diversity. Furthermore, it demonstrated a willingness to create a critical mass of people of color, so that the comfort zone and traditional cultural norms and practices of the majority or nontarget group were challenged.

The conference did, in fact, challenge its members. People of color were prepared to have to push for mandates or policies to ensure compliance by member schools. Many Whites experienced the proposed measures as demands and felt offended by them. These Whites felt that their desire for multiculturalism was evident and that they did not want to be forced. By the middle of the conference, the membership had moved from the good feelings generated by the opening workshop to the tension and conflict inherent in cross-cultural miscommunication. Suspiciousness, mistrust, anger, and hurt were experienced by many.

The conference leadership, however, was able to grasp a sense of the group and, in its parallel process, the leadership was able to work through differences and facilitate some conflict resolution in the group. The process moved forward when conference participants were able to see the conflict as a difference in perception between the target and nontarget groups regarding how effective systemic change occurs.

Summary and Implications

For people of color in this country, long-term change does not occur without mandates, and even mandates do not always make change occur (Ryan, 1981). One of the privileges of nontarget group membership with respect to race is being in the majority and in a position of power, whereby willing a change is likely to make it so. Successful coalitions must take the views of all groups into account (C. R. Brown, 1984).

SPPs can be thought of as a target group within the profession. It is important to remember the legacy inherited by these institutions as they strive to establish legitimacy. Because SPPs are attempting to train practitioners to work effectively in the real world, their mission is much more consistent with a multicultural view than is the mission of a traditional program. The founders of the professional psychology movement, however, are not free from their own inculcation of the monocultural focus of our society. It is no accident that most SPPs do only slightly better than research and academic training institutions in recruiting, training, and graduating people of color and in recruiting people of color as administrators, faculty, and staff. It is also clear that elitism, turfism, academic arrogance, and denial of the validity of the perspectives of, for example, African, Asian, Hispanic, and Native American people on human functioning are highly prevalent.

SPPs, nonetheless, represent a source of hope. They have dared to challenge a strong tradition. They have survived and flourished. Some are exciting models of multiculturalism in action. If SPPs intend to truly prosper as alternatives for all, it is crucial that the hopes, challenges, and processes initiated in Puerto Rico by direct empowerment of people of color and Whites, by attention to mandating and choosing, by committing to process and content, and by the willingness to struggle and to care, be continued again and again.

The late Dr. Martin Luther King explained the process well, in terms of relationships between Blacks and Whites:

> *Like life, racial understanding is not something that we find, but something that we must create and so the ability of Negroes and Whites to work together to understand each other will not be found readymade. It must be created by the fact of contact. (Cited in C. King, 1983, p. 33)*

I would update his words as follows: Like life, racial understanding or multiculturalism is not something that we find. It is, rather, something that we must create. The ability of Blacks, of all people of color, and of Whites—indeed of all target and nontarget groups—to work together to understand each other will not be found ready-made. It must be created by the fact of contact, which means dismantling systemic oppression over time.

3

INVITATIONAL ADDRESS: WHO IS TRAINING OUR ETHNIC MINORITY PSYCHOLOGISTS, AND ARE THEY DOING IT RIGHT?

James M. Jones
American Psychological Association
Washington, DC

In 1974, the American Psychological Association (APA) was awarded a grant from the National Institute of Mental Health (NIMH) to provide training stipends to ethnic minority doctoral students in psychology. The grant was designed as a five-year experimental program, containing stipend support for 10 students per year for three years, or a total of 30 students over the life of the grant. Thus began what we now know as the Minority Fellowship Program (MFP). Since 1974, the MFP has supported more than 600 ethnic minority doctoral students in psychology, of whom more than 300 have earned doctoral degrees. The major premise of the MFP was that the net effect of training ethnic minority mental health providers and researchers would be an increase in the pool of competent and motivated professionals who would provide needed services to underserved ethnic minority populations.

Over the years, however, it has become clear that several other dynamics, with both intended and unintended consequences, are involved in this training enterprise. Psychology programs have varied significantly in their interest and ability to attract ethnic minority students, leading to an informal ranking of programs along general lines of suitability for ethnic minority students. Enrolling significant numbers of ethnic minority students has put pressure on programs to accommodate the students in ways that had not been planned for or, in many cases, in ways that are not seen as desirable by faculty. Recruitment of ethnic minorities is presumed to reflect affirmative action needs as much as, or more than, training needs. Affirmative action is often conceived of as a moral obligation to expiate the past sins of society or, worse, as the bestowal of opportunities on underqualified ethnic minorities.

The moral obligation and social justice basis for affirmative action begs the question of training. As larger numbers of ethnic minorities enter training, questions arise as to what constitutes "proper" or "appropriate" or "good" training in psychology. Are we preparing our students to deliver the services that NIMH has so hopefully assumed graduates would provide?

This chapter frames these complex issues into two questions: "Who is training our ethnic minority psychologists?" and "Are they doing it right?" It is not possible to answer either of these questions fully. Complete data do not exist on ethnic minority enrollments and graduation rates for all doctoral programs, at least in a way that permits public identification. Furthermore, standards for training ethnic minority psychologists do not formally exist, although many people have ideas about what should be involved.

The purpose of this chapter, then, is to provide available information on who is training, who is being trained, and what are the relevant considerations to be addressed in an evaluation of the quality of training programs for ethnic minorities. The discussion aims at directing the reader to consider factors that influence training outcomes for ethnic minorities and suggested strategies for meeting training goals.

Perspectives that Influence Training Outcomes of Ethnic Minority Psychologists

Affirmative Diversity

Affirmative action is an important but insufficient motivation for recruiting ethnic minority students into doctoral training programs in psychology. A better approach is the concept of *affirmative diversity*. Affirmative diversity is defined as the affirmation of the fundamental value of human diversity in society, with the belief that enhancing diversity increases rather than diminishes quality.

Psychology is the study of human thought and behavior. If one believes that there is no difference of significance between Whites and Puerto Ricans, Cubans, Blacks, Chicanos, Asians, Native Americans, and so forth, then one may well assume that all a student need do is enter the program and learn psychology. However, if you believe that there might be relevant human experiences that are not captured by the traditional corpus of psychological knowledge and practice represented in standard materials, theories, and approaches, then you must do something affirmative to bring these experiences into the curriculum and into the training philosophy. To be fully operable, whatever is done must recognize that it is not just ethnic minority students at issue, but also those citizens to whom our graduates provide services. The graduates who provide services are not and cannot all be ethnic minorities themselves. Therefore, if there are important consequences of ethnic, cultural, and racial experience for the practice of psychology, then an affirmative strategy must be adopted to bring these issues into our training programs.

Biologically, genetic diversity increases survival capability. In an old Bill Cosby album, the Revolutionary War was described like a football game, beginning with a coin toss. The British lost and were instructed to wear bright red uniforms and march in a straight line. The referee told the settlers they could wear anything they wanted and hide behind trees. Diversity has its advantages.

McDougall (1921) posed the question in a more sinister way when he asked, in the title of his book, *Is America Safe for Democracy?* His thesis was that the strength of any nation rested with the superiority of its gene pool (the anthropologic argument), rather than with favorable trade routes, natural resources, and so forth (the economic argument). According to McDougall, if we continue to allow citizens of this country to commingle willy-nilly, we risk "contaminating" the superior gene pool that made us a power in the world.

His solution was clearly implied, although he fell short of genocide or sterilization proposals. He suggested that a new factor, "mental anthropology" (i.e., IQ tests), would enable us to ascertain who among us possessed the attributes necessary to preserve our national strength and, of course, by implication, who did not! Thus, according to this view, the social and behavioral sciences were destined to protect the homogeneity and, ultimately, the purity of the gene pool of a democratic society. In psychology, the goals are exactly the opposite. Our challenge is to develop the discipline of human thought and behavior in such a way as to identify the societal strength gained through diversity *within* and *across* people.

Diversity within people. We need to understand how diverse socialization experiences and adaptations to changing environments, particularly those that present competing demands, may be integrated to produce a stronger, more viable human being. With regard to gender, the concept of androgyny has been elaborated as one that capitalizes on masculine and feminine capabilities and tendencies to produce a wider behavioral repertoire and adaptive potential (Bem, Martyna, & Watson, 1976; Spence, Helmreich, & Stapp, 1974). With regard to ethnicity, I have developed a perspective on biculturalism (J. M. Jones, 1986, 1988a) that argues for a similar kind of strength of integration of experience and adaptation. Many other ethnic minority psychologists argue similarly with regard to Asians (S. Sue & Morishima, 1985), Native Americans (LaFromboise & Rowe, 1983; Trimble, 1988), and Hispanics (Padilla & Olmedo, 1977; Ramirez, 1983).

The integrating theme of the bicultural approach is that the cultural basis of the ethnic minority perspective is in competition and often conflict with the majority or mainstream perspective. If those in the majority are unable to recognize the cultural competition or conflict inherent in institutional diversity, then training programs will create environments that stifle, confuse, and frustrate. Most important, training programs will fail to capitalize on the opportunity for growth in our paradigms and our overall knowledge.

Diversity across people. Sampson (1977) has argued convincingly that a failure of American psychology has been its predilection for theories of "self-contained individualism." Sampson would contend that my characterization of diversity within people perpetuates this flaw by locating adaption within a single human being. I do not see diversity as an either/or proposition. The concept of "interdependence" favored by Sampson seems at the heart of our understanding of human diversity.

The full ramifications of the concept of human diversity were explored recently at a conference by that name (Trickett, Watts, & Birman, 1988). People who were ethnic minorities (Blacks, Hispanics, Asians, Native Americans), lesbians, gay men, women, people with disabilities, and elderly people shared perspectives on the characteristics peculiar to their group and collectively shared the perspectives they all had in common. It was a significant learning experience for all in attendance, and it suggested clearly that the paradigms of psychology can be advanced by such collective diversity and interdependence.

In terms of psychology training, human diversity is better embodied in the concept of affirmative diversity than in the concept of affirmative action. Although affirmative action addresses questions of social justice, it fails to acknowledge cultural differences (except in a pejorative way) and usually fails to accommodate to implications of these differences in culture for students, faculty, career goals, and the content and development of basic facets of training. The affirmative diversity approach, however, seeks out cultural differences as a source of program development, which requires active planning and evaluation. The results of this planning and evaluation guide the development of recruitment practices, provide mechanisms for program development and change, and establish goals against which progress can be measured.

Demographic Predictions

The U.S. population is becoming increasingly diverse, which presents issues with psychological consequences, issues for which standard practices of psychology were not developed. For the year 2000, the U.S. Census Bureau projects a population of 281,542,000, comprising about 200,000,000 Whites; 37,602,000 Blacks; 31,208,000 of Spanish origin; and 12,669,000 Asians and other minority groups (U.S. Bureau of the Census, 1986). Asians immigrated to the United States in the 1980s at a rate of 90,000 per year (obtaining residency), Africans at 3,000 per year. Legal and illegal aliens from South America will swell this number considerably. Thus, by the year 2000, we can expect about a 30% ethnic minority population (about 81 million people!). California already has greater than a 50% minority population.

We are a culturally diverse population and becoming more so daily. However, to read our standard texts in psychology, one would think that ethnicity and culture were nonexistent. Although we are speaking of graduate training programs, it is important to note that undergraduate psychology texts, reflecting the first contact with psychology for most undergraduates, offer little incentive for ethnic minority students. A review of six of the major introductory psychology textbooks, averaging 600 pages each, shows that only 3% of the pages contain information relevant to any ethnic group, culture, or race. This includes material on IQ and prejudice, which accounts for about 75% of all textbook topics that deal with ethnicity and race. If, in fact, the standard body of knowledge in psychology is based on a White male therapist and White female client model, how applicable will it be in the 21st century? We have a professional obligation to expand the context of our knowledge and its applicability to the entire population.

Underrepresentation of Ethnic Minorities in Higher Education

Ethnic minority enrollments in psychology do not reach numbers or percentages that reflect the important roles they could play. There is a great need to develop interest in professional psychology careers among the increasing number of ethnic minority undergraduates. In 1984, of 12,524,000 students enrolled full-time in higher education, 1,742,00 were ethnic minorities (13.9%). An additional 4,531,000 students were enrolled in junior and community colleges, where there are surely a larger percentage of ethnic minority enrollments. Thus we can reasonably identify about 2,874,750 ethnic minority undergraduate students in the United States. By the year 2000, we can expect to have some 81 million people of ethnic minority status and a

Table 1

Sex and Race of Doctoral Students Enrolled in Research and Practice
Programs in U.S. Departments of Psychology, 1987–1988

Sex	White	Black	Hispanic	Asian	Native American	Total Non-White	Total
			Research Programs				
Men: N	2,424	119	68	175	7	369	2,793
Ethnic group %	42	45	43	45	41	45	42
Women: N	3,348	145	91	214	10	458	3,806
Ethnic group %	58	55	57	55	59	55	58
Total: N	5,772	264	159	389	17	827	6,601
% of all groups	87	4	2	6	.2	12.5	
			Practice Programs				
Men: N	1,429	82	76	41	8	207	1,636
Ethnic group %	30	34	35	34	29	34	
Women: N	3,336	159	140	78	20	397	3,733
Ethnic group %	70	66	65	66	71	66	
Total: N	4,765	241	216	119	28	604	5,369
% of all groups	89	4	4	2	.5	11.2	

Note: Data represent survey responses from 176 research and 186 practice programs.
From *Characteristics of Graduate Departments of Psychology: 1987–88* by G. Pion, J.
Kohout, and M. Wicherski, 1988, Washington, DC: American Psychological Association,
Office of Demographics, Employment, and Evaluation Research. Copyright 1988 by
American Psychological Association. Adapted by permission.

pool of 3,000,000 undergraduate students to draw from in our efforts to recruit ethnic
minorities to psychology. What do we have to offer them? Why should they choose
careers in psychology? How does your training program address this question?

According to *The Changing Face of American Psychology* (Committee on Employment and Human Resources, 1985), in 1981, 14.6% (5,953) of bachelor's degrees
in psychology were awarded to ethnic minority students. This is a slightly higher
percentage than the overall college minority enrollment rate of 13.9%. Moreover,
from 1976 to 1981, the cumulative percentage change in all awarded bachelor's
degrees was −21% for Whites, but 32% for ethnic minorities! Thus there was an
appreciable growth of interest in psychology at the bachelor's level among ethnic
minorities.

The percentage of doctoral degrees awarded to ethnic minorities was only 10.1%
(247 in 1982). However, from 1975 to 1982, the cumulative percentage increase in
doctoral degrees awarded to ethnic minorities was 88%. The corresponding figure
for Whites was 22%. Recent evidence suggests, however, that this trend has slowed
significantly.

Recent data for graduate enrollments was provided by Pion, Kohout, and Wicherski (1988). Table 1 shows that 604 of the 5,369 graduate students (11.2%) enrolled

in practice programs in 1987–1988 were ethnic minorities. In spite of the popular notion that ethnic minorities are more likely to go into service provider training programs, a higher percentage of ethnic minorities (12.5%, $n = 827$) was found in research training programs.

As was noted earlier, the MFP has supported more than 600 ethnic minority students. Because the large majority of ethnic minority doctoral recipients have earned their degrees since 1975, a profile of MFP recipients may reflect trends over this time period. Table 2 lists the universities and schools where MFP trainees have enrolled over the past 13 years. It is not surprising that some of the larger universities, in or near major urban areas, account for the largest MFP enrollments. However, substantial representation can be found in programs that are not so obviously attached to ethnic minority communities. What promotes the successful recruitment and graduation of ethnic minority students?

I do not have space here to discuss factors that facilitate recruitment of ethnic minorities into psychology programs. A case study analysis is currently being conducted by APA's Committee on Ethnic Minority Human Resource Development, Committee on Graduate Education and Training, and the MFP. The aim of this study is to chronicle recruitment and retention efforts in programs that have been successful in bringing in and keeping ethnic minority students and faculty. However, we already have evidence that the number of ethnic minority students and faculty in a training program strongly influences its nature and quality.

Ethnic Minority Enrollments and Qualitative Differences in Programs

Doctoral programs in practice fields of psychology can be divided into those that have high ethnic minority enrollments and those with low enrollments. Evidence indicates that programs with high enrollment are qualitatively different from those with low enrollment. Table 3 presents data from 76 clinical, 23 counseling, and 16 school psychology programs. Information was taken from special reports submitted by doctoral programs not scheduled for a site visit by the APA accreditation office in 1988. It is judged to be a good representation of the overall profile for accredited programs.

The mean percentage of ethnic minority students was computed for each program. Programs were then divided into those falling above (having a high percentage of ethnic minority students) and those falling below (having a low percentage of ethnic minority students) the mean for the total group within each training specialty. Although statistical tests were not performed, the data suggest that programs with higher percentages of ethnic minority students are somewhat larger (not true for school programs), have a substantially larger percentage of minority students (more than three to one in each case), and have a larger number of ethnic minority faculty (more than two to one in each case) than those with smaller percentages of ethnic minority students. It seems that programs with 20% ethnic minority students fall into one category, and those with less than 10% fall into another. Although the training aspects that may be related to these differences have not been documented, it seems that these percentages may be a good starting point for evaluating progress in this area.

Table 2
Minority Fellowship and Doctoral Recipients, 1975–1988

School	Number Enrolled	Number Graduated	% Graduated
Adelphi U.	4	4	100.0
Arizona State U.	5	3	60.0
Auburn U.	1	0	0.0
Boston College	2	1	50.0
Boston U.	14	6	42.9
Bowling Green State U.	3	0	0.0
California Graduate	1	0	0.0
Catholic U. of America	1	0	0.0
Claremont Graduate School	5	1	20.0
Clark U.	5	2	40.0
Colorado State U.	4	4	100.0
Columbia Teachers	8	5	62.5
Cornell U.	1	1	100.0
CSPP: Berkeley	6	3	50.0
CSPP: Fresno	5	3	60.0
CSPP: Los Angeles	7	6	85.7
CSPP: San Diego	3	1	33.3
Cuny	31	9	29.0
DePaul U.	3	1	33.3
Duke U.	5	2	40.0
Emory U.	1	1	100.0
Florida State U.	1	0	0.0
Fordham U.	6	0	0.0
Fuller Theological Seminary	2	0	0.0
George Washington U.	2	2	100.0
Georgia State U.	2	1	50.0
Harvard U.	13	8	61.5
Howard U.	13	3	23.1
Indiana U.	6	4	66.7
Kansas State U.	1	1	100.0
Louisiana State U.	2	0	0.0
Loyola U.	2	0	0.0
Michigan State U.	4	3	75.0
New School for Social Research	2	0	0.0
New York U.	10	4	40.0
North Texas State	2	1	50.0
Northwestern U.	3	2	66.7
Notre Dame U.	1	0	0.0
Ohio State U.	5	3	60.0
Oklahoma State U.	12	5	41.7
Pennsylvania State U.	11	10	90.9
Princeton U.	2	1	50.0
Purdue U.	2	1	50.0

Table 2 (continued)
Minority Fellowship and Doctoral Recipients, 1975–1988

School	Number Enrolled	Number Graduated	% Graduated
Rosemead School	1	0	0.0
Rutgers	10	6	60.0
Southern Illinois U.	9	4	44.4
St. Louis U.	3	2	66.7
Stanford U.	4	0	0.0
SUNY-Albany	1	1	100.0
SUNY-Buffalo	2	0	0.0
SUNY-Stony Brook	4	2	50.0
Syracuse U.	1	0	0.0
Temple U.	8	2	25.0
Texas A&M	2	0	0.0
Texas Tech U.	2	2	100.0
Tulane U.	1	1	100.0
U. Alabama	2	2	100.0
U. Arizona	2	1	50.0
UC-Berkeley	18	10	55.6
UC-Davis	7	3	42.9
UC-Irvine	1	0	0.0
UC-Los Angeles	22	7	31.8
UC-San Francisco	1	0	0.0
UC-Santa Barbara	3	1	33.3
UC-Santa Cruz	3	0	0.0
U. Colorado	4	0	0.0
U. Connecticut	2	0	0.0
U. Delaware	2	1	50.0
U. Denver	9	7	77.8
U. Florida	2	1	50.0
U. Georgia	7	3	42.9
U. Hawaii	9	4	44.4
U. Houston	4	0	44.4
U. Illinois (Chicago)	2	1	50.0
U. Illinois (Urbana)	9	4	44.4
U. Kentucky	1	1	100.0
U. Maryland	19	12	63.2
U. Massachusetts	2	2	100.0
U. Miami	2	1	50.0
U. Michigan	29	22	75.9
U. Minnesota	3	1	33.3
U. Missouri	1	0	0.0
U. Montana	1	0	0.0
U. Nebraska	15	11	73.3
U. Nevada	4	2	50.0
U. New Mexico	8	5	62.5

Table 2 (continued)
Minority Fellowship and Doctoral Recipients, 1975–1988

School	Number Enrolled	Number Graduated	% Graduated
U. North Carolina	9	6	66.7
U. Oklahoma	2	0	0.0
U. Oregon	7	5	71.4
U. Pittsburgh	14	5	35.7
U. Rhode Island	2	2	100.0
U. Rochester	3	2	66.7
U. San Francisco	1	1	100.0
U. South Carolina	1	1	100.0
U. South Dakota	2	1	50.0
U. South Florida	1	0	0.0
U. Tennessee	6	4	66.7
U. Texas	15	10	66.7
U. Utah	7	4	57.1
U. Vermont	1	0	0.0
U. Virginia	4	2	50.0
U. Washington	8	5	62.5
U. Wisconsin	1	1	100.0
U.S. International	2	1	50.0
Utah State U.	3	0	0.0
Vanderbilt U.	5	3	60.0
Virginia Commonwealth	2	1	50.0
Washington State U.	4	4	100.0
Washington U.	2	1	50.0
Wayne State U.	3	1	33.3
Wright Institute	8	6	75.0
Yale U.	8	4	50.0
Yeshiva U.	3	2	66.7
Totals	585	296	50.6

Note. These figures represent all students who have been supported in the program, including those currently or recently funded. Thus graduation percentages may be misleading. Those that are very high probably represent programs that had more trainees in the late 1970s and early 1980s. Those with low percentages may have more current trainees or a higher noncompletion rate.

Training Issues

As was stated at the outset, there is no definitive answer to the question posed in the chapter's title, "Are programs training ethnic minorities right?" However, a review of some of the factors that are relevant to training ethnic minorities is useful because it facilitates a programmatic self-study of approaches to minority training. The following points are illustrative, not exhaustive, and reflect those issues that have

Table 3

Level of Ethnic Minority Representation Among a Sample of Accredited Programs in Clinical, Counseling, and School Psychology

Program Statistics	Level of Representation		Totals
	High %	Low %	
Clinical Programs			
No. of programs	32	44	76
Program size			
Average no. of students	59.2	66.4	63.4
Average no. of faculty	9.1	11.6	10.6
Minority students			
Total no.	393	211	604
Average no.	12.3	4.8	7.9
% of total students	20.7	7.2	12.5
Minority faculty			
Total no.	33	26	59
Average no.	1.0	.6	.8
% of total faculty	11.3	5.1	7.3
Counseling Programs			
No. of programs	9	14	23
Program size			
Average no. of students	52.1	53.1	52.7
Average no. of faculty	7.9	7.6	7.7
Minority students			
Total no.	104	49	153
Average no.	11.5	3.5	6.6
% of total students	22.1	6.6	12.6
Minority faculty			
Total no.	15	10	25
Average no.	1.7	.7	1.1
% of total faculty	21.0	9.1	14.0
School Programs			
No. of programs	4	12	16
Program size			
Average no. of students	54.0	37.1	41.3
Average no. of faculty	5.0	5.1	5.1
Minority students			
Total no.	54	28	82
Average no.	13.5	2.3	5.1
% of total students	24.8	6.2	12.4

Table 3 (continued)
Level of Ethnic Minority Representation Among a Sample of Accredited Programs in Clinical, Counseling, and School Psychology

	Level of Representation		
Program Statistics	High %	Low %	Totals
Minority faculty			
Total no.	2	3	5
Average no.	.5	.25	.3
% of total faculty	9.6	4.9	6.2

Note. Data are taken from special reports submitted by doctoral programs not scheduled for a site visit by the Accreditation Office in 1988.

surfaced in my many years of travel and interaction with ethnic minority students and program faculty concerned with ethnic minority training issues.

Critical mass of students—voice. As was asserted earlier, affirmative action is an important reason for recruiting ethnic minorities into psychology programs, but not a sufficient reason. A program committed to training ethnic minority psychologists requires a critical mass of ethnic minority students. What is a critical mass of students? A critical mass is defined as enough ethnic minority students to ensure that engaging these issues will result in a healthy, vibrant exchange of information, ideas, and perspective. I suggested that 20% or more ethnic minority students seemed to be the dividing line that describes critical mass. A critical mass, however, is more than mere numbers.

The personal experiences of students matter. Their career goals matter. A critical mass of students gives voice to ethnic minority concerns. Voice can be thought of as the legitimate concern for, and the important role played by, ethnic minority students in their training. One consequence of a critical mass is that the voice must be heard. When a program has a critical mass of students who do not feel that the content of the training is responsive to their interests and expectations, problems arise. Twenty unhappy students is both quantitatively and qualitatively different from one unhappy student. Voice ensures that the unhappiness will be expressed. The presence of a critical mass is important, but it carries multiple obligations, on the part of both trainers and trainees, to build a relevant presence of ethnic minority perspectives into the program.

Obtaining a critical mass of ethnic minority students does not just happen. It is tied directly to the nature of the program being offered and to at least the implicit, if not explicit, assumption that having a significant number of ethnic minority students is desirable both for the ethnic minority students and the program in general. The answer to the question, "Why would a capable and competent ethnic minority student come to my program as opposed to any other?" will help define the basis for attracting ethnic minority students in significant numbers.

Presence of ethnic minority faculty. As was seen in Table 3, programs with a larger percentage of ethnic minority students also had larger numbers of ethnic minority faculty. This is not a surprising finding. However, numbers do not tell the whole story. The presence of ethnic minority faculty is important for several different reasons. Ethnic minority faculty have research or practice interests and expertise that serve the training interests of the program and the students, both ethnic minority and majority. Minority faculty keep the intellectual life of ethnic minority issues vibrant and sustain the legitimate interest of ethnic minority students in them.

All ethnic minority faculty need not be working actively in research on ethnic minority issues to contribute substantially to the quality and success of training ethnic minority students. The ability of ethnic minority faculty to share the culture of ethnicity and the strategies of successfully negotiating the graduate experience can contribute to the ethnic minority student's ability to do well in a program. Where cultural barriers to communication exist between ethnic minority students and White faculty, minority faculty may well be the ombudspersons needed to help things work.

We must be careful that ethnic minority faculty are not overburdened with the entire responsibility for ethnic minority training. For affirmative diversity to work, it must be a value to which the entire program is committed. It is certainly appropriate for ethnic minority faculty members to take the lead, but they should not be expected to carry the entire weight. It is also entirely appropriate for someone else to take the lead and for the ethnic minority faculty member to take a secondary role.

Ideally, it should be possible for ethnic minority faculty to exist in sufficient numbers that they may make choices about the roles they wish to play. Except for rare situations, however, it is common that the undersupply of ethnic minority faculty members demands that they will be expected to play multiple roles. Whatever their roles, it is highly important that ethnic minorities be central to the business of scholarship, training, science, and mentoring. This visibility, training input, teaching, and scholarship is an integral part of ethnic minority training.

Courses and perspectives.   There is always the debate about the relative merits of integrating ethnic content into standard or core courses versus developing specialty courses on ethnic minority issues. This debate always sees the two as an either/or option. However, both are necessary and possible. In structuring ethnically diverse curricula, the first consideration is that race, ethnicity, and culture present issues that are fundamental to training in psychology. Ghettoizing ethnic minority mental health courses with ethnic minority faculty and students does a disservice to quality teaching and training in psychology.

There are specialized content courses that focus attention on patterns of culture, behavior, and life-style that implicate the therapeutic context, including methods, assumptions, assessment, strategies, and so forth. For example, a comparison of successful and unsuccessful lower-income Black and Hispanic men showed that what distinguished successful Black men from unsuccessful Black men depended on their attitudes toward and relationship with their mothers. For Hispanics, success and failure turned on relationships with the fathers. This kind of observation suggests the need for focused training on the content of cultural patterns of behavior for different ethnic groups. Determining which courses are appropriate will depend, in part, on the critical mass of students, their interests, and the nature of the available client population.

Conversely, there are fundamental questions that implicate race (or sex, or other parameters of difference) in psychotherapy. Recently, I heard a case presentation (K. White, 1989) in which a White male client was treated by a Black female therapist. Among many problems experienced by the client was that he identified with being

Black and spent many hours in Harlem going to clubs, chatting with people on their stoops, and even going to the church of the Holy Rollers. He was most comfortable and alive in these settings. The Black female therapist described him as a Black-identified White man. He shot back that her highly educated, analytically trained professional style certainly put her equally into a cross-racial identification mode, suggesting that she was a White-identified Black woman. Thus transference and countertransference processes evoke myriad questions and analytical themes that are not limited to peculiarities of ethnic minority concerns but may be fundamentally important to the basic processes of psychotherapy.

As a second curriculum consideration, standard psychology knowledge should be responsive to fundamental questions of culture and ethnicity. If there are real cultural, racial, and ethnic differences in socialization, behavioral styles, language capacity, family organization, parenting styles, and so forth, what are the implications for training? Is cultural understanding a prerequisite for trust in therapy? The transference and countertransference issues must turn, in part, on these issues. Do poor people have different outcome requirements from therapy than do middle- and upper-income people? If the experienced problems are system generated, does that differ from inner-generated problems? Is it necessary to label the locus of problems in order to fashion approaches to solutions? Along what dimensions do therapist–client differences matter and how? We already consider that sex, race or ethnicity, and sexual orientation matter. What else matters?

There is much for us to learn about mental health and how our profession can serve a positive role. However, we must also recognize that we have gone too long without systematically paying attention to the myriad questions that are asked of our theories, empirical knowledge, and practical applications. Answers to these questions will help to determine whether or not your program is doing it "right."

Integration of research findings. It is critical to integrate research findings on ethnic minority issues into the training program. There is now a growing body of theory and research on ethnicity, race, and culture. These research findings and theoretical ideas deserve to be carefully evaluated for their implications for practice.

For example, in a study of Black and White police officers in Cleveland, N. D. Henderson (1979) collected personality measures, using the Edwards Personality Preference Schedule (EPPS) and the Sixteen Personality Factor Questionnaire (16 PF), and performance evaluations by superior officers and peers. Data indicated that EPPS personality ratings of Black police officers on dominance, heterosexuality, and aggression and 16 PF scores that showed them to be outgoing, enthusiastic, free-thinking, and self-sufficient were *negatively* correlated with performance ratings by superior officers and peers. Correlations for Whites on these factors hovered around zero. Conversely, EPPS personality measures of Black police officers on deference, order, autonomy, and endurance were *positively* correlated with performance ratings. Again, no such relationship was found for White police officers. There were no differences between Black and White police officers on any of the personality measures.

These data suggest that the world experienced by Black police officers, as related to the major domains of performance, evaluation, and motivation, is fundamentally different from that of Whites. How does coping with such a subtly biased experience manifest itself in psychological adaptations? How well do our therapeutic approaches equip us to detect and treat such psychological processes?

A wide variety of conceptions about the content and characteristics of different cultural groups is now represented in research journals that focus on ethnic minority mental health (e.g., *Hispanic Journal of the Behavior Sciences, Journal of Black Psychology, Journal of Black Studies, Asian American Psychology,* and *American Indian and Alaska Native Mental Health Research*). In addition, authored and edited books on ethnic minority mental health identify theoretical, empirical, and process issues that represent the content of a vibrant training program for ethnic minority students (e.g., Atkinson, Morten, & D. W. Sue, 1983; Boyd-Franklin, 1989; E. E. Jones & Korchin, 1982; Ramirez, 1983; S. Sue & Morishima, 1985; Turner & Jones, 1982).

Practicum and supervision. Practicum and supervision experiences should allow for the inclusion of cultural considerations and their practical consequences in the therapeutic relationship and process. To prepare students to provide mental health services to ethnic minority populations, it is essential to build practicum clinical experiences into the training concept. To do this, relevant clinical populations are a precondition. In addition, supervision that guides trainees through the experience, as well as benefits from creative approaches to the presenting problems and successful elements of treatment, is critical. It is also essential that this described supervision be carried out by supervisors who can impart it in a relevant way.

Much theorizing and research on processes of therapy with ethnic minority clients has appeared in the recent literature of psychology. In general, it is widely accepted that treatment prognoses and outcomes are poorer for ethnic minority clients. Why this is so is a subject of much debate.

Evaluation of assessment instruments. Assessment instruments should be evaluated constantly for their utility with ethnic minority clients. Do we know that extant assessment instruments work in a non-biased way with minority populations? Do diagnostic categories work? Does the *Diagnostic and Statistical Manual of Mental Disorders—Third Edition* (DSM-III; American Psychological Association, 1980) capture the dimensions of mental ill health? Does it overinterpret illness? Does the System of Multicultural Pluralistic Assessment (SOMPA; Mercer & Lewis, 1978) work to the advantage of better diagnosis? What role does language play? Do assessment courses and supervision systematically address these issues? Does the Wechsler Intelligence Scale for Children—Revised (WISC—R) produce the same results when translated into Spanish? Are the cultural assumptions spelled out in assessment devices? Do they operate comparably across cultural groups?

To the extent that such questions now do not have answers, and to the extent that the answers will make a real difference, we are shortchanging our students and the populations that they and we serve. Ethnic minority concerns are, in a basic sense, general concerns about the practice of psychology. Engaging these issues in our training programs, our scholarship, our practice, and our science enriches our discipline and its relevance to society.

Treatment. S. Sue and Zane (1987) have provided an excellent summary of the ways in which ethnic differences enter the therapeutic situation. They made a distinction between distal and proximal variables as they affect the therapeutic process. Distal variables are those associated with cultural phenomena such as values, meanings, experiences, and the associated characteristics such as race, ethnicity, age, and so forth. Somewhat more proximal are the process variables that define the therapeutic tactics and strategies that guide the course of therapy. Most proximal are the intimate variables that are fundamental to the therapy outcome. S. Sue and Zane defined the most prominent of these as "credibility."

Credibility can derive from "ascribed" status such as race, ethnicity, age, and so forth, or it can be "achieved." The advantage of a therapist–client match on relevant characteristics is that such a match often confers credibility on the therapist. Absence of an ascribed credibility may be compensated for, in this analysis, by manifestation of sensitivity to and understanding of the client through the following:

- *Conceptualization of the problem*—These must be congruent with the client's belief system and patterns of shared goals.
- *Means for problem resolution*—Required responses must be culturally compatible with the client's behavioral preferences.
- *Goals for treatment*—Treatment goals must take into account what the client thinks is important.

Thus, through effective sensitivity to these proximal process factors in the therapy relationship, a therapist can achieve credibility. Conversely, by failing to be responsive to these factors, a therapist with ascribed credibility can lose it.

The critical point for training is that, through coursework, and particularly through supervision, such models of the therapy process can be promulgated. A course on ethnic characteristics of particular groups is certainly helpful, but it is insufficient. We need to know how that knowledge translates into therapeutic credibility via the mechanisms I just outlined. S. Sue and Zane have given us an excellent model to drive such training objectives.

Similarly, E. E. Jones (1984) argued for a more molecular analysis of the therapy situation than the molar level offered by a simple consideration of race or ethnicity. E. E. Jones suggested that empathy enables one to overcome racial dissimilarity and to use countertransference processes effectively to improve therapeutic outcomes in cross-racial situations. Block (1984) called for the application of race-specific knowledge to the understanding of process in therapy with Black clients.

Training paradigm. A paradigm of disadvantage, resilience, stress reactions, and culturally based problem solving should be developed and made a core feature of training. For the most part, consideration of the circumstances of ethnicity and race have lead psychologists to a problem-centered focus on the mental health consequences of ethnic minority status in America. Nowhere is this better demonstrated than in the classic Kardiner and Ovesey (1951) analysis of Negro personality:

> *The Negro, in contrast to the White, is a more unhappy person; he has a harder environment to live in, and the internal stress is greater. By "unhappy" we mean he enjoys less, he suffers more. There is not one personality trait of the Negro the source of which cannot be traced to his difficult living conditions.* There are no exceptions to this rule. The final result is a wretched internal life [*emphasis added*]. (p. 81)

This dismal portrayal of the inner life of Black Americans is wildly discrepant from, and gyrates 180 degrees out of phase with, other stereotypes about the happy-go-lucky, carefree personalities of Black people (Gilbert, 1951; D. Katz & Braly, 1933). We have such conflicting portrayals of Blacks because we have no models that understand how one can cope with oppression, disadvantage, and denial in ways that permit any degree of normalcy. Psychology's interest in ethnic minorities should cover the full range of minority experiences, oppression as well as opportunity. Each ethnic group struggles with and suffers from oppression, physically and psychologically. Each group has developed adaptive coping mechanisms for dealing with this duality of existence. Psychology seems to sit on the sidelines, watching with interest, but contributing very little as an organized discipline of science and practice.

G. Miller (1969) challenged us to "give psychology away." He believed that we should empower members of society to define their own problems, and to use our tools (the instruments of our science and practice), with our help, to solve their problems. Psychologists can play a constructive role in society by (a) recognizing the basic paradigm of oppression-driven stress, which is adapted to via culturally based problem solving, and (b) developing training and intervention models from this paradigm. Ethnic minority students and faculty are a necessary part of this process.

Multicultural focus. A multicultural focus or concentration should tie all of these facets together in an integrated training program. There is an opportunity to learn much more about human capabilities and sources of conflict and strain by systematically addressing issues of cultural, racial, and ethnic difference. Tying together the issues of critical mass of students, ethnic minority faculty, courses, research, practicum and supervision, evaluation of assessment instruments, and treatment is the bottom line of a focused program. We have much to learn about the relevance of psychology to culturally different people.

All training programs need not become dominated by a multicultural focus, but any program that ignores this reality is doing a disservice to its students (of any race or ethnicity) and to the members of society they are trained to serve. If psychology is to be a relevant discipline in the 21st century, a multicultural training component is vital. It is not merely a matter of social justice or affirmative action; it is a matter of human relevance and affirmative diversity.

Where Do We Go From Here? A Summary of Possible Actions

Affirmative Diversity—Not Just Affirmative Action

The message of this chapter is straightforward. Training ethnic minority psychologists involves a commitment to the proposition that human diversity is a valued goal; its achievement enhances program performance. One aspect of diversity is represented by the experiences, insights, cultural perspectives, and career paths of ethnic minority students and faculty. The inclusion of this significant source of diversity in our training programs will move psychology generally, and clinical training specifically, toward greater relevance and usefulness in the diverse society that is the United States.

This commitment must incorporate the principle of affirmative diversity, and we must find ways to balance the inalienable academic freedom of faculty with the coordinated goals of a training program. The beneficiaries will be all students, most faculty, and, above all, the clients we serve. Although affirmative action details a commitment to diversify the student and faculty representation, the commitment proposed here goes well beyond numbers and representation. It speaks to program, to training, and to product. Self-study is the first step toward determining whether such a commitment is desirable. Each program must make its own determination.

The Critical Role of Research in Formulating Clinical Approaches

A subtheme of this chapter is that valid and crucial researchable questions abound, the answers to which play a key role in determining the content of curriculum and training. The formulation and evaluation of the questions themselves are a critical part of the training process. Although much work needs to be done, the number of psychologists currently collecting data and evaluating the entire mental health approach to ethnic minority populations is adequate for developing courses and launching lecture series. The developing body of knowledge helps to guide the content of supervision and assessment courses and the formulations of therapy processes. The affirmative action approach argues for inclusion of ethnic minorities from a social justice perspective. The affirmative diversity approach, based on systematic empirical analysis and demonstrations, specifies the substantive reasons *why* inclusion is important and *how* it can be implemented.

Broader Visibility and Potency of Ethnic Minority Issues

Part of what needs to be done is the systematic pursuit of the issues represented by ethnic minority involvement in psychology. There are several avenues by which such visibility and development can take place. APA's Division 45, the Society for the Psychological Study of Ethnic Minority Issues, provides one avenue. Division 45 is chartered to study the whole range of issues outlined in this chapter. Membership in this division should be mandatory for anyone who presumes to participate in the affirmative diversity directions outlined here. The division is not a forum for ethnic minorities to share experiences and plan political action, although surely that is one important role it plays. But as its name clearly suggests, Division 45 envisions the study of ethnic minority issues and the application of that knowledge to the broad questions of mental health service delivery and research. Each program should have established relationships with the division, and joint programs should be commonplace.

In addition, there exists the Office of Ethnic Minority Affairs in the Public Interest Directorate of APA, as well as the MFP. The Public Interest Directorate, along with the developing Education Directorate, provide a broader organizational context for pursuing these issues. There are surely many relevant issues of interest to groups within the Practice Directorate as well. We must take advantage of organizational opportunities in order to advance collectively this important training goal. Planning, commitment, and energy are the catalysts necessary to energize these extant human and material resources.

A Leadership Role for the National Council of Schools of Professional Psychology

By focusing on ethnic minority training issues at its midwinter 1988–1989 Puerto Rico conference, the National Council of Schools of Professional Psychology (NCSPP) has asserted the importance of ethnic minority training. Some of the actions taken at the conference further indicate the resolve of NCSPP to follow through and make a difference. I have outlined some of the resources available, as well as some of the program elements necessary for a successful training approach. NCSPP can serve as the catalyst for these diverse elements. As an organized and focused group of program trainers in psychology, NCSPP has the wherewithal to pursue these ideas with consistency, direction, and purpose. I am confident that if NCSPP makes a collective commitment to significant achievement in ethnic minority training programs, it will provide a major service to all of psychology, and to the human populations that psychologists serve.

PART II
INSTITUTIONAL CHANGE

4

ADDRESSING
INSTITUTIONAL CHANGE

James McHolland

Illinois School of Professional Psychology
Chicago, Illinois

The 1989 National Council of Schools of Professional Psychology (NCSPP) Conference in Puerto Rico initially was structured to present the work of the four subcommittees of the Committee on Minority Participation and Service to Underserved Populations (faculty/administration recruitment and retention, student recruitment and retention, curriculum, and service to underserved populations). As the conference program evolved, however, the planning committee recognized that subcommittee reports and recommendations were tied inexorably to changes in institutional status quo at host schools. It became clear that ethnic diversification could occur only in the presence of positive changes in institutional climate. And, once the process of ethnic diversification was set in motion, it, itself, would initiate profound transformations within the institution. Perceiving this essential relationship between institutional change and ethnic diversification, the planning committee added this topic to the conference program and arranged for invited presentators to address it. Part II of this volume (chapters 5, 6, 7, and 8) is a compilation of those papers. The central perspectives of the authors are discussed briefly in the following paragraphs.

In "Working Against Prejudice in a Large State University," chapter 5, Peterson chronicles the efforts of a large state university to work against prejudice. First acknowledging "a surge of racist expression" at such prestigious colleges and universities as Purdue, Columbia, Dartmouth, Stanford, Wisconsin, and the University of Colorado, Peterson argues persuasively that college campus incidents and other forms of bigotry are "rooted in a deeper strain of general prejudice that pervades our entire society." Although a longitudinal study of racial attitudes in America (Schuman, Steeh, & Bobo, 1985) shows a striking increase in public support for principles of equal treatment over the last 20 years, Peterson recognizes accurately that "implementation has often lagged behind principle." More important, he reminds us that "no social scientist I know ever predicted that the transformation from a restrictively segregated university society to the competing diversities we see today would occur without conflict."

When racial incidents occurred at Rutgers—The State University, the president convened a group of faculty and administrators to consider the problem. Peterson was in that group and encouraged the involvement of the community psychology program at Rutgers. As is often the case when one has a good idea, Peterson was put in charge of the committee to work against prejudice. Although the project only recently was underway when Peterson's chapter was written, the Rutgers group posed three questions that other institutions might find useful:

1. From your position and in your experience, what do you see as the main expressions of prejudice, discrimination, or bigotry on this campus?
2. What do you see as the main conditions that produce and maintain these expressions?
3. What do you think we ought to do about it?

Equally important, the Rutgers approach to the problem of prejudice emphasizes *listening* to the answers to these questions given by a wide diversity of campus groups. In asking its various constituencies to respond to its questions, Rutgers is opening itself to the possibility (some would argue the inevitability) of institutional change. More, from a psychological perspective, Rutgers is gathering assessment information before intervening in the problem.

Peterson describes other activities with which the committee was charged in order to coordinate moving Rutgers toward a more pluralistic society and to reduce prejudice. An important contribution of chapter 5 is the statement of 10 principles from community psychology theory, which hold particular personal meaning for Peterson as a result of Rutgers's efforts to reduce prejudice.

In chapter 6, Persico focuses on "Creating an Institutional Climate That Honors Diversity." Persico begins with "the assumption that, through education, citizens can develop the means of ensuring mobility and access to the power and control necessary to influence directly the course of their lives is fundamental to the existence of a democratic society." Then he summarizes the educational establishment response to this premise. He determines that, in our attempts to create an institutional climate that honors diversity, there are no historical models to consider. Lacking models to emulate, Persico argues that we must engage in pioneer efforts "to alter the culture and consciousness of the higher education setting if we are to create institutions that support diversity." The challenge, as he sees it, is more than reallocating resources. Rather, when a culture is created that honors cultural diversity, resources will be found and allocated appropriately.

Why should schools create a climate honoring diversity? According to Persico, social purpose and public responsibility require it. Graduate programs in psychology generally define their primary goal as educating and training doctoral-level psychologists who are able to meet the mental health needs of the population. Thus, Persico reminds us:

> *Now, our population is so culturally diverse that in our lifetimes we will experience only the second period in American history when White people are not in the majority. ... If we are to meet our public responsibility, we must address the issues raised by this unprecedented diversity and we must alter our climates to honor the changes and consequences inherent in living within a diverse culture.*

How is a climate created that honors diversity? Persico defines and discusses eight steps to build and maintain the necessary climate.

1. Establishing institutional commitment.
2. Creating a culturally diverse faculty.

3. Creating a culturally diverse administration.
4. Creating a culturally diverse student body.
5. Creating student-faculty support systems.
6. Generating financial aid funds.
7. Altering the core curriculum.
8. Preparing for the consequences of change.

Persico is helpful in reminding us that not everything must change. Rather, for the necessary change in climate to occur, we must become critically aware of who we are and what we intend to be as an institution, so that our hirings and policies fit into the environment we seek to establish. The author speaks from the position of experience and successful leadership in building a climate and training program (California School of Professional Psychology: Los Angeles) that facilitates and honors ethnic diversity. His chapter is essential reading for program leaders who are seriously committed to improving their institution's climate for diversity.

In chapter 7, "Institutional Change and Leadership: Challenges in Education," Santiago-Negrón discusses the kind of leadership needed "to maximize our performance as agents of social change" and asks us to consider what concrete activities graduate program leaders can undertake to provide impetus to optimize the accessibility of higher education for minorities. Santiago-Negrón's argument for institutional change is based on an economic, rather than a value-oriented or moral, premise. For example, in 1950, 17 workers paid the benefits of one retiree (Hodgkinson, 1985). By 1992, it is predicted that only three workers will provide funds for each retiree and one of the three will be a minority person. The Commission on Minority Participation in Education and American Life, sponsored by the American Council on Education (1988), predicted that, between 1985 and 2000, minority workers will constitute one third of the net additions to the U.S. labor force. By the year 2030, it is projected that two workers will be supporting the Social Security benefits of one person. According to Santiago-Negrón,

> *If this demographic profile is accurate, it is in the self-interest of all Americans to improve substantially minority citizens' competence, education, employability, and earning power. Only by addressing this plight can we hope to provide the income support and health care needs of the future aging population.*

Santiago-Negrón summarizes several studies on the current enrollment of minority groups in graduate and professional schools that underscore the generally low proportion of minorities, except for Asians, in higher education. At the same time, general enrollment rates for nonminority students continue to increase. Significantly, the American Council on Education (1988) surveyed college administrators of 367 colleges and universities to determine the main challenges seen for the next 5 years. Only 1 in 10 administrators regarded the improvement of racial and ethnic diversity as one of the most important challenges ahead. Santiago-Negrón states:

> *This survey indicates that the need to incorporate racial diversity into our institutions of higher learning is only superficially acknowledged by academic leaders. Failure to develop skill-building assets in minority populations ignores an important human resource and reduces America's ability to compete economically with other developed nations.*

Santiago-Negrón outlines specific strategies that graduate program leaders might consider to improve outreach for, and retention of, racial and ethnic minorities. Among his suggestions are (a) think-tanks, (b) inclusive support systems known as "webworks," (c) charging institutional committees with a mission, (d) involvement of minority representation at *all* levels of the institutional infrastructure, and (e) linkages with historically minority colleges. To improve ethnic diversity in higher education, Santiago-Negrón encourages institutional leadership from NCSPP and similar organizations to pose a challenge to regional and national accreditation bodies:

> Diversity *among college students, among university faculty and administrators, and among the curricular contents is crucial for achieving excellence in the American educational system. Achieving institutional excellence without addressing the needs of minorities is tantamount to an inconclusive agenda in the field of higher education.*

Essentially, he suggests active influence to change accreditation criteria so that institutions of higher education *must* include the issue of ethnic diversity in the planning and implementation of their educational programs.

In chapter 8, "Barriers to Minorities in the Field of Psychology and Strategies for Change," Diaz identifies academic, personal, and institutional barriers that affect the optimal functioning of minorities in psychology. Diaz believes that these barriers are a reflection of socioeconomic and sociocultural factors or a lack of commitment, by American academic institutions and governmental agencies, to provide access to higher education for minorities. Among academic barriers is the use of the grade point average (GPA) as a major criterion on which to base graduate school admission. The GPA represents a serious barrier for many minority students because of the inferior quality of the public school districts from which many come. Likewise, standard admission tests such as the Graduate Record Examination (GRE) and the Scholastic Aptitude Test (SAT) become barriers for minorities because "virtually every test . . . reveals that the mean of the scores of minority students is about one standard deviation below the mean of the scores of the rest of the American population."

Personal barriers for minority student achievement include (a) dissonant values and belief systems when compared to the majority American culture; (b) identity conflict with one's cultural group when educational programs encourage assimilation to the dominant culture at the expense of rejecting the uniqueness of one's own cultural identity; and (c) lack of aspiration or motivation as a result of the lack of role models and culturally relevant psychological theories, training, and practices. Diaz believes several institutional barriers also exist. Among these are (a) ineffective recruitment practices, (b) discriminatory admissions criteria, (c) limited financial assistance, and (d) lack of faculty and administration support for ethnic minorities.

Governmental institutions also constitute a significant barrier for minorities in education. She asserts, "the Federal Government's low-key participation in and enforcement of equal opportunity and affirmative action legislation have reduced an opportunity to take substantial corrective action to match the nation's higher education system with the society it serves." To reduce these barriers, Diaz reviews 19 strategies found in the literature. The strategies vary with regard to difficulty in immediate implementation. The list of references, in itself, constitutes a helpful resource for our use.

What will happen if NCSPP and its member schools are successful in creating institutions that value and promote ethnic and racial diversity? Persico describes a future reality many of us will experience. He predicts:

> *The institution, as we have known it, will be different. People will know, understand, and behave differently from you. They will wonder why you do what you have always taken for granted. They will want things you do not want, and ask for things you do*

not want to give. You will have to remember that you want your institution and this society to be different. ... A truly integrated society, and even truly integrated institutions, do not exist. ... We have to be comfortable, standing firmly in nothing but our will and commitments, in creating a new institution that enables everyone to share in the knowledge that empowers them to create a healthy and supportive new society.

5

WORKING AGAINST PREJUDICE IN A LARGE STATE UNIVERSITY

Donald R. Peterson

Rutgers—The State University
New Brunswick, New Jersey

Racial Unrest at American Universities

In October 1986, following a World Series game in which the New York Mets defeated the Boston Red Sox, a fight broke out at the University of Massachusetts. The trouble began with the usual taunts of opposing sports fans, but soon some racist feelings began to show. The Sox are seen as mainly a White team. The Mets's stars are Black, and the sympathies of the crowd tended to divide on racial lines. In the bitterness of loss at the last moment, with a lot of alcohol flowing through the viscera of the mob, the jeers of the Blacks were too much for the Whites to take. Long-suppressed racial anger was expressed in shouts and shoves, then punches, kicks, and the swinging of clubs. The Black students were outnumbered. By the end of the fracas, one Black student was beaten unconscious, and at least 10 people were treated for injuries.

At first, university administrators denied any racial basis for the episode. All that was involved, they claimed, was the impulsive behavior of a few overly enthusiastic sports fans who might have been drinking too much. A later inquiry, exceptionally thorough in its scope and penetration, showed that racist feelings were deeply involved. Only when the basic nature of the conflict was acknowledged did constructive resolution begin.

Many related incidents have occurred at other colleges and universities. At Purdue University, a cross was burned on the lawn in front of the university's Black Cultural Center. At The Citadel in South Carolina, White students dressed as Ku Klux Klan members and terrorized a Black cadet. At Smith College, someone scrawled "Niggers, spics, and chinks, stop complaining or get out" on the door of a cultural center building. At Columbia University, a racially motivated demonstration led to a fight between groups of Black and White students that spilled out of a building onto Broadway. At the University of Colorado, a fraternity used a photo of an obese, nude Black woman in a flier designed to attract pledges. Black students were not amused.

An angry demonstration followed. At the University of Michigan, a disagreement arose over use of a student lounge, and a flier insulting Blacks was slipped under the lounge door where Black women were meeting. The next week, the disc jockey at the student-run radio station mixed a laugh track with some racist jokes told by an anonymous caller. At Dartmouth College, staff members of the *Dartmouth Review* entered the classroom of a Black music professor to demand that he stop using his classroom as a forum for his personal political views and focus instead on the education they were paying high prices to obtain. A bitter, spreading controversy has continued ever since. Incidents at Stanford University, the University of Wisconsin, and numerous other institutions show with alarming clarity that the racial tensions in our colleges and universities are widespread in extent and dangerously virulent in form and effect.

A good deal of speculation about the causes of these events can be seen in the popular media. The rise in racial incidents has sometimes been attributed to a loss of national leadership in the protection and advancement of civil justice. According to some observers, concern for minorities was replaced by economic greed in the political agenda. In 1986, addressing the American Psychological Association convention in Washington, DC, journalist Carl Rowan described Ronald Reagan as the "most racist president since Woodrow Wilson." That is not entirely fair. Wilson's racism was active and deliberate. He was fond of telling jokes about Blacks in cabinet meetings and was instrumental in segregating the federal civil service. Reagan's racism took a passive form. His attitude was one of denial and neglect. Black leaders who met with him said that Reagan simply seemed incapable of understanding the pain and helplessness that Black people experience and had no real sympathy for their plight. If, as I believe (Peterson, 1988), the natural social forces that encourage prejudice are very strong, constant vigilance and unrelenting action by public leaders is required to reduce prejudice. When people are comfortable with their biases, as they were allowed to be during the Reagan administration, the ever-present forces of bigotry increase. President Bush appears to be more deeply concerned with civil rights than Reagan was. We shall see whether our nation grows kinder and gentler as a result.

In a longer view and apart from ad hominem considerations, however, it is clear that some turmoil was bound to occur as a delayed effect of the civil rights movement itself. Among the central actions in the movement was the opening of American universities to minorities. Black, Hispanic, Asian, and Native American students were actively recruited through affirmative action programs. As a result, universities that had once solved the problems of prejudice by discriminatory exclusion were converted within a very short time into complexly mixed societies. The universities of the 1980s include students of every race, color, and creed. Many of these students grew up in segregated communities with their own cultures of prejudice. In the university, they are thrown together in an inherently competitive situation. For the first time, many students are required to confront others whom they were taught all their lives to hate, fear, and despise.

The visions of chaos projected by early opponents of access and integration have not materialized. In fact, the massive longitudinal study of racial attitudes in America by Schuman, et al. (1985) shows a striking increase, over the past 20 years, in support for principles of equal treatment. Jim Crow laws that once were taken for granted are now almost universally repudiated. Implementation has often lagged behind principle, however, and no social scientist I know ever predicted that the transformation from a restrictively segregated university society to the competing diversities we see today would occur without conflict.

Whatever the causes and whoever may be to blame, a surge of racist expression is clearly washing through American universities right now, accompanied by other forms of bigotry, and rooted in a deeper strain of general prejudice that pervades our entire society. At Rutgers expressions of bigotry have taken many forms and found many victims. So far, we have seen no physical violence, but other kinds of attacks have been vicious enough, and the range of abuse has been so wide that few are left untouched. Posters advertising Black and Hispanic events have been defaced and torn down. Counterattacks on "punk racists" are seen in bathroom graffiti. Swastikas have been painted on walls at the Hillel Foundation and elsewhere. "Boot power," "kill Jews," and other chilling slogans arouse feelings of the Holocaust. Several incidents of acquaintance rape were reported, and women organized a protest. As they marched down College Avenue at Rutgers, some fraternity brothers sat on their porches and shouted obscenities. A survey conducted by gay and lesbian students showed that many of them had been threatened with physical attack, but they did not appeal for protection from the police because they feared they would only meet another form of prejudice there.

Taking Action at Rutgers

When the earliest of these incidents occured at Rutgers during the spring of 1987, Edward J. Bloustein, the president of Rutgers University, called together a group of administrators and faculty leaders to consider ways of dealing with the problem. The group produced a document entitled "Toward a Pluralistic Community Free of Prejudice" that laid out a broad agenda for constructive action. As a basic premise, the seriousness of the condition was openly acknowledged. Rather than denying the problem or trying to remove symptoms, basic changes were proposed. The agenda suggested ways of reducing prejudice through (a) course work, (b) honors programs, (c) faculty and staff development, (c) student relations, (d) improved communications, (e) honoring excellence, (f) needs assessment, and (g) research. The President then wrote an open letter to the 60,000 members of the Rutgers community to encourage thinking, discussion, and action on these concerns.

Among other initiatives, he brought the agenda for reducing prejudice to the annual retreat of vice presidents, provosts, and deans. What Bloustein said to us, essentially, was "We have a serious problem here, as well as an opportunity to take advantage of our diversity. What are we going to do about it?" That is when I took my first step toward a new form of community involvement. I had just helped edit a book entitled *Assessment for Decision* (Peterson & Fishman, 1987) that laid out a strategy for designing assessment systems at all levels of human functioning from biopsychology to community organization. The proposal for "needs analysis" in the president's agenda seemed naive to me. I wrote a note to that effect prior to the retreat and offered to help design a better process for community assessment.

Then, at the retreat itself, I took another step. During an evening break in the proceedings, President Bloustein and I found ourselves standing on opposite sides of a couple of drinks and I said something like the following:

> *You know, Ed, we have a school of professional psychology at Rutgers University that we keep bragging about as the best of its kind in the world. One of the things we do is community psychology. We try to figure out what is going on in communities, and then we put everything we know about social organization, intergroup conflict, per-*

formance engineering, and human psychology of every kind to work in helping the community function better. We try to prevent problems from arising rather than only reacting to them after they have gotten out of hand. We try to go after these conditions at a deep, systemic level so that any solutions we come up with can have general and lasting effects. We try to evaluate everything we do so that we can extend the programs that work and drop the ones that do not work. I wonder if there is any way our community psychologists could turn their talents back upon our own community.

Two days later, I was in President Bloustein's office hearing him ask me if I would organize a committee to oversee the campaign. I said I would be honored to try but made no promises to solve our problems. Since then I have spent at least one quarter of my time (my wife thinks it is closer to one half) in an effort to improve the cohesion of the Rutgers University community, in part through reducing prejudice and bigotry on campus.

At first, we called ourselves the "Committee on Human Relationships," but some people were uneasy with the connotations of that term. Maybe they feared that we would start running nude marathon groups or indulge in some of the other foolish excesses of the human potential movement. In any case, we are now known as the "Committee to Advance Our Common Purposes," a title that sounds more grand than any of our accomplishments to date can justify, but it strikes the right note in several ways. Instead of stressing our problems, we move toward opportunities. Instead of emphasizing our conflicts, we emphasize the common goals we all share. The title expresses the well-known principle that the best possible way to unite people with competing interests is to get them working together in attaining superordinate goals.

The Committee to Advance Our Common Purpose

The committee is composed of about 20 members, including the president and me. Representatives were chosen from several administrative offices, including the offices of the vice president for student affairs, the vice president for minority affairs, the vice president for personnel, the provost, and the deans of some of the undergraduate colleges. Faculty were chosen to extend minority representation, as well as for their known interests and experience. The first year, I packed the committee with several community psychologists from our school because we needed their technical knowledge, but this year I have asked some of those people to retire from the committee to make room for broader representation from other units. No one objected to relief from a committee assignment, and the community psychologists in our school continue to perform essential services as staff consultants.

I have felt considerable pressure to enlarge the committee to include currently underrepresented constituencies, but I have never seen a committee larger than 20 members function effectively as a work team, however it might appear as a political organization, so I have resisted pressures to expand. A parallel student committee to advance our common purposes was established at the same time the faculty and staff committee was formed, and the chair of that committee serves as liaison between the two groups. The committee meets as a whole only two or three times each year to set general directions and define policy. A smaller executive committee meets much more frequently to manage operations and deal with the inevitable crises that arise in activities of these kinds.

Community needs assessment. Our charge included several specific responsibilities as well as a very general mission. First among the specific responsibilities was the needs analysis, or community assessment, that I had offered to help conduct. When consulting firms are brought in to do this job, they usually begin with some surveys, and proceed with interviews to see what people say is going on. Then they write a report, receive a fee, and move on to the next job. When an organization is in serious turmoil, when anger and distrust are running high, it is probably wise to seek outside consultation of this kind, because the outsiders are more likely than any group of insiders to be seen as objective and politically neutral. Of course they are neither of those. In my view, objectivity is a myth, and so is political neutrality. So if an inside group can be composed that has no obvious stake in anything except finding out what is going on and trying to improve conditions, it may be possible to maintain a measure of political credibility, save some money, and at the same time institutionalize an assessment and monitoring operation that is built into the structure of the organization.

I have avoided the kinds of attitude surveys that are often used for needs analyses and are the most commonly used procedures for research on prejudice, such as the F-Scale (Adorno, Frenkel-Brunswick, Levinson, & Sanford, 1950) and the social distance scales (Bogardus, 1928). Those instruments might show that engineers admit to more racism than social workers, for example, but I see little value in that kind of information, except to provide grist for the theory-driven research mill. In *Assessment for Decision* (Peterson & Fishman, 1987), my co-editor and I present an alternative technological paradigm that emphasizes helping people (rather than serving the needs of the assessors) as the central purpose of assessment, linking assessment with change in a systematic, thorough-going way, and studying psychosocial functions by multiple procedures, in natural settings, as a process over time.

Fishman and Neigher (1987) laid out a generic five-stage sequence of operations that can be used in designing assessment systems for any kind of biopsychosocial system, from the rehabilitation of stroke victims to the operation of a community mental health center. In practice, the ideal paradigm can rarely be followed with perfect rigor. In Fowler's (1987) Alabama prison project, for example, where he and a team from the University of Alabama reclassified all the inmates in the Alabama prison system, the methodology was constrained by a court order and the political realities of the state correctional system. When Hackman and Helmreich (1987) set out to assess the team performance of aircraft crews, in order to reduce the risks of deadly crashes, they were limited not only by the inherent complexity of the problem but also by the political restrictions of the pilots' union. Under the real-life, real-time conditions of practical assessment, one simply does as well as one can, and in some cases, such as Paul's (1987) methodology for assessing staff and resident performance among severely disturbed patients in mental institutions, the results can be impressively dependable and useful.

No one who contributed to *Assessment for Decision* (Peterson & Fishman, 1987), nor anyone anywhere else so far as I know, has attempted thorough, decision-focused assessment of a university community with special reference to racial, sexual, and religious prejudice, although the consulting groups that make a living doing this kind of thing have worked out some interview and survey procedures that are not without merit. I spent a great deal of my own time last year interviewing people, mainly administrators who had also been faculty members and had been at Rutgers for a long time, to get an idea of the lay of the land and, at the same time, to bring the issues we were confronting more sharply into focus among some people in positions to support our programs in the long run. I asked each person three general questions: (a) From your position and in your experience, what do you see as the main expressions of prejudice, discrimination, or bigotry on this campus? (b) What do you see as the main conditions that produce and maintain these expressions? (c) What do you think we ought to do about it? Many interesting replies were voiced, and some patterns began to take shape. I cannot describe specifics in this brief chapter, but reports are listed among the references to this volume (i.e., Committee to Advance Our Common Purposes, 1988b, 1988c).

This year, we will send out teams of interviewers to meet with the leaders of student organizations, in their home territories, to hear their answers to these three questions, as well as some other questions. This is not an easy task, and it is politically volatile. There are 625 registered student organizations at Rutgers. Some are politically active, some less so, but they all have an agenda of some kind, and prior decisions about which groups to see and how to match interview teams with the various constituencies is an interesting challenge in its own right. Among the politically active groups, anyone who is not seen first is likely to feel offended. We need to ask people what they think should be done to improve the social and educational climate of the university, but we must be careful about raising expectations unrealistically or making promises that cannot be kept.

The routine we have worked out is described in another statement listed in the references to this volume (Committee to Advance Our Common Purposes, 1988a). It includes a lot more than just getting out into the community to encourage group catharsis. We have tried to construct a procedure that will bring the students' views and suggestions to the administration for such action as may be feasible and constructive, and then another meeting to provide feedback to each student group following whatever action we may take. There is no such thing as "no response" to a proposal or demand. No response *is* a response, and we need to be accountable for it. In the longer run and at a deeper level, we hope to establish new lines of communication among students, faculty, and administration, so that people who claim that "nobody listens" to them will have somebody readily available to listen and help whenever possible. In all this, we need to be sensitively mindful of the risks of offending or getting in the way of others with official responsibility, such as deans of students and officers in charge of minority affairs, for doing the same kinds of things we will be doing. That is one of the reasons why I asked the overworked and underfunded staffs in these offices for their nominations of people who might help with the interviews.

Although I have some reservations about surveys, if well designed they can provide certain kinds of comprehensive, low-cost, and confidential information that cannot be obtained in any other way. Many surveys are to be found in the attitude research literature. For our purposes, we plan to modify an instrument prepared by the National Institute Against Prejudice and Violence and the Office of Human Relations at the University of Maryland at Baltimore (Erlich, Pincus, & Morton, 1987). One of the modifications will be a request for detailed reports of critical incidents of prejudicial expression along lines of the interaction record procedure that I developed originally for the study of marital interactions (Peterson, 1979a, 1979b). In the case of prejudicial expressions, we will ask for detailed, blow-by-blow, narrative accounts of incidents that people have experienced or observed. We want to know who did or said what, to whom, under what conditions, and to what effect, with full reports about the way people felt, thought, and acted as the episode ran its course.

This kind of naturalistic description of a process provides a better basis for preventive intervention than does the kinds of state or trait data that most attitude surveys provide. At the end of the interviews with student leaders, we shall ask them if they are willing to work with their organizations to provide the survey information we are seeking, and if we run the interviews right we should get a reasonably good response. Ultimately, our community assessment procedures should provide some key performance indicators, on-line, managed routinely by the University's Bureau of Institutional Research, to provide an early warning system for any troubles that may be brewing, to help identify targets for preventive or meliorative intervention, and to provide a running record of the patterns of prejudice that flow through our community as well as the effectiveness of the programs we are developing to improve the social and educational environment of the University.

Financial support. Besides needs analysis, our committee received another specific charge. Although I did not feel we were quite ready to do the job, the president initiated a grant program that offered financial support to students and student organizations for programs that promised to advance our common purposes. Forty-three applications came flooding in, from all three campuses of the university, from women's groups and men's groups, straight groups and gay groups, from Asian groups, Hispanic groups, Black–Hispanic coalitions, Jewish groups, and interfaith organizations. Within a very short time, our committee was required to manage the program, which demanded the definition of criteria and a technically sound, equitable, politically credible procedure for review. Competitive grant programs offer valuable incentives for cooperation, but they also carry the danger of offense among rejected applicants, and the risk that resentments will overbalance any gain to be had from the positive activities of favored beneficiaries. The community psychology class of our school, under the direction of Daniel Fishman, offered essential help in designing an effective review procedure, and in conducting a technical evaluation of each proposal.

Information clearinghouse. The committee was also charged with general responsibility for coordinating a wide range of related activities, all designed to move us toward pluralistic cohesion and reduced prejudice, but often initiated directly by the president or growing out of the grass roots activities of people elsewhere in the community. Coordination often comes to mean bureaucratic control. We do our best to avoid that. I made clear to everyone on our committee, and tried to show everyone else in the university who had any contact with us, that everybody who had sensible, constructive ideas for improving our community should not wait for any signal from us, but should go ahead on their own. We told people that our committee would appreciate being informed, we would advise if asked, and we would support where possible, but we did not want to be seen as another committee that everybody had to report to in order to get good things done. As a coordinating agency, a committee like ours can serve mainly as an informational clearinghouse for related programs, a few of which I will now mention.

One of the things that has to be done in any systematic effort to reduce prejudice is to improve multicultural education. We want to help men understand women better, Whites understand Blacks, Blacks understand Whites, heterosexual males understand lesbian women, everybody understand everybody else a little better than they did before they came to the university. We have a long way to go in this regard. As I get older, I am more and more impressed with how young our students are. Few of them lived through the civil rights movement, and many of them know next to nothing about it. For that matter, a shocking number of our students know next to nothing about our history of slavery and the Civil War. Changes in the curriculum are needed not only to reduce prejudice, but as a fundamental component of a sound college education.

But look out. Bloom (1987) and others have shown the dangers of sloppy liberalism in the design of curricula. And look out again. Faculty, not administrative committees, control curricula, so our committee cannot directly initiate a change in the educational canon. What we can do is encourage and support activities initiated by others. Last year, as an example, a member of our English Department obtained a grant to conduct a summer institute titled "Integrating Scholarship on Gender." The vice provost for undergraduate education suggested that teams of instructors in large undergraduate courses be encouraged to attend the institute, and our committee furnished financial incentives to faculty members to provide the necessary encouragement. The faculty members who attended report that basic changes have been made in the English composition courses that every Rutgers student is required to take, and in the large introductory courses in philosophy, political science, and psychology as well.

One often hears proposals for a required course in non-Western cultures to replace the Western civilization courses that many universities have required in the past. Contents based on cultural assumptions other than those of White, male, heterosexual, Judeo-Christians are usually suggested. So far, we have resisted the illusion that we can solve our main problems with a single course and have favored suffusion of basic courses in all pertinent disciplines with the substance and the spirit of multicultural understanding.

The model developed by the team on gender issues appears to be useful and lends itself readily to other aspects of diversity, such as race, class, sexual orientation, and ethnicity. The model also offers a means of approaching the very difficult issue of faculty development. To me, that is one of the toughest problems of all. I have yet to meet a faculty member who wants to be "developed." They think they already are developed. The idea of development by way of reducing an assumed prejudice is especially repugnant to many faculty. Most of them do not believe they harbor any prejudices, and the worst of them would be least receptive to any effort to relieve them of their biases. If, however, opportunities and incentives are offered to provide knowledge that will improve teaching skills, and in some cases provide new orientations and ideas for scholarly inquiry, at least some of the faculty will be attracted to the programs. Then, as word gets around about their marvelous courses and exciting research, other faculty members may be inspired to join the movement.

A similar challenge and a comparable strategy holds for staff development. We have to start working with secretarial staff, security police, dining hall supervisors, residence hall receptionists, custodial personnel, and other members of our complex work force if we hope to do any lasting good. However, this is also a tough problem. Police are tired of being told they are not "sensitive" enough and are scornful of the kinds of workshops that have often been attempted in the past. Union problems and scarcity of resources also constrain us. I cannot say we have done anything substantial in examining, much less reducing, the levels and forms of prejudice among the staff of our university. As policy, the one clear agreement we have reached is that sensitivity needs to be taught as a tacit element of professional skill. Most people want to do their jobs well, and everybody wants to stay out of unnecessary trouble. So, if we can teach people skills that really help them perform more effectively, and support them as they learn, we all will be better off.

The most important program along these lines at Rutgers is an adult literacy program. Large numbers of our staff do not know how to read and write. Many of them are unwilling to admit that, either because they claimed otherwise when they took their jobs or because they cannot bear the humiliation that goes with the term *illiterate*. Comfortable ways must be found to bring these people into situations where they can gain some knowledge of general value to them, and without which any other kind of training we might attempt is either severely handicapped or doomed to failure.

Other activities. Many other activities in the general program on common purposes could be described in a longer narrative, but all I can do is mention them in this chapter. Active recruitment of minority faculty, administrators, and students is obviously essential to the success of our efforts. Aggressive recruitment programs have been in effect for many years at Rutgers, and in some respects our record is among the best in the country. Within professional psychology, the active initiatives of our ethnic minority alumni have been very important in bringing students into the school. Recruiting and retaining minority faculty has been a much more difficult job, and we cannot claim much success there.

A select committee on lesbian and gay concerns has been formed by the president. One of their members is on our committee, and I invited the chair of the select committee to report on their activities at the last meeting of the common purposes group. If they want any more help from us, we will do what we can to support them.

Next year marks the 20th anniversary of some serious turbulence at Rutgers that led to formation of the Equal Opportunity Fund and numerous other affirmative action programs. A planning group, of which some of our committee are members, has organized a major commemorative event for next spring. Students and faculty who were part of the process will discuss where we were, where we are, and where we need to go in confronting the social conditions that concerned us then and concern us still. A course called "Racism and Rutgers" is currently in progress and has drawn a large enrollment.

Conclusion

For his commencement address last spring, President Bloustein (1988) spoke on the topic "Community Service: A New Requirement for the Educated Person." He proposed that the campaign against bigotry be placed again at the center of our national agenda, and at the center of our university agenda as well. To do so, he said, required abandonment of the "shallow image of individualism," rediscovery of the satisfaction of caring for others, and the deliberate, systematic teaching of civic responsibility as a liberalizing art. Since then, he has formed still another committee, the Committee for Civic Leadership, that extends its membership throughout and beyond the university community. The program, housed in the university's Walt Whitman Center for the Culture and Politics and Democracy, is designed to encourage the students, faculty, and administrators of Rutgers to accept responsibility for improving the surrounding community of which they are a part. The work of the civic leadership group complements the work of the common purposes group, and several of us are active members of both organizations.

Community action, as every community psychologist knows, is not a peaceful pursuit. In an interesting way, our committee has gotten itself caught between the Rutgers Association for Zionism and Israel and some of the Palestinian groups on campus. I have suggested to both groups that they are unlikely to solve the problems on the West Bank by fighting with each other in New Brunswick, and now, on the initiative of some of the leaders of those groups, we have an opportunity to support a series of programs known as the "Israeli–Palestinian Forum."

We have seen some well-intentioned efforts backfire. The third session of a series of discussions on the "Roots of Racism" at one of our undergraduate colleges, was interrupted by a protest in which a large group of Black students slowly filed in, surrounded the audience, and demanded that the president explain why one of their counselors had been discharged. The president disclaimed any knowledge of the affair and declared that he would be unable, for reasons of confidentiality, to discuss the matter, even if he knew about the case. The students persisted in their demand, the president maintained his silence, and the meeting was finally adjourned by the faculty member who had arranged the series. I said nothing during the episode, but later responded to some questions from a newspaper reporter about my interpretation of the event. I was misquoted in a damaging way, and the paper did not print the correcting letter to the editor that I submitted the next day. The dean of the college and the assistant vice president for minority affairs met with the students for nearly two hours after the protest, and they tell me that some moves toward resolution have taken place but, as near as I can tell, the main effects of the incident have been further misunderstandings, a hardening of positions on both sides, and continuing resentment.

The president later invited leaders of some minority organizations to dinner at his home to hear what they had to say. The next day the leaders of some of those and other organizations wrote a letter of protest claiming that the meeting was nothing more than a public relations gesture, and that meeting over food and drink trivialized the serious issues the students wanted the administration to face. The president did not respond immediately. I decided on my own that an early reply was needed and wrote a soft answer to everybody who had signed the letter of protest, indicating that the meeting had been productive for those who attended, despite the misgivings of those who protested, and told the protesters of our plan for interviews and action next semester. By now, I may be in trouble not only with the students, who wanted an answer from the president, but with the president, for failing to clear my letter with him before sending it out.

So it goes. I have learned many lessons in the course of this effort. Everything I have learned is thoroughly discussed in the lore and literature of community psychology, but the following principles have new meaning for me now.

1. Our assessment strategy is sound, but assessing the function of a community is much easier to write about than to do.
2. Effective action based on the assessment is tougher still.
3. Even effective actions are sure to have unintended effects, some of which will be adverse.
4. Whenever you help somebody, somebody else will be offended.
5. Do not even think about a community action program unless you have firm

support from top administration and reasonable prior credibility in the community.

6. Even with full support and reasonable credibility, every action undertaken will meet with some resistance and will be misunderstood by somebody.

7. Reporters hardly ever quote anybody accurately.

8. There is not a damn thing you can do about that.

9. For all their problems, the challenges of community action are exciting and some are worthwhile.

10. Schools of Professional Psychology have special opportunities not only to celebrate diversity within their own organizations but to use their collective knowledge about human behavior in the service of the larger community.

Anyone who takes on a community program of the kind I have described will sooner or later be in strange and surprising circumstances. Last fall, I was asked to give a sermon at Kirkpatrick Chapel, the church on the campus of Old Queens where the Dutch Reformed students of Rutgers were once required, as a moral duty, to worship. To a secular psychologist like me, especially one whose religious views have sometimes been described as those of a fallen-away Unitarian, the invitation was a considerable challenge. I never had more trouble in my life preparing a talk. However, I finally got the sermon ready (Peterson, 1988), and I closed with a prayer.

Lord, let me find the light to see the world, in all its ugly sadness and all its beauty, through the eyes of my brothers and sisters.

Let me gain the sense to know the difference between outer appearance and inner reality, and to reach the common good in all people.

Let me have the heart to care for the loved ones of others as I care for my own. Amen.

6

CREATING AN INSTITUTIONAL CLIMATE THAT HONORS DIVERSITY

Connell F. Persico

California School of Professional Psychology
Los Angeles, California

Historical Overview

The assumption that, through education, citizens can develop the means of ensuring mobility and access to the power and control necessary to influence directly the course of their lives is fundamental to the existence of a democratic society. As the Industrial Revolution propelled the move from farms to urban areas, education was defined as the instrument by which the social, political, and economic needs of the society could be met (Newman, 1985; Vermilye, 1977). First, through compulsory elementary education, and on through the creation of the land grant colleges and universities, American society responded to changing priorities and populations by focusing on education as the means by which these changes could be understood, harnessed, and made productive.

After the end of World War II, higher education assumed a more critical role in meeting national objectives. In the postwar period, educational opportunities enabled returning veterans to reintegrate into a changed society. In the 1950s, education provided the science and engineering strength that enabled our society to create and maintain a level of affluence that supported the survival of democratic capitalism in a changed and often hostile world.

In the 1960s, several societal needs forced higher education to pursue conflicting priorities. As a surge in applications to colleges and universities developed, the funding of higher education shifted toward graduate-level, research-focused university programs (Newman, 1985). College students of this decade, the first postwar group of children old enough to attend college, reacted negatively to the elitism and the narrowing of concentration and opportunity inherent in these funding patterns.

The relevance of educational process and content to the values and ideological, political, economic, social, and cultural realities of the time were called into question by many. The fundamental issue was whether or not higher education would continue to be a vehicle by which citizens could gain access to, and share in, the burgeoning wealth of their society (Benson, 1968). Would educational opportunity for all be severely constrained by the need for control inherent in the creation of new technology, the need for loyalty inherent in the ideological struggle between democratic capitalism and communism, and the need for only a small number of competently trained technicians and leaders who would operate the new socioeconomic structures?

Evidence was rampant that, in fact, educational opportunities were being limited. Although increasing numbers of high school graduates were entering college, increasing numbers were also facing compulsory military service, unemployment, and poverty. The differences were most profound along racial lines. The college students of the 1960s began to challenge the questionable relevance and apparent elitism of the higher education system (Persico, 1974). Concurrent concerns articulated outside the educational establishment by leaders of the civil rights movement helped to nurture the concerns voiced from within higher education institutions. Those leaders asserted that American society was essentially racist; throughout its history, it had acted to deny equal opportunity to people of color by denying them the right to vote; it had withheld, from minorities, access to education that was available to the majority; and it supported oppression by allowing discrimination on the basis of race to remain a cornerstone of social policy (Persico & McEachron, 1971).

The efforts made in the 1960s and early 1970s to increase access to higher education and to alter its content and purpose provide the context within which one must address the current issue of creating an institutional climate that honors diversity. It is important to understand that one cannot create such a climate now without recognizing that, in the historical development of our institutions, there are no models. Thus we must act as pioneers. As the 1980s end, the access issues remain critical, and the content and purpose of the enterprise are still exclusive. We must lead the effort to alter the culture and consciousness of the higher education setting if we are to create institutions that support diversity.

Why Do We Need a New Institutional Climate?

The Climate of Traditional Institutions

As many major universities came to understand that their future and their development depended on generating scientific research to support governmentally determined objectives, university leaders organized their human and material resources to create a climate to support that scientific research. They recruited the best researchers they could find, forgave them teaching responsibilities, organized the political and community support necessary to support the higher levels of expenditure required, built laboratories, and recruited research assistants needed to accomplish the projects. They also redefined curricula to enable those who were students in this context to become degreed. Thus, a new form of institution with a new climate that supported this new culture and consciousness was created. Many, if not most, people who attended or who are now attending these institutions are not directly involved in the research activities. Yet, when people speak of or define these institutions, they are classified as major research universities. The climate of these institutions honors scientific research.

We also need to consider the undergraduate liberal arts college. Although many of its students may have specific career interests that are met through training curricula, the liberal arts college is usually known and supported for its focus on general education. Whereas some of its classes may possess the same impersonal qualities characteristic of the research university, the liberal arts college, nonetheless, is valued for its intimate climate as defined by the student–faculty relationship.

The research university and the liberal arts college do not create climates based on recognition of what the majority of their constituents do. Instead, climates are based on institutional recognition of social purpose and public responsibility to achieve that purpose. The research university creates a climate that enables it to play a role in ensuring that the society is technologically competent and current in areas that create public good (Newman, 1985). The liberal arts college defines itself as fulfilling a social need by educating questioning and challenging generalists, thereby offsetting the limitations of specialization.

The Climate of Culturally Diverse Institutions

There exists a social purpose and its corollary, apparent for 25 years in education, for which no supportive climate yet has been developed. The purpose is to create institutions that enable culturally diverse people to share in the knowledge, attitudes, and skills that are attainable only through education, and to enable them to do so without a loss of culture or self. The corollary is to redefine, as a consequence of the participation of a culturally diverse population in the educational process, the knowledge, skills, and attitudes to be shared.

Although this purpose was delineated in the 1960s, and efforts to support it were set in motion in the 1970s and 1980s, the society experienced both severe economic problems and lost confidence in the notion that education was a solver of social problems. As resources were trimmed back, so was the commitment to equal opportunity and access for all people. At all levels of education—elementary, secondary, baccalaureate, and graduate—the commitment to achieve higher levels of equality was de-emphasized as support funds and other resources for this purpose were reduced. In 1975–1976, minorities accounted for 7.9% of doctorates awarded, but in 1983–1984, they accounted for 5.5% of doctorates (Adams, 1988; Clewell, 1987). Equal opportunity, without a climate of support, declined in emphasis and priority. Today, the challenge goes far beyond the reallocation of resources. We need to create a culture and a consciousness that honors cultural diversity. Within such a climate, resources can and will be generated, found, and reallocated to ensure that the climate is maintained.

Why would schools of professional psychology (SPPs) undertake the creation of such a climate when other levels and kinds of institutions have tried and failed, and when such schools grant terminal degrees available only to those who have successfully completed all other levels of education? Why would SPPs want to alter their current climate (e.g., training competent therapists to deliver services in a long-term dynamic therapy mode) to create a climate honoring diversity? I suggest that the answer lies in the social purpose and public responsibility constructs. What social purpose is achieved by educating and training doctoral-level psychologists? We educate and train psychologists in order to ensure that a regular supply of competently trained clinicians is able to meet the mental health needs of the population. How do we accomplish this in a socially responsible way? We train our students in the current understanding of theory, application, and research, as well as the knowledge, skills, and attitudes that will enable them to respond in ethical and professional ways to the problems presented. We, in fact, certify to the public that our graduates will perform their responsibilities based on these standards.

Now, our population is so culturally diverse that in our lifetimes we will experience only the second period in American history when White people are not in the majority in the United States. As professional psychologists, we must certify ourselves to different people who have different standards of ethical and professional behavior and different performance expectations. If we are to meet our public responsibility, we must address the issues raised by this unprecedented diversity and we must alter our climates to honor the changes and consequences inherent in living within a diverse culture. Only then can we ensure that our students and our graduates will be able to deliver competent service to people in need.

Eight Steps to Creating a Diverse Institutional Climate

How does an institution go about creating a climate that honors diversity? Eight steps must be taken in order to ensure continuity of a climate in which early problems can be solved and the successes that follow can be maintained.

1. Establishing institutional commitment.
2. Creating a culturally diverse faculty.
3. Creating a culturally diverse administration.
4. Creating a culturally diverse student body.
5. Creating student–faculty support systems.
6. Generating financial aid funds.
7. Altering the core curriculum.
8. Preparing for the consequences of change.

Establishing Institutional Commitment

Clearly, the first step is the establishment of institutional commitment, because it provides the foundation for all else that follows. Institutional commitment requires policy, procedures, and agreements at all levels of decision making (i.e., the governing board, the administration, and the faculty) that establish that the institution wants to and will alter its population and programs so as to create an environment that reflects increased diversity. At a policy level, it requires an affirmative action policy that goes beyond the one published in catalogs. It is a policy that states that we will become diverse; therefore, all actions taken will be measured against a standard that requires regular gain in implementing the policy. It is a board-level procedure that requires administrators to report regularly on their progress. It is a faculty constitution revision that says that the faculty body must reflect the diversity that exists in the culture. Perhaps, most critically, institutional commitment is an agreement that nonachievement of the goal is unacceptable, and unanticipated consequences and unforeseen problems will not be resolved by the extant traditional processes.

There must be an acceptance of the premises that decision makers may act from bias and institutions may have elements of racism. This acceptance is not proposed to induce guilt, or to reduce standards, or to abrogate responsibility for achieving excellence. It is a plea to accept the role of learner—to consider that the basis for current response and action modes are based on an understanding of how our systems currently work and how the effects of our decisions are perceived and received. Remembering that our systems have been created based on monocultural premises and that our populations have reflected majority values, we must retest hypotheses and reexamine the assumptive bases for our strategies and decisions. The task is to use each situation arising from diversity as a potential learning situation in which the change inherent in the situation may be good for all members of the institution.

Consider a situation in which a minority faculty member complains about being asked to do double duty as faculty member and minority person. There are multiple ways to respond, such as (a) this is a plea for special treatment because the person is a minority, (b) this is normal overload near the end of a term, (c) doing more than desirable is a shared concern on the part of those most committed to helping the institution achieve its objectives, or (d) this is a resource allocation issue requiring serious attention. If the institution uses such a situation to examine and consider all the possibilities and responses in its institutional reality, it has taken a giant step toward creating a climate that honors diversity. Does the reward and promotion system work to enable those who give more to get more? Does the institution have effective means for coping with excessive stress? Does the institution critically review its expectations and accompanying resources? Do individuals who undertake extraordinary responsibilities receive special treatment?

The institution must identify and understand its reality before responding. The fact that a minority faculty member is treated like a majority faculty member is important. But, it is equally important that an issue, which originally arose specific to a minority faculty member, be considered in a broader context. If the faculty member is being asked to do more, amend the workload or provide more support. If the workload is more stressful, reduce the stress. If this faculty member has to be shown that the workload, although heavy, is common and a consequence of limited resources to support unlimited ambition, then show it.

Those who lead in creating the environment must suspend their accustomed processes and procedures. They need to reconsider the unique vantage point of the different or the minority, which can contain an important truth about the organization. Reacting defensively can obscure this truth and destroy the climate construction process itself.

Creating a Culturally Diverse Faculty

The second most critical aspect of climate development is faculty recruitment, retention, and development. As educators and trainers, the faculty defines the quality of our institutions. As in any developmental process within education, those who are to deliver the services and ultimately determine the environment are our faculty. Once the institutional commitment is made, the first arena in which the promise will become reality is in the selection of faculty.

In entering into the faculty selection process, it is wise to review (with as much objectivity as possible) the current state of hiring practices, the salary and benefit practices, and the state of planning around faculty development. If faculty hiring is in the hands of a few senior faculty, they must be imbued with the new commitment, or the hiring methodology must change. If current salary and benefit levels are not understood in relation to market conditions, competition for minority faculty will be at a distinct disadvantage. If there is no support for faculty development, obviously, newly hired minority faculty will be short-changed.

It is not necessary to restructure everything in order to create a climate that honors diversity. However, an institution must become critically aware of who and what it is, so that the newly hired faculty will fit into the environment and will not be given false illusions or false expectations. An old axiom of organizing for social and institutional change says, "You must start with people where they are." By design, superstars, extreme differences, or special treatment notions, are built-in promises of failure for any program.

The process of recruiting minority faculty involves a combination of different elements: (a) competition for a scarce resource with a limited budget, (b) an uncertain future, (c) a broadly fleshed out program, and (d) a serious commitment. It is most helpful to find a knowledgeable expert and respected mentor who will give guidance, support, and direction. To cite one example, James M. Jones and Joe Martinez initially were my mentors when they served as site visitors for the American Psychological Association (APA) Minority Fellowship Program. One of our students at the California School of Professional Psychology: Los Angeles (CSPP: Los Angeles) was a fellow, and they came to site visit. I shared with them our developing commitment and my need for faculty. Within one week, I had my first list of referrals, and within three months I was able to hire a bright young Hispanic faculty member who is now perhaps our best faculty member in the area of dissertation design and mentoring. Since then, CSPP: Los Angeles has hired an internal mentor.

In the early stages of minority faculty recruitment, it is critical to find an ally who, once convinced of the seriousness of institutional intent, will introduce the recruiters to the informal network. Once the minority faculty member is hired, it is important to acknowledge his or her uniqueness and provide a method through which he or she will be confident of support. In the early phase of building faculty, it is critical to remember that individuals who are in a significant minority often experience their environment as anywhere between nonsupportive to hostile, and because they do not have a critical mass they are not comfortable expressing their minority viewpoint. Therefore, until a critical mass does exist—Kanter (1977) said it occurs when minorities make up about 15%—certain and clear support of the development of that mass has to exist.

All aspects of the minority faculty hiring process must be carefully controlled. Faculty who display unusual insensitivity to their colleagues are best omitted from search committees, regardless of what claims to service they might have. Clear charges to committees must be made, clear criteria of acceptability must be stated, and adherence to the goals must be mandated. The first minority hired must soon see the next minority hired, and those two must soon be in a position to influence the next set of decisions. This is the way all programs are built, and cultural diversity should be no exception.

Creating a Culturally Diverse Administration

Creating a culturally diverse administration is necessary in and of itself and is critical to the stage of development following the establishment of a culturally diverse environment (where race, sex, class, or other socioeconomic variables are no longer relevant because a shared consciousness exists). Although it is acceptable and desirable to delegate responsibilities for the growth of minority programs to some minority faculty members, it is mandatory that minority administrators be part of the team that assumes institution-wide responsibilities. The administration must reflect the diversity being created in order to ensure that minority issues become institutional issues and that *each* member of the institutional community knows that his or her reality is part of the institutional reality. Equally important, a diversified administration serves as a role model for faculty and students. White men have always known leadership roles were possible. Women recently have begun to believe they are possible. Ethnic minorities are still trying to enter academia at the faculty level. Minority administrators demonstrate that leadership roles for minorities are possible and establish that competence and vision, not race, are the critical factors.

Creating a Culturally Diverse Student Body

The fourth essential element in establishing a climate that honors diversity (and on which institutions most often concentrate their first efforts) is the creation of a diverse student body. Consider for a moment the following construct. Minority students per se, or minority students who are qualified to meet standards, are a scarce resource. Therefore, competition to enroll the minority students will be intense and an institution may not want to or be able to compete. On the other side of the coin is the pool of minority college graduates who want to pursue further education and training. They consider graduate school to be a scarce resource and the competition to be stiff, and they may not want to or be able to compete.

How can we meet goals set for recruiting minority students? First, the notion of minority students as a scarce resource must be eliminated, and minority students must be defined as a plentiful and desirable resource. In 1982, there were nearly 2 million minority students enrolled in undergraduate programs (Newman, 1985). Second, the institution needs to learn how minority students behave vis-à-vis graduate education and training. Third, a marketing strategy that is designed to attract minority students must be developed. Most of what is presented here is based on what is known in the literature and in experience about attracting and retaining minority students (Adams, 1986; Atelsek & Gomberg, 1978; Banta et al., 1983; Clewell, 1987; Newman, 1985). Any institution that strategically plans for minority recruitment will meet its objectives. Although there is plenty of room for experimentation and variation in a student recruitment strategy, three elements—student—faculty support systems, financial aid, and curriculum—are important for all students and, thus, are important for minority students.

Creating Student–Faculty Support Systems

Because institutions developed out of the majority culture and serve to support that culture, support for majority students is endemic to the institution. Without thinking about it, majority students expect to find others like themselves, familiar rituals and processes, and a faculty who will understand the graduate experience and be willing to embrace the insecurity, anxiety, and despair that students know they will manifest. The minority student, as pioneer, dares not make such assumptions, and we, too, would be foolish to do so. If we accept support systems as natural institutional phenomena, and the natural state of our institutions is support of majority students, then we can create the special support systems required to enable minority students to pursue graduate education in the same fashion as majority students do. Two points need to be clarified. First, although special support systems are required, they are not extra or extraordinary. They are a necessity in order to create equal conditions so that all students operate from the same level of advantage. Second, the support systems must be managed by people from the minority experience so that they are designed to respond to the unique cultural, social, educational, and psychological experiences of minority students.

Generating Financial Aid Funds

The institution must be able to help fund minority students throughout their education. As Newman (1985) noted:

> The rate of persistence and completion of a degree for students with heavy loans is lower than for students who receive other forms of student aid. . . . Minority students, in particular, are less likely to use loans and therefore less likely to enter or stay in college. (p. 77)

As all majority students do not need full support, all minority students will not need full support. As some majority students are willing to invest a portion of their future earnings in current educational pursuits, so are minority students. And, as institutions have always been able to find those extra dollars to attract particularly desirable majority students, so the institution can allocate resources to support its commitment to attract desirable minority students. An institutional commitment of specific funds to support minority students is a clear indicator of purpose and intent.

California School of Professional Psychology, which has historically committed a percentage of tuition revenue to a general scholarship fund, found it logical to increase that percentage and specifically earmark the increase for minority students. The logic was simple: The institution is committed to recruiting minority students, and recruitment of minority students historically has been the school's most difficult problem; therefore, additional resources must be allocated in order to redress the problem. Remember, resource allocation is the clearest indicator of actual institutional commitment.

Altering the Core Curriculum

The creation of a new climate must occur in the curriculum arena because it is here that personal experience, theory, tradition, and thinking all interplay, adjudicate, and educate. The biggest challenge to environmental restructuring is inherent in curricula change. Tension always resides in curricula. How does a curriculum define what is known? What part of what is known is to be formally taught? In what ways can what is unknown be addressed? Within the framework of the majority perspective, these issues are not resolved completely because the knowledge base is too broad and too deep to be reduced to a curriculum. When we add the minority perspective, which at its best challenges basic theoretic assumptions and modes of practice, we have problems of sizable proportions. There are no definitive curricula that encompass the minority perspective. Curricular models for integrating some minority content into core courses have been developed, specific and discrete courses about minorities have been developed, and combinations of these and others have been developed, yet they are always additive or correcting.

At a minimum, it is necessary to the climate creation process that minority perspectives be given credibility and potency in the curriculum. Space must be allocated in the core curriculum for minority issues and points of view. Fertile ground exists to create a program that starts from the premise that the curriculum must flow out of a synthesis of majority and minority experience, theory, and practice. Such an undertaking would enable the discipline to better articulate the ferment currently underlying conflicting demands for curricular reform.

Preparing for the Consequences of Change

There is no easy way to prepare for the consequences of change in institutional climate. The institution, as we have known it, will be different. People will know, understand, and behave differently from you. They will wonder why you do what you have always taken for granted. They will want things you do not want, and ask for things you do not want to give. You will have to remember that you want your institution and this society to be different. You will have to constantly return to value levels to assess your own feelings and attitudes in respect to the issues that come before you. You must confront new issues and forms of politics, ethics, collegiality, and loneliness on a daily basis. Remember, too, loss of will and a desire to return to more comfortable and secure ground historically have been the sources of failure in efforts to create new climates.

A truly integrated society, and even truly integrated institutions, do not exist. The task before us is to follow the image Sarason (1972) invoked in *The Creation of Settings and the Future Societies*. We must move into new uncharted waters and pull the old institution along. We have to be comfortable, standing firmly in nothing but our will and commitments, in creating a new institution that enables everyone to share in the knowledge that empowers them to create a healthy and supportive new society.

We have to create the new setting that supports and honors cultural diversity because the degree and kind of social change occurring demands it. We are faced with the need to do this, together. No matter how good a single institution may be in creating an appropriate climate, its singularity will ultimately doom it to failure. We know that minority issues and needs do not get addressed until there is a critical mass of minorities within an institution. And, we know that until a critical mass of institutions commits to creating a climate, that climate will not exist in any one place with any permanence. Until the new support systems, until the new faculties, until the new curricula, and until the financial support is collectively massed, any and all of our efforts will be precarious. Yet, it is time to start and to start with the knowledge that it is an achievable objective. Let that achievable task continue to shape the agenda of the National Council of Schools of Professional Psychology.

7

INSTITUTIONAL CHANGE AND LEADERSHIP: CHALLENGES IN EDUCATION

Salvador Santiago-Negrón
Caribbean Center for Advanced Studies
San Juan, Puerto Rico

Minority Rights in the Last Three Decades

If we take a glimpse at the historical evolution of minority civil rights in America in the last three decades, we can conclude, without hesitation, that progress has been achieved. There is no doubt that real access to opportunities for minorities has been enhanced. The times when a member of a minority constituency was the first to be accepted into an institution of higher education seem to be in the distant past, yet it was only as recently as the mid-1960s that opportunities for minority members started to expand as a result of civil rights activism.

There seems to be a consensus among scholars that the American community, as a whole, is becoming a more mature, civil, and tolerant society. Although significant pockets of institutional prejudice still exist, the long-term direction of change toward real equality of opportunity continues to develop in spite of the apparent stagnation of the recent years. The collapse of the Jim Crow institutions in the 1960s, the proliferation of minority city mayors in geographic areas that seemed untenable two decades ago, and the acceptance of minority leaders in cities such as Birmingham, Richmond, Atlanta, Chicago, Los Angeles, Philadelphia, and Miami are examples of the direction that social change has taken toward more tolerance and pluralism. According to Blumberg (1980):

> *Even the ever-vigilant, never-complacent American Civil Liberties Union said in its sixtieth anniversary in 1980 that "... it is fair to say that we have won many important victories and established many new rights during our first sixty years. There is more liberty today than there was in 1920, and more people have more rights now than they did then." (p. 16)*

Undoubtedly, this statement can be extrapolated to the 1980s as compared to the

1970s, for we can say decidedly that we enjoy more civil liberties today than we did 10 years ago.

The National Council of Schools of Professional Psychology (NCSPP) devoted its midwinter 1988–1989 Puerto Rico conference to the pursuit of ways in which educational opportunities for minority constituencies can be improved. This effort was undertaken at a time when the organization was hard pressed to attend to other pertinent issues, such as the formulation of a response to the challenge of the National Conference on Graduate Education and Psychology (American Psychological Association, 1987). NCSPP's actions can be construed as an indication of today's zeitgeist, a strong undercurrent that is influencing our generation to turn the American fantasy of maximized opportunities for all into an attainable reality.

The 1960s and the 1970s brought a new awareness of the need to help bootstrap our minority constituencies into the arena of full participation in all the essential affairs of our society. Unfortunately, the 1960s and the 1970s also left us without a clear articulation of the concrete challenges that we have to face in the quest for greater accessibility to higher education for minorities. Thus the decade of the 1980s has challenged us to reexamine our current ability to maximize the human potential of our society, including our ethnic communities, in view of our diminishing competitive edge in the international arena. What are the present challenges? What are the most appropriate ways in which we can respond to the challenges without jeopardizing our quest for excellence? How can we organize our collective energies to target the present challenges? What kind of leadership do we need in order to maximize our performance as agents of social change? What concrete activities do we have to undertake as leaders of our respective universities to provide impetus to the need for widening the door of our organizations to optimize the accessibility to higher education for minorities?

Governmental Budgetary Constraints and Minority Education

The issue of attaining ethnic diversity in higher education, in an era when the nation is faced with a mammoth budgetary deficit, poses a tremendous challenge to our generation. Following World War II, American society was rich enough to afford huge expenditures both in military and educational activities. Currently, however, as a direct result of the largest deficit in the trade balance in the history of the country, budgetary priorities are being rearranged as special interest groups compete for pieces of the smaller pie. As educators, we will have to voice our concern so that military expenditures are not made at the expense of cuts in the education budget.

There is concern that attempts to balance the national debt at the expense of education will pose a security issue in that we risk eroding our competitive edge vis-à-vis the lack of adequately prepared human resources. One dramatic illustration of how our competitive edge is eroding can be observed in the field of engineering. Consider the numbers of engineers graduated on the average each year in the following countries: Japan—72,000; France, the United Kingdom, and the Federal Republic of Germany (FRG)—31,000; the United States—78,000; and the Soviet Union—325,000 (American Council on Education, 1983). Thus the Soviet Union graduated almost twice as many engineers as did Japan, France, the United Kingdom, the FRG, and the United States combined—and more than four times as many engineers as the United States alone. The impact of further cuts on educational budgetary allocations

Figure 1
Projected Minority School-Age Population

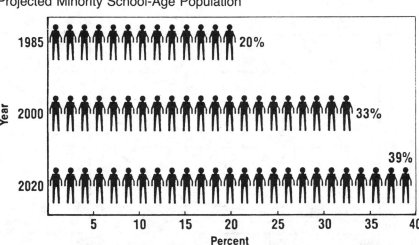

Note. From *Current Population Reports* (Series P-25, No. 1022, Table 1: 12 and No. 955, Table T: 14). Washington, DC: U.S. Bureau of the Census.

will be felt more intensely by minority populations due to the already scarce resources available to them.

Minority Demographics and Educational Opportunities

The School-Age Population

An analysis of the minority constituencies' current potential for achieving access to higher educational opportunities seems warranted. Ethnic minorities are defined as groups of people who, for reason of race or national origin, have been barred from full participation in our educational system. Blacks, Hispanics, Asians, and Native Americans are these constituencies. The Commission on Minority Participation in Education and American Life, sponsored by the American Council on Education (1988), reported that gaps still persist or are widening between members of the minority groups and the majority population in areas such as employment, income, health, longevity, education, and other basic measures of well-being. Furthermore, they stated that the minority population will soon constitute one third of the nation's total population.

The current U.S. census indicates that 14% of adults, and 20% of children under 17, are Black, Hispanic, Native American, or Asian American. At present, in 25 of the nation's largest cities, one half or more than one half of all public school students are minority group members. Figure 1 shows the nationwide trend toward greater concentrations of minority students in our public school system. By the year 2000, 33% of all American public school students will be minority children.

The Labor Force

The Commission on Minority Participation in Education and American Life (American Council on Education, 1988), stated that "between 1985 and the year 2000 the

Figure 2
Projected Number of Social Security Beneficiaries per 100
Covered Workers

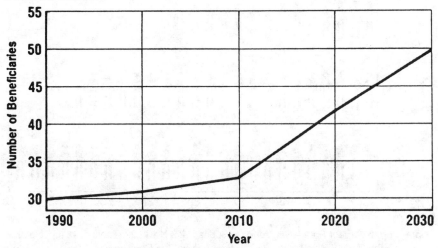

Note. From *1988 Annual Report of the Board of Trustees of the Federal Old-Age and Survivors Insurance and Disability Insurance Trust Funds* (Table 30:80), 1988, Washington, DC.

minority workers will make up one-third of the net additions to the U.S. labor force" (p. 3). Furthermore, Social Security projections indicate that, over the next four decades, increasingly more retirees will be supported by the Social Security contributions of increasingly fewer workers. As is shown in Figure 2, by the year 2030 there will be 50 retired beneficiaries per 100 workers currently contributing to Social Security, as compared to the year 1987 when there were 30 retired beneficiaries per 100 workers currently contributing to Social Security. According to Hodgkinson (1985), in 1950, there were 17 workers paying the benefits of each retiree. However, it is expected that, by 1992, there will only be three workers providing funds for each retiree. It is estimated that one of the three will be a minority member.

If this demographic profile is accurate, it is in the self-interest of all Americans to improve substantially minority citizens' competence, education, employability, and earning power. Only by addressing this plight can we hope to provide the income support and health care needs of the future aging population. If we do not raise the educational level of minority constituencies, the leading role of America as an industrial colossus is doomed.

College Students

If we examine the patterns of college entrance and study the economic and social class origins, we can observe that the low-income working class, in which the incidence of minority members is high, reports the lowest percentage of college entrants. As is shown in Figure 3, the 1986 U.S. Bureau of the Census reported that approximately 15% of full-time college students between the ages of 18 and 24 years came from families with an annual income of less than $10,000. The percentage of college students from families with higher incomes was significantly greater than of students who came from lower socioeconomic backgrounds.

In 1970 there were almost six times as many college entrants from upper- and

Figure 3

Percentage of Families with One or More Members 18 to 24 Years Old Attending College Full Time By Income Level

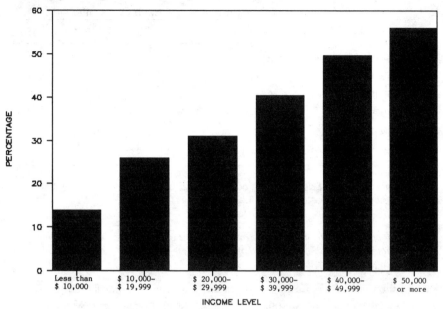

Note. From "School Enrollment Social and Economic Characteristics of Students: October 1986" by the U.S. Bureau of the Census, (in press), *Current Population Reports* (Series P. 20), Washington, DC: U.S. Government Printing Office.

upper-middle-class families than there were college entrants from lower income working-class families. The high incidence of potential, but not enrolled, college minority students from lower class families is one of the hurdles that the government, the private sector, and the educational institutions will have to overcome if we want to make educational opportunities a viable alternative for minority constituencies. It is important to remember that the best predictor of employment is high educational achievement.

Graduate Students

What is the current status of minority group enrollment in graduate and professional schools? In 1984, according to the Office of Civil Rights (U.S. Department of Education, 1976–1986),

Overall, minority enrollment in graduate and professional schools appears to have peaked in about 1976–77. Gains made after this date, have begun to suffer some erosion. ... Information on minority groups indicates their substantial underrepresentation in graduate and professional schools. Non-Black minorities comprise 5.2

Table 1
Social Class Origins of College Entrants, 1920–1970

	Percentage of Each Class Attending				
Social Class	1920	1940	1950	1960	1970
Upper and upper-middle	40	70	75	80	88
Lower-middle	8	20	38	45	64
Upper-working	2	5	12	25	40
Lower-working	0	0	2	6	15
% of total age group entering college	6	16	22	33	47

Note. From *Society and Education* (4th ed., Table 5.2, p. 93) by R. J. Havighurst and B. L. Neugarten, 1975, Boston: Allyn & Bacon.

> *percent of all graduate enrollments and 5.0 percent of first professional enrollments. The relative number of minority students entering the graduate arts and sciences has declined steadily since the mid-seventies. (p. 21)*

Table 2 shows the 1984 enrollment of graduate students by ethnicity as prepared by the U.S. Department of Education; 86% of all graduate students were White, whereas all other groups combined constituted 14% of all graduate students.

The Carnegie Foundation for the Advancement of Teaching (1987) reported that the proportion of minorities in higher education, with the notable exception of Asians, does not reach the level of their presence in the population. The disparity is likely to increase, as population projections indicate that the number of minorities in the American population will continue to grow. Frank H. T. Rhodes, president of Cornell University and chair of the Commission on Minority Participation in Education and American Life, (American Council on Education, 1988) said, "bringing the minority

Table 2
Enrollment of U.S. Graduate Students by Ethnicity, 1984

Ethnicity	Number Enrolled	Percentage Enrolled
White	216,339	86.0
Black	11,298	7.1
Nonresident alien	10,471	2.5
Asian	7,048	1.5
Hispanic	4,844	2.5
Native American	529	0.4
Total	250,529	100.0

Note. Data are from *Minority Enrollment in Graduate and Professional Schools* by U.S. Department of Education, 1984, Washington, DC: U.S. Office for Civil Rights.

citizens into the mainstream of American life is a matter of basic social justice. It also is a matter of national survival" (p. 6). In other words, if educational opportunities are not significantly enhanced for minority constituencies, the future of the minority and the majority populations are at stake. For most of us, opening new options in the area of higher education for minorities is a need that cannot wait until the 21st century.

Opportunities for the Future

In contrast to the stagnation of minority college enrollment, the 1988 Higher Education Panel Report of the American Council on Education (El-khawas, 1988) indicated that the general enrollment picture for American colleges and universities has been a positive one throughout the 1980s, despite predictions to the contrary. Demographers had predicted lower enrollment as the baby boom generation passed the age of becoming potential college students. Nevertheless, El-khawas (1988) surveyed a total of 372 university centers and reported the following:

1. *The majority of institutions—54 percent—had net increases in enrollment since 1980.*
2. *Progress regarding enrollment of minority students was quite modest in 1987–88: about* one in four *institutions had increased their enrollment of Blacks, Hispanics, or Asian students.*
3. *Two thirds of campus administrators rated their institution's performance in attracting minority students as "fair" or "poor." (p. 1)*

According to a survey of 367 colleges and universities, conducted by the American Council on Education (1988), college administrators identify the main challenges for the next five years as follows:

1. How to strengthen the curriculum.
2. How to implement effective assessment of programs.
3. How to maintain program quality with limited resources.
4. How to serve new needs and populations. (However, only *1 in 10 institutions* specified improvement in racial and ethnic diversity as one of the most important challenges in the years ahead.)

This survey indicates that the need to incorporate racial diversity into our institutions of higher learning is only superficially acknowledged by academic leaders. Failure to develop skill-building assets in minority populations ignores an important human resource and reduces America's ability to compete economically with other developed nations.

The Academic Agenda for the Leadership of the Next Decade

NCSPP

Because only 1 in 10 higher learning institutions considers improving racial and ethnic diversity as a priority, the need for a leadership role in the patriotic mission of making the field of higher education a viable alternative for all minority constituencies has arisen. In order for leadership to be effective, it must follow these steps:

1.   Identify collective needs.
2.   Promote awareness of perceived needs in groups of interest that are being affected by them.
3.   Translate needs into challenges to be tackled by a constituency powerful enough to satisfy them.

NCSPP has the potential for assuming institutional leadership in the quest for expanding racial and ethnic diversity in institutions of higher learning.

NCSPP has already processed step 1 by identifying its collective need as the improvement of ethnic diversity in the field of higher education. It is currently working on step 2 by promoting awareness among the groups of interest that are being affected by the perceived need, that is, the disenfranchised traditional minority population, as well as the majority population. The agenda of NCSPP's Puerto Rico conference is an example of its commitment to raise the level of national awareness of the need for improved ethnic diversity in higher education.

Another way for NCSPP to promote national awareness is to influence the priorities that make up the agendas of the majority of the higher education institutions. This can be done by appealing to the accrediting institutions that regulate academic activities. As part of assuming a leadership role, NCSPP should pose the following challenge to the accrediting national bodies: *Diversity* among college students, among university faculty and administrators, and among the curricular contents is crucial for achieving excellence in the American educational system. Achieving institutional excellence without addressing the needs of minorities is tantamount to an inconclusive agenda in the field of higher education.

Conservative leaders such as Hirsch (1987) and William Bennett have contributed significantly to the idea that the quest for excellence alone should be the main goal of our educational system. This tunnel view might have contributed to the present stagnation in outreach, admissions, and retention of minority groups that we are facing in our educational system. We have to change the proportion of higher education institutions interested in improving ethnic diversity within their campuses from 1 in 10, as the American Council on Education (1988) reported, to at least 9 in 10, before the end of this century.

If the Puerto Rico conference achieves the second step—the promotion of national awareness—step 3—the powerful constituency's satisfaction of the identified needs—should follow. In this instance, it is increasing minority access to higher education. Step 3 will be easier to achieve if NCSPP develops task forces that will extend the efforts initiated in the Puerto Rico conference and begin to influence the influencers. These influencers are the large constituency of accrediting bodies that regulate the higher education institutions across the nation.

Addressing the plight of minorities by partially opening the door, by admitting an insignificant number into institutions of higher education, was labeled as tokenism in the 1960s. Tokenism emerged as a way of publicly expressing institutional concern from a conservative perspective. This was the way of unilaterally helping *them* and never thinking that in that fashion, we were helping *us*. The psychology of *them* versus *us* has become old-fashioned now that the whole nation is at stake if we do not address the educational needs of the less privileged members of our society. This time we have to go beyond tokenism if we want to achieve the goal of maintaining a competitive edge as an industrial power in the world.

Academic Institutions

The leadership of the 1990s can be conceptualized in two fundamental dimensions: the individual and the collective. At the individual level, the leaders of the 1990s will have to go beyond the tendency to indict the system as a whole and to start visualizing ways in which to develop different networks of people and institutions that will join forces to enhance the potential for increasing outreach, admissions, and retention of minorities in all the higher education institutions of America. The creation of think-tanks in the area of outreach, recruitment, and retention of minorities in our educational system is the most crucial agenda for the formidable challenge that we are facing before this century ends. These think-tanks should address the need to develop institutional support systems for the potential minority candidates whom our collective efforts might entice to enter college or pursue a career in psychology.

We have to create think-tanks to develop new ways to improve outreach, recruitment, and retention of minority members in the area of higher education, and also to devise strategies for anticipating the reactions that those in positions of power might exert to slow the movement toward diversity. The recommendations reported in "Minority Enrollment in Graduate and Professional Schools" (U.S. Department of Education, 1984) are good examples of what think-tanks can accomplish if given opportunities to function. Culler and Diaz-Guerrero (cited in Ramisey, 1983) used a definition of support systems that is more inclusive than those used in previous research. They refered to this expanded support network as the "webwork." The webwork is composed of people, organizations, institutions, and an ambiance conducive to collective support for an increased integration of minority constituencies in the field of higher education. The concept of webwork seems to be a useful tool for conceptualizing how the leadership of the 1990s will have to move in order to achieve success in increasing the number of minority students in the area of higher education, and for ensuring that the survival rate of those already enrolled improves substantially.

The webwork approach can be used by individual academic institutions to identify and make an inventory of what constitutes sources of support for the different minority student groups that it intends to recruit to its campus. Not all minority groups respond in the same fashion to different support systems. Thus each institution needs to do its own research among its faculty members, administrative personnel, student body, and potential minority students to identify support systems that will enhance the probabilities that admitted minority students will have a fair fighting chance to overcome barriers to the successful completion of their studies.

Permanent institutional committees that address the issues of outreach, admission, and retention of minority students, with appropriate adjustments of the work loads of the members of such committees, are essential if we want to succeed in the challenge of increasing diversity in higher education. According to the U.S. Department of Education (1984), "Minority recruitment programs should be institutionalized so that they have the same legitimate status as other viable university programs" (p. 46). One may add that this principle also applies to outreach and retention efforts. College presidents need to validate the importance of these committees by organizing them under their direct jurisdiction. Such appointments give the committees the necessary leverage and prestige needed within the institution to do an efficient job, and they also provide committee members with needed visibility to exert influence on other webwork members.

As part of the webwork needed to sustain the path toward ethnic diversity, there must be minority representation at all levels of the university infrastructure, including the board of trustees. The available psychological literature has provided ample evidence of the importance of role models for our minority students. Ethnic diversity in the board of trustees is critical in developing and supporting permanent institutional policies that specify minority representation at all levels of institutional life. If we want to immerse our institutions of higher education in a significant commitment toward tackling the issue of ethnic diversity, we have to have impact on their organizational structure at four levels:

1. The appointment of minority members to boards of trustees or to the governance bodies of the institutions.
2. The hiring of minority members at the administrative level (from middle management up).
3. The hiring of minority members at the faculty level.
4. The implementation of a long-range plan for outreach, admissions, and retention of minority students.

The Commission on Minority Participation in Education and American Life, in its landmark report, "One Third of a Nation," (American Council on Education, 1988, pp. 21–28) presents seven challenges that, if taken seriously by all leaders of our educational institutions, will result in major changes in the representation of ethnic diversity on American campuses. These challenges are paraphrased as follows:

1. For America's institutions of higher learning to renew and strengthen their efforts to increase minority recruitment, retention, and graduation;
2. for national leaders to identify and implement policies to stimulate economic growth and restore national solvency;
3. for the nation's elected officials to lead efforts to ensure minority advancement;
4. for private and voluntary organizations to initiate new and expand existing programs designed to increase minority participation and achievement;
5. for each major sector of our society to contribute to a new vision of affirmative action around which broad national consensus can be formed;
6. for minority public officials, institutions, and voluntary organizations to expand their leadership roles; and
7. for education leaders to improve coordination and cooperation among all levels and systems.

Schools of Professional Psychology

Because of their administrative agility and flexibility, schools of professional psychology (SPPs) are in an excellent position to consider the seven challenges just outlined. Furthermore, they are less prone to suffer from the classic inertia that is created by the complex bureaucracies usually present in big organizations. Among SPPs, one key concept is the use of pooled resources in order to accelerate particular projects of mutual interest. Faculty and student interchange is only one of myriad projects that can be developed to enhance ethnic diversity in respective campuses.

The promotion of linkage with historically minority colleges and schools seems of particular importance, because of their privileged position of accessibility to a larger than usual pool of minority students and professionals. Accessibility to their pool of graduates provides a unique opportunity to extend a hand to an incipient professional. The possibility of creating faculty trainee positions for young graduates provides career opportunities for minority graduates and opportunities for faculty diversification for the institution. Sharing resources or providing financial or technical help to these historically minority schools and colleges is a feasible plan than can be implemented immediately.

The record of educating minority professionals by ethnic minority institutions is significant when compared with typical higher education establishments. The Caribbean Center for Advanced Studies, a historically Hispanic school of professional psychology, has graduated more Hispanics with doctorates in psychology than have most graduate schools in America. Through August 1986, this institution has graduated 612 Hispanic students in both its masters and doctoral programs. Through August 1988, The Caribbean Center has graduated 154 Hispanic students in its doctoral program alone, far exceeding the record of any other psychology program in either the United States or Puerto Rico. It is noteworthy that the average cost of training 154 students in an SPP is equivalent to the cost of a single missile sold by the Reagan administration to the Ayatollah in Iran.

If the goal for the educational leaders is to increase accessibility of minority members to our educational system at all levels, the financial aspects of this agenda will have to enter into consideration at a national level. It is important to recognize that the conservative message will stress quality and accountability as the only legitimate issues in academe, a message that could prevent the necessary budgetary allocations that are needed to increase diversity in our educational system from being made part of the national agenda.

We should be prepared to present the message that without diversity, quality, and accountability are incomplete ingredients for facing the challenges that we will have to endure as a nation that wants to keep a competitive edge in the 21st century. Without ensuring appropriate diversity in higher education, our national security will be at stake. We should insist that quality, accountability, and *diversity* is the trilogy needed to achieve justice and security for all in America.

8

BARRIERS TO MINORITIES IN THE FIELD OF PSYCHOLOGY AND STRATEGIES FOR CHANGE

Evelyn Diaz

Caribbean Center for Advanced Studies
Miami, Florida

Minority Students in Psychology

Underrepresentation of minority students in the field of psychology and in higher education in general is a fact of American life. Minorities constitute more than 20% of the population of the United States, but in 1984–1985 they earned only 7.9% of the doctoral degrees awarded in psychology (National Center for Education Statistics, 1988). As the minority population rapidly expands, this dramatic underrepresentation in psychology will have a progressively more serious effect on the capacity of psychology training institutions to meet the demand for culturally sensitive psychologists and culturally sensitive mental health services. In this chapter I review the status of Hispanics, Blacks, Asians, and Native Americans in the field of psychology during the 1980s. I then discuss the barriers that exist for minorities in the field of psychology in the United States, and recommend ways to provide access for this population to psychology and higher education.

Hispanics

According to Orum (1986), Hispanic Americans are at once the oldest and the newest immigrants to the United States. The U.S. Bureau of the Census has shown a steady growth in the Hispanic population from 9.1 million in 1970 to 14.6 million in 1980. There were nearly 16.9 million Hispanics in the United States in 1985. Hispanics represented 7.9% of the nation's mainland population in 1985 and are expected to increase to at least 11% by 2010 (Fields, 1988). Despite the dramatic growth of the Hispanic population in the continental United States, a serious gap and underrepresentation exists in higher education.

Table 1
Percentage of Psychology Degrees Earned by Minority Students
in all U.S. Institutions, 1984–1985

Race/Ethnicity	Percentage of Degrees		
	Bachelor's	Master's	Doctoral
Blacks	6.7	5.1	3.9
Hispanics	3.4	3.3	2.2
Asians	2.1	1.5	1.8
Native Americans	0.5	0.4	0.2
Whites	85.9	86.1	88.8

Note. Data are from *Racial/Ethnic Data for Fall Enrollment and Earned Degree Recipients* by National Center for Education Statistics, 1988, Washington, DC: U.S. Department of Education.

The National Center for Education Statistics (1988) presented significant statistics relating to degrees conferred in the field of psychology. As is seen in Table 1, Hispanics accounted for only 3.4% of the bachelor's, 3.3% of the master's, and 2% of the doctoral degrees in psychology during 1984–1985. According to the National Research Council (1987), as is shown in Table 2, Hispanics earned only 3.4% of all the doctorates in the areas of clinical, counseling, and school psychology in the nation in 1986. Furthermore, demographic research indicates that less than 2% of all psychologists in the United States are of Hispanic origin (Stapp, Tucker, & VandenBos, 1985). It is estimated that, from a total pool of 130,000 psychologists in the mainland during 1986, between 1,200 and 1,500 were Hispanics. Thus there were less than 1,500 Hispanic psychologists in the nation to serve a growing population of 16.9 million Hispanics. It is important to mention that the statistics just cited do not include the doctoral recipients of the Caribbean Center for Advanced Studies, a school of professional psychology (SPP) dedicated to the training of Hispanic psychologists, which has conferred 34 doctorates in clinical psychology at the Miami campus from 1980 to 1988, and 154 doctorates in clinical psychology at the Puerto Rico campus from 1971 to 1988.

Blacks

Historically, for many generations Black Americans were excluded from quality education. Despite the steady growth of the Black population, the academic enrollment rates for Black Americans have dropped dramatically. There were nearly 30 million Blacks in the United States in 1987 (U.S. Bureau of the Census, 1988). They accounted for approximately 12% of the nation's population and are expected to increase to at least 17.5% by 2020 (Hodgkinson, 1985). Yet, from 1976 to 1985, although the percentage of Blacks completing high school increased from 67.5% to 75.6%, the college enrollment rates for Blacks dropped from 33.5% to 26.1%.

From 1980 to 1986, however, Blacks, in comparison to the other three ethnic groups discussed, obtained the highest percentage of doctorates in clinical, counseling,

Table 2

Percentage of Doctoral Degrees Awarded to Minority Students in Clinical, Counseling, and School Psychology, 1980–1986

Race/Ethnicity	Degrees Awarded			
	1980	1982	1984	1986
Blacks				
Percentage	4.0	4.0	4.9	4.6
Total	(63)	(67)	(85)	(79)
Hispanics				
Percentage	2.3	2.7	3.2	3.4
Total	(36)	(45)	(55)	(58)
Asians				
Percentage	1.7	0.9	1.2	1.9
Total	(27)	(15)	(21)	(32)
Native Americans				
Percentage	0.2	0.6	0.2	0.4
Total	(3)	(10)	(3)	(7)
Whites				
Percentage	91.7	91.9	90.5	89.7
Total	(1,450)	(1,545)	(1,562)	(1,532)

Note. Data are from *Summary Report 1986: Doctorate Recipients from United States Universities* by the National Research Council, 1987, Washington, DC: National Academy Press.

and school psychology (see Table 2). Between 1975 and 1984, the number of Black psychologists who earned doctoral degrees grew (American Psychological Association, 1986b; J. M. Jones, 1988b). Blacks earned 6.7% of all bachelor's degrees, 5.1% of all master's degrees, and 3.9% of all doctoral degrees in the field of psychology in 1984–1985 (see Table 1). Although the number of Black psychologists increased, only about 2.2% of all psychologists in the nation were Black as of 1985 (Stapp et al., 1985). It was estimated that there were less than 2,000 Black psychologists in the United States to serve a population of nearly 30 million Blacks as of 1985.

Asian Americans

Demographics also show a steady growth in the Asian American population. Asian Americans constituted 2% of the nation's mainland population in 1980 (U.S. Bureau of the Census, 1984). They represented 3.1% of the total undergraduate enrollment in higher education in 1984. The American Council on Education (1987) noted that Asians achieved the greatest increase in the fields of engineering, biological and life sciences, and business and management in 1984–1985 in proportion to any racial or ethnic group.

Unfortunately, psychology is highly underrepresented as a career choice for Asian Americans. By 1985 only 1% of the psychologists in the United States were Asian Americans (Stapp et al., 1985). There were approximately 805 Asian American psychologists to serve a population of more than 3.7 million Asians in the nation. In 1984–1985, Asian Americans earned 2.1% of all bachelor's degrees, 1.5% of all master's degrees, and 1.8% of all doctoral degrees in psychology in the United States (see Table 1). The National Research Council (1987) reported that Asian Americans have consistently obtained a nominal number of doctorates in clinical, counseling, and school psychology in the United States (see Table 2).

Native Americans

The Native American population has been increasing for the first time since the 16th and 17th centuries. The U.S. Bureau of the Census reveals an increase of more than 50% in the Native American population since 1970, and the population is expected to continue to increase. Similar to other minorities, the representation of Native Americans in higher education is disproportionate to the Native American population in the United States. Indeed, Native Americans are the most underrepresented minority group in higher education: 0.6% in education, 0.4% in business, 0.4% in social sciences, 0.4% in health professions, 0.6% in public affairs, and 0.3% in engineering (American Council on Education, 1987). Moreover, Native Americans gained fewer degrees than any other group during 1984–1985.

Stapp et al. (1985) suggested that Native Americans represented only 0.2% of the psychologists in United States as of 1985. There were only 180 Native American psychologists to serve a population of approximately 2 million Native Americans in the nation. During 1984–1985, Native Americans obtained 0.5% of all bachelor's, 0.4% of all master's, and 0.2% of all doctoral degrees in the field of psychology (see Table 1). Historically, they have earned less doctoral degrees in clinical, counseling, and school psychology than has any other group in the nation (see Table 2).

Barriers to Minorities in Psychology

Some of the factors that account for minority underrepresentation in the field of psychology may be associated with socioeconomic issues, sociocultural differences, and a lack of commitment by American academic institutions and governmental agencies to provide minorities with access to higher education. These factors contribute to creating academic, personal, and institutional barriers that affect the optimal functioning of minorities in psychology.

Academic Barriers

Numerous researchers appear to have identified academic deprivation and poor academic preparation as major barriers to higher education for minority students. J. C. Vaughn (1985) claimed that minority underrepresentation has its roots in the socioeconomic disadvantages that characterize disproportionate numbers of minorities in American society. Factors such as poverty, unemployment, poor neighborhoods, single-parent families, and others combine to produce a poor learning environment. From the very beginning of the educational process, the poor learning environment negatively affects the successful completion of advanced education. J. C. Vaughn (1985) stated the following:

> Since each higher level of education builds on what was mastered at the preceding level, early deficits grow more severe at each succeeding level. More often than Whites, minorities receive a poor-quality elementary and secondary education, with a lower proportion of students completing high school. Fewer minority students completing high school have taken college-preparatory courses than is the norm among high school students in general. These factors compound each other, reducing the numbers of minorities eligible for college. Of those enrolling, minority students are less likely than White students to complete college. Education is often regarded as a mechanism for escaping from poverty and from its consequences, which makes poverty self-perpetuating. The unfortunate irony is that the actual education acquired by the children of low-income families in which minorities are represented at a disproportionately high level is likely to be inferior to that received by the children of middle and upper-income families. Inferior education is more likely to perpetuate than to eliminate poverty because it places students at a competitive disadvantage. (p. 155)[1]

Crossland (1971) emphasized that the quality, nature, and extent of prior schooling are major factors in determining who is likely to go to and succeed in college. Astin (1982) stressed that the quality of the student's academic preparation proved to have a more frequent and stronger relation to college success than did any other academic variable. He listed the following variables as measures of academic preparation: grade point average (GPA), aptitude test scores, study habits, preparatory curriculum, and the perceived need for tutoring.

Grade point average. According to Astin (1982), the student's high school grades prove to be, by far, the most important predictor of the college grade point average (GPA). However, careful consideration must be given to the fact that many minority students are likely to live and attend school in poor districts where less money is spent per student, teachers are the least experienced, guidance counselors are in scarce supply, and students spend fewer years studying academic subjects (Wilson & Justiz, 1987–1988). Therefore, college and graduate admission based solely on GPAs may represent a serious barrier to minority education.

Aptitude test scores. Astin (1982) reported that a student's academic aptitude, as measured by standard admission tests, does not show a substantial relation to success in higher education. But, similar to the GPA, standard admission test scores may act as a serious academic barrier to higher education for minority students. J. C. Vaughn (1985) reported that minorities tend to score below the national average on the Scholastic Aptitude Test (SAT), Graduate Record Examination (GRE), and other standardized tests frequently used as admission criteria. Crossland (1971) pointed out the crucial fact that virtually every test measuring educational aptitude or achievement reveals that the mean of the scores of minority students is about one standard deviation below the mean of the scores of the rest of the American population. He asserted that test scores, if used without discrimination and without reference to subgroup

[1]From *The State of Graduate Education* (p. 155) by J. C. Vaughn, 1985, Washington, DC: Brookings Institution. Copyright by Brookings Institution. Reprinted by permission.

within the total population, constitute a major obstacle for minority students seeking access to higher education.

The literature reveals numerous debates about the validity of standardized achievement or intelligence measures with minority populations. There is concern because these tests are constructed using the norms determined by the largest segment of the population, which is White and middle class (Wilderson, 1983). Wilderson (1983) stated:

> The basic assumption of such tests then is that there is a commonality of experiences shared by all those who take the test. The assumption ignores the reality of distinctly different arrays of cultural and social experiences that each ethnic group in this country enjoys or is subjected to by virtue of that ethnicity. Further, it ignores the fact that not all have equal facility with the English language and that not all have been exposed to the same quality and level of written or verbal communication in the English language. Implicit in these assumptions is the expectation that all who take the test will comprehend the word usage and the context of the questions in exactly the same way and that all students share the same value system. There is no recognition then, that differences in cultural background, the economic conditions of one's life, and the value of one's family and culture will influence responses to such questions. (pp. 81–82)[2]

Other variables. Astin (1982) suggested that good study habits are positively related to persistence and to GPA. The socioeconomic status of parents seems to play a crucial role in the development of study habits and, therefore, academic achievement. Many poor families cannot afford to provide the home environment conducive to the development of good study habits and academic performance, thereby placing their children at a competitive disadvantage in the educational system.

Poor curriculum, frequently experienced by minority students at earlier stages of their educational history, may limit their opportunities, motivation, and ability to achieve, thus creating another barrier. A perceived need for remedial help in reading and composition has also been found to be positively related to GPA and to persistence among minority students (Astin, 1982). Nevertheless, minorities with a prior history of low self-esteem may be affected by the stereotypes associated with tutoring or remedial programs for minorities and ignore opportunities for remediation.

Personal Barriers

Dissonant values and belief systems, identity problems, lack of aspiration or motivation, poor interpersonal skills, adjustment problems, and lack of coping or problem-solving skills are among the most common factors associated with academic difficulties. Too often, they are found to be related to sociocultural factors.

Dissonant values and belief systems. Minority students come from different sociocultural backgrounds that influence their worldviews, values, and belief systems. Lazarus, Bild, and Diaz (1985) emphasized that the development of personality and the individual's psychological processes can be understood only within a cultural context. They asserted that biological, historical, geographical, political, economic,

---

[2]From *Perspectives in Immigrant and Minority Education* (pp. 81–82) by R. J. Samuda and S. L. Woods (Eds.), 1983, Lanham, MD: University Press of America. Copyright 1983 by University Press of America. Reprinted by permission.

and sociocultural factors, among others, interact to influence the development of personality.

Minorities may experience cultural dissonance with many mainstream American values and life-styles. For instance, American society places enormous emphasis on success, accomplishments, achievements, and competition. Indeed, American culture has been described as the epitome of the individual-centered approach that cherishes uniqueness, independence, and self-reliance (Gillin, 1955). Pragmatism, individualism, power or control over others, and achievement in higher education are considered important in American society.

Because of their own historical, socioenvironmental, and cultural realities, many minorities do not subscribe to some of these attitudes and beliefs which places them in a dissonant position in American society.

Identity problems. Minority students may be concerned with whether or not a college education will place them in a state of dissonance with their cultural groups. Furthermore, they may feel pressure to reject their ethnic identities and experiences in order to function within, and be accepted by, the American college environment. Banks (1983) stressed that the common curriculum in the nation's educational system has been historically dominated by assimilationist forces in American life, largely because the assimilation of millions of immigrants and indigenous ethnic groups has been a major national goal.

Assimilation was foreseen as the outcome for the millions of European immigrants who peopled the United States before 1960. It is important to note that Europe, by and large, supplied most of the early immigrants. Although they came from different countries, these early European immigrants forged a new American culture based on their community traditions and cultural identity. Since the 1960s, nearly half of all immigrants have come from Central America, South America, and Asia.

These latter immigrants face rejection because they are new to an already established community and their culture is alien to the European-rooted American society. Assimilation for culturally distinct people may engender identity conflicts, confusion, self-denial, and self-rejection. Identity-related conflicts could very well be too much of a price to pay for economic, political, and social mobility (Banks, 1983).

Lack of aspiration or motivation. Three major factors that seem to be associated with lack of aspiration or motivation create a personal barrier to minorities seeking to become psychologists: (a) lack of role models, (b) socioeconomic conditions, and (c) lack of culturally relevant psychology training. The lack of role models is substantiated by research indicating that many minority students have little opportunity to observe what psychologists do and consequently may not show interest in psychology as a career (P. J. Woods & Wilkinson, 1987). Socioeconomic factors also influence aspiration or motivation. Lower class students, in spite of their capabilities or potential, may be less motivated to perform academically. Fernandez (1979) suggested that students from lower-class levels do not seem to believe that they will benefit from education as much as students from higher social classes.

Finally, many minority group students seem to view psychological theories and practice as alien and irrelevant to their culture. Indeed, psychology training and practice in America have been greatly influenced by the European worldview and seem to be based on a White, middle-class culture designed for a White, middle-class people (Giorgis & Helms, 1978; Ivey, Ivey, & Simek-Downing, 1987; Ramirez, 1983).

Many psychology programs in the United States do not seem to be equipped to train psychologists to deal effectively with people who are from low socioeconomic classes or who are culturally distinct.

Adjustment problems. Because they come from different environments, minorities frequently confront problems in adjusting to college life. However, many of the adjustment problems that minorities face in the field of psychology are not associated with inferior cultural values, as some have proposed. They are not related to low intelligence, as others have suggested, or to inherent racial traits or dysfunctional child-rearing practices (Nieves, 1978). Rather, the problems that minorities confront seem to be very similar to problems that other people would confront if they were expected to survive in an environment for which they have not been prepared.

Institutional Barriers

The American higher education system, as well as federal and state policy-making institutions, are highly influential in the quality and quantity of ethnic and racial minority participation in the economic and social mainstream of the nation. Academic institutional barriers, such as ineffective recruitment and marketing practices, discriminatory admission criteria, limited financial assistance, lack of faculty and administrative support, and an inhospitable academic community, have been identified in the literature as major deterrents for minority education (Astin, 1982; Crossland, 1971; U.S. Department of Education, 1984; Wilson & Justiz, 1987–1988). In addition, the federal government's low-key participation in and enforcement of equal opportunity and affirmative action legislation have resulted in lost opportunities for taking substantial corrective action to match the nation's higher education system with the society it serves (Wilson & Justiz, 1987–1988).

The serious underrepresentation of minorities in higher education will have severe repercussions for minorities as well as for future generations of nonminority Americans. America risks developing an educational and economic underclass whose contributions to society will be limited and whose dependency on others will grow (Wilson & Justiz, 1987–1988). Furthermore, according to Wilson and Justiz (1987–1988), this educational neglect occurs at a time when the nation clearly needs more, not fewer, highly educated individuals to sustain its competitiveness in the world economy.

The Commission on Minority Participation in Education and American Life, in its seminal report, "One Third of a Nation" (American Council on Education, 1988), advocates and challenges American institutions to increase minority participation in higher education. Indeed, the Commission alerts American society to recognize that, shortly after the turn of the 21st century, minorities will constitute one third of the nation's population. Schools of professional psychology (SPPs) and psychology departments of all universities in the nation are confronted with these changing demographics and are challenged to increase minority access and successful degree completion because future pools of potential students increasingly will be minority in composition. Psychology programs are urged to review existing policies, expectations, and curricula offered to culturally distinct populations. The American Psychological Association's (APA) Committee on Employment and Human Resources

(APA, 1986b) stressed that, although psychology has made progress toward increasing minority participation, it must continue to recruit and retain talented minorities at all levels of the educational process.

Strategies for Change

As Figure 1 shows, access to and success in psychology and higher education for minorities will be determined largely by the decrement of barriers and the strengthened commitment of policy-making institutions to minority education. Socioeconomic, sociocultural, and political factors have been affecting the equal participation of culturally distinct people in the educational pipeline, in general, and in the field of psychology, in particular. Special attention to recruitment, admission, retention, and degree completion of minority group students is essential in order to increase their participation in the field of psychology. Because minority underrepresentation in higher education and psychology seems to be rooted in complex and longstanding societal problems, the attention of state and federal as well as academic policy makers is essential to making education accessible to all Americans. Based on a review of the extant literature, I recommend the following strategies for change, which should be implemented at the societal level and by policymakers in academic settings, SPPs, and financial institutions.

Societal

- American society, as well as all institutions of higher education, should demonstrate acceptance and respect for cultural differences.
- American policymakers, both in institutions and in government, should develop procedures to reduce the educational and economic underclass that threatens America's future stability and socioeconomic welfare and that perpetuates the nominal participation of minorities in society.

Academic

- The American education system should make a coordinated effort to improve the quality and quantity of education for minorities from early childhood programs to graduate school (Wilson & Justiz, 1987–1988).
- Cultural, sociological, and demographic factors must be researched to explain the underrepresentation of minorities as well as their differences in adapting to and succeeding in educational settings in the United States (Cox & Jobe, 1987–1988).
- Institutions of higher education must demonstrate commitment to minority education in four main areas (Rendon & Nora, 1987–1988):

Mission—A mission statement must be instituted that reflects concern for cultural diversity.

Action—Activities and strategies must be developed to promote the participation and success of minority students.

Figure 1
The Path to Success for Minorities in Psychology and Higher Education

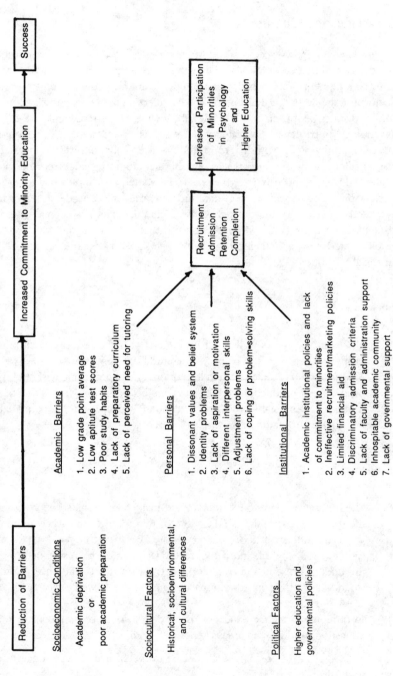

Budget—Funds must be allocated to develop and implement minority programs.
Support services—The academic, social, and emotional needs of minority students must be included in the goals, objectives, and priorities of the institutions.

- Faculty and administration should contribute to making American campuses more humane, more collaborative, and more welcoming to diverse students. The ivory tower isolation of campuses accustomed to having homogeneous student bodies needs to be reduced. There is a need to reevaluate the academic institution and its mission in light of the new demographic realities (McKenna, 1988).

- Academic institutions should maintain effective retention programs that identify academic deficiencies early enough so that they can be reversed. Programs must be developed not only to enhance or improve basic academic skills and language barriers, but also to review theoretical foundations and clinical skills.

- Academic institutions should coordinate a minority peer counseling program to help students feel comfortable on campus, eliminate feelings of isolation, provide a support system, and improve interpersonal skills.

Schools of Professional Psychology

- Psychology training programs should pursue the scientific study and understanding of human behavior from bio-, psycho-, and sociocultural perspectives. Contemporary psychology in the United States has become essentially a discipline that addresses White, middle-class Americans (Albizu-Miranda, Schwartz, & Snyder, 1988). American psychology should provide a degree of attention to, and systematic study of, the role of the sociocultural environment in determining psychological patterns of behavior (Feshbach, 1978).

- Psychology programs must keep in mind that, by the turn of the ensuing century, minority as well as nonminority psychologists will be challenged to provide mental health services necessary to an American society of which one third will be minorities. Demographic changes in American society must alert psychology training programs to train professionals who will be competent to treat the psychological and mental health service needs of the increasing minority population as well as the majority population.

- Psychology programs should establish cooperative linkages with Black and Hispanic psychology schools, as well as coordinate the interchange of information from Asian and Native American psychologists. There is a great need for a joining of forces in a combined effort to increase competency in the application of psychological treatment and assessment procedures with culturally distinct populations.

- Psychology programs should take a leadership position in training psychologists to become aware of their own prejudices, biases, and stereotyped attitudes in reference to the acceptance, understanding, and tolerance of minority populations.

- Psychology programs and academic institutions should reexamine the responsiveness and relevance of their curricula to culturally diverse populations.

- Psychology programs should develop and implement effective recruitment and marketing strategies.
- Minority admissions to psychology programs must not be based solely on traditional measures such as GPA, GRE, previous research experience, and so forth. Instead, innovative methods, such as noncognitive measures and culturally sensitive admission committees that consider qualitative as well as quantitative data, must be considered.
- Minority psychologists should take a leading role in the treatment and assessment of minority populations as well as becoming role models and mentors for minority students in the field of psychology.

Financial

- State and federal support in assisting economically disadvantaged students of different ethnic and racial backgrounds should be increased rather than reduced. Quality education must be a national priority for all members of American society.
- Sources of state and federal funds should be explored to subsidize minority enhancement programs that could reduce previous academic deprivation and poor academic preparation.
- Academic institutions should make available all pertinent information regarding institutional and financial resources so that minority students can make informed decisions concerning their education. Financial aid in the form of grants and work-study programs, rather than loans, should be promoted so students do not need to work more than half-time (Astin, 1982).

PART III
FACULTY–
ADMINISTRATION
RECRUITMENT AND
RETENTION

9

RECRUITMENT AND RETENTION OF ETHNIC MINORITY FACULTY IN PROFESSIONAL SCHOOLS OF PSYCHOLOGY

Billy E. Vaughn
California School of Professional Psychology
San Diego, California

The Importance of an Ethnic Minority Faculty

It can be concluded from previous chapters that traditional White ethnic schools of professional psychology (SPPs) must focus on increasing ethnic diversity at the faculty and administrative levels before undertaking recruitment of minority students. With Part II (Institutional Change) as background, the chapters in this section take on special importance in terms of understanding how recruitment and retention of ethnic minority faculty and administration are critical for achieving ethnic diversity within an institution. There are several reasons for starting ethnic diversification at the faculty and administrative levels of an institution.

1. Ethnic minority faculty are pivotal in the creation of an institutional ideology that encompasses the sociocultural perspectives of minorities. They can be instrumental in interpreting multicultural perspectives for the institutional mainstream (chapter 12, this volume).
2. "Ethnic minority faculty are critical in meeting the specific training needs of ethnic minority students because of their ability and commitment to teach courses that relate culture or ethnicity to professional practice" (chapter 12, this volume).
3. Institutions must demonstrate sensitivity to the needs of ethnic minority students in order to maintain them. When minority students experience the presence of faculty and administrators with whom they share sociocultural history, they perceive the institution as being sensitive to their special concerns (chapter 14, this volume).

4. Ethnic minority faculty play a critical role in bridging the gap between students and administration. They can, for example, provide both the faculty-at-large and the administration-at-large with insight into programmatic changes needed to train minority students effectively.

5. Senior ethnic minority administrators and faculty serve as mentors and role models for junior faculty, and the totality of ethnic minority administrators and faculty serve as mentors and role models for students.

6. "Ethnic minority faculty also serve as resources for White students who are interested in an ethnocultural training component" (chapter 12, this volume).

Each chapter in this part speaks to the importance of the presence of a significant ethnic minority faculty in SPPs, its lack therein, barriers to recruitment and retention, and recommendations for change. Although each of the authors approaches the issue from a different perspective, they all conclude that the need for more ethnic minority faculty is critical and begs to be addressed by those institutions that profess to have made a serious commitment to ethnic diversity.

In chapter 10, "Minority Faculty Development: Issues in Retention and Promotion," Olmedo stresses the need for institutions to assume the responsibility for establishing a comprehensive approach to minority faculty development. Olmedo describes the lack of adequate minority faculty representation at all academic levels and states that there is no indication of any increase in the foreseeable future. The actual percentage of minority faculty is very low, and the percentage of minority faculty with tenure or high academic rank is even lower.

According to Olmedo, the major barrier to the retention and promotion of minority faculty is the attitude of the White ethnic majority that the nature and significance of research conducted by minority faculty "is . . . 'soft' and not sufficient to survive the scrutiny of tenure and promotion reviews" (chapter 10, this volume). When determining criteria for retaining and promoting ethnic minority faculty, one must be sensitive to the ethnic minorities' contributions, which are likely to include services that assist in the institution's commitment to achieving diversity. Evaluation of the research interests of ethnic minority faculty should reflect sensitivity to diversity. In order to control for all potential sources of bias, ethnic minority participants should be part of the evaluation process when ethnic minority faculty are being reviewed.

Olmedo states that a comprehensive approach to minority faculty development requires establishing and operationalizing a sound commitment to ethnic diversity, which is reflected in the organization's climate. This comprehensive approach must include an aggressive recruitment strategy, the establishment of appropriate criteria for retention and promotion, the design and implementation of review procedures that honor cultural diversity, and the recruitment and retention of senior minority faculty and administrators to serve as mentors and role models for the young minority faculty to be hired. Olmedo believes that it is difficult for organizations to undergo the cultural changes needed to create an environment that is sensitive to ethnic diversity because institutions tend to engage in rhetoric rather than in the clear articulation of the specific goals and actions that are needed to put commitments into operation.

In "Qualified Minorities are Encouraged to Apply: The Recruitment of Ethnic Minority and Female Psychologists" (chapter 11), Hall emphasizes the importance of aggressive recruitment strategies as the first and critical step in promoting equal opportunities for ethnic minority and female psychologists. According to Hall, the fact that the pool of ethnic minority and female psychologists is small, "is not justification for the low percentage of ethnic minority and female tenured and tenure track faculty teaching in graduate psychology programs" (chapter 11, this volume). In order to recruit ethnic minorities successfully, institutions must make a clear commitment to achieving ethnic diversity and support this commitment with aggressive action. Hall suggests that a positive recruitment strategy necessitates gaining access to informal minority networks instead of relying solely on advertisements in professional journals, and contacting associations with a high percentage of ethnic membership.

In addition, Hall suggests that the White ethnic faculty misperceives affirmative action, which acts as an institutional barrier to the recruitment of ethnic minority faculty. According to Hall, the term *affirmative action* is viewed by White ethnics as being synonymous with *less than qualified*. Therefore, affirmative action candidates often feel stigmatized as unqualified and do not seek out positions that invite affirmative action candidates to apply.

Hall offers specific suggestions for recruiting minority students: enlarge the pool of potential candidates by increasing scholarships, modify the curriculum to include ethnic perspectives, increase the number of minority faculty members, and expand employment opportunities. In order to recruit and retain minority faculty, Hall recommends raising salaries so that they are competitive with those in the private sector, restructuring the tenure review process so that special consideration is given for the unique offerings that minority faculty members bring to a university, and providing the necessary resources to support faculty development and opportunities for promotion. Extra effort must be made to demonstrate that the institution is genuinely supportive of ethnic diversity.

In "The Problem of Organizational Culture in Ethnic Diversity in Professional Psychology Training: Implications for Recruitment," (chapter 12), I provide a framework for understanding how institutional barriers resist change. Vaughn points to the role of an institution's organizational culture in creating barriers for achieving ethnic diversity. I define organizational culture as one in which assumptions about what makes an institution unique and successful are deeply held and longstanding. Three key elements of organizational culture vitiate against change: cultural influence on perceptions and behaviors of its members, cultural unconscious control of members' behavior, and cultural potential for creating subcultures.

I argue that it is imperative that an institution study its culture in order to understand what is needed to fulfill its commitment to achieve diversity. Because the assumptions about how to behave and to evaluate the behaviors of group members tend to be deeply held and unconscious, members of an institution must become aware of how these factors may result in an ethnocentric perspective of professional training and evaluation. Awareness of an institution's ethnocentrism is preliminary to moving toward an ethnically diverse perspective. Because most SPPs were founded and developed by White ethnics to train White ethnic students, the culture of SPPs is necessarily ethnocentric in scope.

Institutional leaders play a critical role in effectuating institutional change. Leaders are responsible for identifying cultural factors that resist change, determining how the nonhuman elements in the organization create obstacles to change, and developing an awareness of how culture controls management. The recruitment and retention of ethnic minority faculty should be considered one of the key responsibilities of SPP's leadership. As I state in chapter 12, the recruitment of ethnic minority faculty is the most productive place to begin meeting the challenge of creating diversity in

SPPs. Ethnic minority faculty members are instrumental in recruiting and retaining ethnic minority students, are able to assume teaching responsibility for those areas of the curriculum that relate culture or ethnicity to professional practice, and serve as advocates of cultural diversity to the university-at-large. Olmedo, Hall, and I, individually and collectively, provide convincing evidence for the importance of an ethnic minority faculty, the institutional barriers that obstruct the recruitment and retention of this faculty, and the rewards to be reaped if determined efforts meet with success.

National Council of Schools of Professional Psychology: A Model System

In the remainder of this chapter I will concentrate on a model system that embodies many of the ideas expressed in the chapters of this section. The focus will be on the ways in which one institution, the National Council of Schools of Professional Psychology (NCSPP), developed an ethnically diverse perspective and integrated it into its cultural structure. Nationally recognized, NCSPP comes as close as any, and closer than most comparable institutions, to achieving ethnic diversity.

Founded in 1974, NCSPP made its first formal commitment to ethnic diversity at its midwinter 1986–1987 meeting, the Mission Bay conference. The primary purpose of the conference was to arrive at specific resolutions that could be applied to standards and evaluations for professional psychologists in training. However, Persico and Troy of the California School of Professional Psychology: Los Angeles (CSPP: Los Angeles) proposed that training issues could not be addressed adequately if they lacked a consideration of and a commitment to ethnic diversity. In response, the NCSPP conference participants voted overwhelmingly, if not unanimously, to include the following as one of three general resolutions:

> *As an expression of their professional and social responsibility, NCSPP and its member schools commit themselves to:*
>
> a. *Initiating a recruitment strategy designed to increase significantly the proportion of ethnic minority students and faculty in professional schools by developing articulated programs designed to attract and support ethnic minority students and faculty.*
> b. *Developing curriculum offerings designed to prepare all students in professional schools in relevant aspects of the delivery of human services and health care to ethnic minority and other underserved groups and populations. (Bourg et al., 1987, pp. 32–33)*

In addition to making the resolutions, NCSPP formed the Committee on Minority Participation and Service to Underserved Populations (CMPSUP). Its responsibilities were (a) to develop and recommend strategies for increasing ethnic minority participation in SPPs and (b) to discover ways to monitor service delivery of psychological services in order to gain insight into and disseminate information about intervention strategies. Because there were only two ethnic minority representatives at the Mission Bay conference, both Black men, the CMPSUP initially was composed of Whites, predominantly. The number of ethnic minority committee participants, however, increased considerably during the next year and a half.

Much of the committee's efforts to operationalize the resolutions came under the guidance of Elizabeth Davis-Russell, who became active at NCSPP's summer 1987 meeting. Assigning an ethnic minority woman to chair the committee was an important action taken by the NCSPP Executive Committee. Davis-Russell undertook her role as chairperson with vigor and seriousness of purpose. With the assistance of Thomas Titus at Spalding University, a questionnaire was developed to survey ethnic minority students' participation and needs. NCSPP member schools were asked to complete and return a copy of the survey, and the committee analyzed the results.

The CMPSUP presented its findings at the NCSPP midwinter 1987–1988 meeting in Scottsdale, Arizona. The report showed that the committee had undertaken and had accomplished a considerable amount of work. As a result of the committee's efforts and the disposition of the membership-at-large, NCSPP decided to dedicate its forthcoming annual agenda to issues in minority education and training. The increase in the number of ethnic minority participants at the Scottsdale meeting was further indication that NCSPP was attaining some measure of success in ethnic diversification.

In addition, at Scottsdale, CMPSUP was divided into four subcommittees in order to address specific training issues: (a) faculty recruitment and retention, (b) student recruitment and retention, (c) curriculum, and (d) service delivery. Four subcommittee chairs were chosen, each being held responsible for one of the areas. The goals were to develop strategies for identifying issues relevant to each area and to share this knowledge with member school representatives during the summer and winter meetings of the following year.

The subcommittee chairs met during the spring of 1988 at the Chicago School of Professional Psychology. Along with two executive committee members, James McHolland and George Stricker, the committee developed a program for the summer 1988 conference, which was to take place in Atlanta. This was the first time a NCSPP committee was made up primarily of minorities, although power remained vested in White members (i.e., the ex officio members of the executive committee).

The program committee decided that, at the Atlanta conference, member school representatives might benefit from consciousness-raising exercises. The aim was to provide opportunities for White members to develop insight into the ways in which they think about education and training and how these views might create barriers for including ethnic minorities in professional schools. It was hoped that the exercises would give members insight into their own biases and that, in turn, they would share this insight with faculty and administrators at their respective institutions.

The committee drew up plans that included group simulation exercises focusing on the application review process for ethnic minority students in one simulation, and for ethnic minority faculty in another. A T-group model, with a few people role playing a review committee and observers participating through the use of open seats, was employed. When the simulation was presented at the Atlanta meeting, it seemed to be well received. Although it was difficult to measure how much the members benefited from the exercises, there was a clear sense that everyone felt that the experience was worthwhile.

Another outcome of the Atlanta conference gave further evidence of NCSPP's expanding ethnic diversification. Kenneth Polite, one of the two ethnic minorities who had attended the Mission Bay conference, was elected as treasurer of NCSPP—a position that made him the first minority member of the executive committee. This was, indeed, history in the making for NCSPP. Polite's position on the executive committee would prove to be instrumental in giving ethnic minorities a strong voice at the forthcoming Puerto Rico conference.

The theme of the midwinter 1988–1989 Puerto Rico Conference concerned issues in minority education and training. This conference was designed to be the conduit through which member schools would demonstrate their commitment to creating ethnic diversity. It was the responsibility of the conference steering committee to guide the participants toward a formalized commitment to ethnic diversity in education and training. This committee comprised eight members: five ethnic minorities (each of the four subcommittee chairs and Polite) and three White ethnics (the other three members of the executive committee). For the first time in NCSPP history, the majority of the steering committee was composed of ethnic minorities. Furthermore, ethnic minorities made up one third of the total number of representatives attending the conference, also a first-time occurrence for NCSPP.

The conference program consisted of the presentation of position papers, formulation of resolutions, and voting on resolutions. The position papers, under the aegis of each of the four subcommittees, were intended to provide member school representatives with insight into the issues from the points of view of experts. After each set of position papers was presented, the participants met as a group to develop resolutions that would be presented to the entire conference for a vote.

After 2 days of presentations, discussions, and development of resolutions, 40 resolutions were finalized for presentation to the membership-at-large for discussion and vote. In order to structure and give meaning to the subsequent voting, the steering committee decided that it was necessary to change the mission statement of NCSPP's bylaws. It was considered imperative that the mission statement reflect sensitivity to diversity in order to demonstrate a commitment to changing those attitudes and behaviors that create barriers to achieving diversity. Although there was considerable discussion prior to the vote, this resolution passed unanimously after a few minor changes were made in its wording.

There was not sufficient time left to discuss and vote on the full set of 40 proposed resolutions. In order to present as many resolutions as possible for deliberation and voting, the steering committee decided to trim the number to a smaller set that could be addressed during the remaining time. The strategy was to present the most controversial resolutions at the conference and save the least controversial resolutions for ballot by mail.

There was debate over a few resolutions, but eventually all were approved. It is insightful to discuss, from an organizational perspective, the complicated nature of the interactions surrounding the passage of one resolution. This serves to illustrate how certain negative perceptions and ideas about the meaning of achieving ethnic diversity can create division within a diverse group of people. The purpose of this resolution was to suggest that each member school engage in activities that would make its faculty and administrators more aware of their ethnocentric behaviors. Disagreement centered on the implications of the specific wording of the resolution, rather than on the objective contained therein. A White ethnic argued that the resolution's use of the term *consciousness raising* was too reminiscent of the tone of 1960s activism. The concern appeared to be that the psychological community would perceive NCSPP as assuming a radical position. However, an ethnic minority participant contended that, in order for the resolution to specify the agreed-on goal of encouraging activities similar to those used in the NCSPP meetings, it was necessary to retain the terminology.

An initial vote on the resolution with the original terminology (consciousness raising) did not pass. White ethnics predominantly voted against the resolution, whereas ethnic minorities tended to vote for it. Polite, who was responsible for counting the votes, noticed the division along ethnic lines and pointed it out to the group. With this in mind, Stricker, the leader of the conference, requested that another vote be taken after a recess, during which designees would reword the resolution. The new wording was to include the controversial term but, in addition, it was to emphasize that a range of exercises was considered important for an institution to include in its efforts to become sensitive to ethnic minority issues. When the group reconvened, the resolution was overwhelmingly accepted and *consciousness raising* remained as part of the terminology.

This book is an outgrowth of the NCSPP Puerto Rico conference. Although the content is informational, it goes beyond facts and captures the spirit of the Puerto Rico conference. The occasion of a national, professional organization devoting its annual agenda and conference to issues in minority education and training is testimony to the preeminence of NCSPP as a leader in ethnic diversification in professional psychology training. NCSPP's commitment to increasing ethnic minority participation in its organization and its member schools serves as a model. It has ethnic minority representation throughout the system, from the executive committee to subcommittees to conference participants. The conference steering committee was committed to making the conference a success and projected this to member school participants. Considerable work remains to be done. However, among traditional, national, White ethnic organizations, NCSPP has established its place as a leader in addressing ethnic diversity.

10

MINORITY FACULTY DEVELOPMENT: ISSUES IN RETENTION AND PROMOTION

Esteban L. Olmedo
California School of Professional Psychology
Los Angeles, California

The importance of a culturally diverse faculty in graduate psychology programs in the United States has been recognized for some time and recently emphasized in major national conferences on graduate education and training (American Psychological Association, 1987; Bourg et al., 1987). Minority representation is viewed as desirable from the perspectives of equity and social justice, and necessary due to ethical imperatives pertaining to the competence of graduates to provide service to, conduct research with, and teach members of culturally diverse populations. I have three objectives in this chapter: (a) to show that, despite much rhetoric, minority faculty representation remains minimal and has leveled off at unacceptable levels, (b) to describe barriers to the retention and promotion of minority faculty, and (c) to propose a comprehensive approach to minority faculty development.

Minority Representation in Academe

Data from a variety of surveys indicate that there are few minority faculty, and they are concentrated in the junior ranks. Non-Hispanic Whites represent 92% of all faculty, 94.5% of full professors, and 93.4% of associate professors (Menges & Exum, 1983). In 1981, the composition of the faculty of graduate departments of psychology was as follows: Whites, 93.8%; Blacks, 2.9%; Hispanics, 0.8%; Asians, 1%; and Native Americans, 0.2%, for a total minority representation of 4.9% (Russo, Olmedo, Stapp, & Fulcher, 1981). The latest available data from the American Psychological Association is for 1985 (Hall, personal communication, October 1988) and reflects no substantial improvement: Whites, 92.3% of faculty; Blacks, 2.9%; Hispanics, 1.1%; Asians, 1.1%; and Native Americans, 0.2%, for a total minority representation of 5.3%.

With respect to tenure status, it is apparent that minorities are also at a disadvantage. As of 1981, in doctoral departments of psychology, minorities constituted 3.1% of the tenured faculty, 8.8% of the faculty on tenure track, and 7.4% of the faculty not on tenure track (Russo et al., 1981). In terms of academic rank, it is clear that minorities are concentrated in the lower ranks in doctoral departments of psychology, as they are in academe at large. As of 1981, minorities constituted 2.7% of the full professors, 3.8% of the associate professors, 8.4% of the assistant professors, and 13% of the lecturers and instructors (Russo et al., 1981). Minority representation is somewhat higher in schools of professional psychology. A recent survey by the National Council of Schools of Professional Psychology (1987) indicated that, out of a total of 397 faculty in 22 professional schools, 90% were White, 7% were Black, 2% were Hispanic, 0.3% were Native American, and 0.7% were "other."

The magnitude of minority underrepresentation can be better understood in the context of the overall minority population in the United States. The current minority population is over 20% and is expected to constitute at least 25% of the overall U.S. population by the year 2000 ("40 Years On," 1982). A particularly troubling aspect of minority underrepresentation in academic settings is that there may be a "revolving door" phenomenon. White men are the most likely to receive tenure, whereas minorities (as well as White women) have a much higher frequency of leaving a department before a tenure decision is made. The specific reasons for this phenomenon remain unclear (Stapp, 1979); however, the negative implications for the retention and promotion of minority faculty are obvious.

The Issue of Salaries

A common myth in higher education circles is that qualified minority applicants are so rare that they are in a position to command top salaries and are thus beyond affordability for many institutions (Wilson, 1987). In fact, at least in graduate departments of psychology, there are no significant salary differences between minorities and nonminorities once academic rank and years in rank are accounted for by analysis of covariance (Russo et al., 1981). In other disciplines, for example, schools of management (Ford, 1986), White faculty have been found to receive higher salaries than minority faculty after controlling for length of service and academic rank.

Suinn and Witt (1982) reported results of a survey of graduate departments of psychology that focused on minority faculty recruitment and retention. Department chairs reported that, among the reasons why minority finalists refused employment offers, a higher salary elsewhere ranked first. Other important reasons, however, were geographic location and higher concentration of minorities in the community (ranked second and third, respectively).

There is no reason to believe that salaries are any less important for nonminorities, so institutions must be prepared, among other things, to offer competitive salaries if they expect to be successful in recruiting and retaining minority faculty. Furthermore, there is no evidence to indicate that minority faculty are, on the average, receiving salaries that are significantly different from those of their nonminority colleagues with similar levels of professional experience.

Barriers to Retention and Promotion

Suinn and Witt (1982) also asked department chairpersons to identify obstacles that minority faculty face when they are up for tenure. The item ranked first was "too much minority service." This finding provides empirical support for what minority faculty have experienced all along. They tend to be hired because of their commitment to minority issues and are expected to be heavily involved in various activities related to minority service, such as advising minority students, developing minority curricula, serving as liaisons to the minority community, and so forth. These activities are usually *in addition to* other faculty duties expected of all faculty. However, when the time comes for tenure or promotion review, these activities are not viewed as sufficiently "scholarly" or "research oriented" to facilitate retention and promotion. So there is, in a sense, a mixed message or double jeopardy situation facing minority faculty. They are told, in effect, "The reason you are hired is the reason you will be fired."

The other obstacles to tenure identified in the Suinn and Witt (1982) survey complement the aforementioned finding. Ranked second, third, and fourth, respectively, were "insufficient publication due to insufficient research activity," "insufficient publication due to inexperience in writing research," and "insufficient data-based publication." Other obstacles that are commonly suggested, in fact, were lower down on the list: "Insufficient teaching efforts" was ranked 8th, "overly militant" was ranked 12th, and "not political enough" was ranked 17th.

Therefore, it is clear that, with respect to tenure (and, by inference, retention and promotion), the major barriers for minority faculty have to do with research. It may be argued that this is true for all faculty; however, it also may be argued, rather convincingly, that many minority faculty face unique and special issues in the area of research and scholarly productivity. As was noted by Menges and Exum (1983):

> *Higher education has been dominated by White males; consequently, their definitions of learning and scholarship prevail. Charging that those definitions are incomplete, women and minorities sometimes offer their own scholarship to compensate for what is missing and sometimes radically redefine issues, research paradigms, and approaches to teaching. (p. 134)*

Menges and Exum pointed out that by the late 1970s, women and minorities had challenged the content of conventional scholarship, particularly in the social sciences and humanities, because it did not provide for a satisfactory explanation of their experiences. They created an "intellectual core of feminist, and to a lesser extent minority, political ideology" (Menges & Exum, 1983, p. 134). Minorities have also challenged traditional research paradigms (Sampson, 1978), particularly the naturalistic and ahistorical paradigms predominant in the social sciences, and proposed alternative paradigms that seek "conclusions that are historical, context bound, concrete, and particularistic" (Menges & Exum, 1983, pp. 134–135). A third challenge involves the philosophy of teaching and learning. "Academic feminists and minorities have espoused an ideal of collectively generated learning, the student as an active participant in the learning process, and egalitarian and personalized student-faculty relations" (Menges & Exum, 1983, p. 135).

The result of these challenges to the academic status quo is often perceived by senior academics as provocative and threatening. The scholarly work of minorities is devalued and, particularly when it involves "ethnic" or "cultural" topics, is seen as "soft" and not sufficient to survive the scrutiny of tenure and promotion reviews. A related issue is that, because of its focus, minority-oriented research is often not accepted for publication in mainstream journals. These journals, incidentally, are likely to be edited by the same senior academics. Thus the status of the journals in which minority-oriented research usually appears also compounds the problems facing minority faculty who are up for tenure or promotion.

A Comprehensive Approach to Minority Faculty Development

Given the magnitude of minority underrepresentation among faculty and the multitude of barriers to the promotion, retention, and tenure of minority faculty, it is clear that it is the *responsibility of the institution* to retain the minority faculty it has been able to attract and employ (Wilson, 1987). There is, however, a paucity of systematic empirical research addressing the issue of effective approaches to retention of minority faculty. The approach discussed here is based on (a) personal and institutional experience, (b) identified obstacles to the progress of minority faculty (Menges & Exum, 1983; Suinn & Witt, 1982), and (c) other specific recommendations found in the literature (Wilson, 1987).

Establishing Institutional Commitment

It is clear that the first step to the development of minority faculty has to be the establishment of a demonstrable institutional commitment to cultural diversity, equal opportunity, and affirmative action. This commitment must begin at the top with the governing board, the president of the institution, and the local chief executive (for multicampus institutions). Top administrators must be held accountable for achieving institutional goals with respect to the recruitment and retention of minority faculty. They must also be capable of designing and implementing the tough measures necessary to achieve these goals (Wilson, 1987).

Institutional commitment also needs to exist at the level of faculty and students. The academic setting is one in which peer and student evaluations and perceptions are a key to the professional future of faculty. These major constituencies need to be engaged in the effort to develop minority faculty if that effort is to be successful. Overt and covert prejudice and racism must be identified and dealt with in an open and constructive way. The anonymity associated with peer and student evaluations can provide a fertile ground for subtle discriminatory processes that undermine the institution's commitment to retain and promote its minority faculty.

The institution's commitment to its minority faculty and students is also manifest in its support for and fostering of programmatic and curricular components that reflect cultural diversity and respect cultural differences. It is clear, especially in professional psychology training programs, that the development of courses, subspecialties, and programs designed to incorporate minority issues reflect the degree of value that the institution places on minority populations and their experiences. For minority faculty, these programmatic components provide a key indicator of whether or not they are welcome at the institution.

Finally, institutional commitment is also reflected by the general organizational climate. Tangibles such as minority representation among students, faculty, and administration, and in the curriculum, as well as the presence of subtle cues, are indicative of a climate supportive of minority faculty. Sensitivity to cultural differences is reflected by the pattern, level, and content of communications within the institution. Accessibility to top administrators and circles of power by minority faculty is a key ingredient of a supportive organizational climate. Conversely, suspicion, resentment, and social isolation send a clear message to minority faculty that they are not wanted, respected, or appreciated.

Conducting Appropriate Recruitment

Conducting appropriate recruitment is essential to subsequent success in the retention and promotion of minority faculty. The first step involves assessing the adequacy of institutional resources to mount and sustain an effort to recruit and retain minority faculty. Are there financial resources to offer competitive compensation packages? What are the available support systems and links to the minority communities? Are there adequate library and other research support resources necessary for specialized minority-oriented research and teaching? Are there clear, distinct, and identifiable support mechanisms for the development of minority faculty?

An objective assessment of these institutional resources, together with a careful evaluation of applicants, provides the basis for creating realistic expectations, both on the part of the institution and on the part of the successful applicant. It is essential that both parties understand well the expectations concerning research, teaching, institutional and professional service, and special minority-related activities. It is also essential that the institution be explicit about its level of support on behalf of these activities.

A third aspect of appropriate recruitment is the matching of the applicant's qualifications and expectations to the institution's expectations and resources. For example, a minority candidate with little research experience who expects rapid advancement would be a poor match for an institution where research is the major factor for promotion and tenure but where little resources are available for research in the applicant's area, which may involve minority populations or topics. Most situations call for some modification of expectations; however, it is necessary that these issues be resolved up front, rather than later, after much frustration and pain for both applicant and institution.

Establishing Appropriate Criteria for Retention and Promotion

Perhaps more racism and discrimination are perpetrated under the cloak of maintaining high academic standards than under any other guise in the academy. As Menges and Exum (1983) have pointed out, "the overriding value in academia is merit, and academics proudly characterize their institutions as meritocracies" (pp. 138–139). However, meritocracies are predicated on clear standards, whereas there is usually a great deal of ambiguity in complex academic criteria and standards, as well as in the assignment of weights to the various components used in the academic evaluation process.

In promotion and tenure reviews, merit, which ignores local context, tends to be emphasized over worth, which is defined in relation to the local context (Menges & Exum, 1983). If cultural diversity is an important value of the institution, then this value should be properly reflected in the institution's criteria and standards for retention and promotion of faculty. This means that recognition of cultural diversity and minority issues should permeate the typical criteria pertaining to research activities, teaching, professional service, and service to the institution.

Designing and Implementing Review Procedures that Honor Cultural Diversity

It is not sufficient to have criteria for retention, promotion, and tenure that reflect the values of cultural diversity. Academic institutions must also design and implement review procedures that honor cultural diversity and respect cultural differences.

With regard to procedures, the input of minority faculty members is essential. They need to be involved in the development and review of documents that specify review procedures in order to ensure that issues specific to minority faculty are properly reflected. For example, it is often the case that the senior faculty conducting reviews are White and may have little knowledge of minority research, teaching, or service. The procedures, then, must provide explicit means to ensure that criteria and standards concerning these areas are properly applied. If there is no minority representation in the review committee, then the institution should arrange for ad hoc participation of minorities in the evaluation of minority faculty.

It is common in academic reviews to solicit the input of scholars outside the institution. However, as Menges and Exum (1983) have pointed out, "the 'old boys' network important for hiring is replaced at promotion and tenure time by an 'old referees' network" (p. 136). Minorities are, of course, underrepresented in both networks. Thus, it is the responsibility of deans and other administrators to ensure that the external reviewers involved in the evaluation of minority faculty have an adequate level of expertise in the specific field of the faculty member being reviewed. In addition, it is important to include reviewers who have an understanding of research paradigms that typically underlie scholarly work on minority-related topics.

Finally, it is not sufficient that review procedures be fair to minority faculty. They must also be *perceived* as fair by the faculty member being reviewed. This is important because many minority faculty, through painful experience, have developed distrust of White-dominated academic bureaucracies. The secrecy with which academic reviews are usually conducted contribute to feelings that one is not being given a fair shake by the system, and that racism and discrimination flourish under the cloak of anonymity. Thus, it is important for review committee chairs, department heads, and deans to make every effort to ensure that minority faculty are thoroughly briefed about the nature of review criteria and procedures, and how these criteria and procedures are fair and sensitive to minority faculty.

Ensuring the Availability of Mentors and Role Models

No discussion of minority faculty development is complete without mention of the crucial role of mentoring and the availability of role models. Every effort needs to be made by the institution to recruit and retain senior minority faculty and administrators who can be role models and provide mentoring for the junior minority faculty who are hired. The presence of minorities at the top of the academic hierarchy sends a clear message concerning the institution's commitment to equity. For junior minority faculty, it also signifies access to those who have undergone similar experiences and "have made it" within the system and to those who can provide guidance in professional development and advise on learning the ropes in the academic environment—in other words, those who embody the institution's commitment not only to recruit minority faculty but to ensure that they benefit from every opportunity for a long and productive academic career.

11

QUALIFIED MINORITIES ARE ENCOURAGED TO APPLY: THE RECRUITMENT OF ETHNIC MINORITY AND FEMALE PSYCHOLOGISTS

Christine C. Iijima Hall
American Psychological Association
Washington, DC

The 1960s was a revolutionary time for advancements in affirmative action policies. Federal laws were enacted that required employers and educational institutions to make efforts at reversing the effects of discrimination by promoting equal opportunities. Equal opportunities begin with recruitment activities. Specific recruitment practices must be directed toward those groups that do not have equal access to education or job opportunities. In this chapter I discuss the recruitment of ethnic minority and female professionals within the field of psychology. Topics included in this discussion are the existence of and access to the pool of professionals, barriers to recruitment, and suggestions for successful recruitment.

Is there really a pool of women and minorities out there? The statistics from the National Research Council (NRC, 1987) and from the American Psychological Association (APA, 1986b) show that only 8.6% of the PhDs awarded in psychology in 1984 were awarded to ethnic minorities (Blacks, 4.1%; Hispanics, 2.8%; Asians, 1.5%; Native Americans, 0.2%); women received 50% of the PhDs. The relative percentage of PhDs awarded to ethnic minorities has remained fairly constant throughout the past 10 years, although the raw numbers have increased slightly. The pool is small and needs to be increased; nonetheless, its small size is not justification for the low percentage of ethnic minority and female tenured and tenure track faculty teaching in graduate psychology programs. Data for the 1984–1985 academic year (American Psychological Association, 1986b) showed the ethnic composition of psychology graduate faculties to be as follows: Black, 2.9%; Hispanic, 1.1%; Asian, 1.1%; and Native Americans, 0.2%. In 1984–1985 psychology graduate faculties were composed of 77.5% men and 22.5% women.

Barriers to Recruitment

Recruitment is the first step in the employment process during which discrimination may occur. The other two barriers, as delineated by Braddock, Jomills, and McPartland (1987), appear in the job entry stage and the job promotion stage. Obviously, the recruitment stage is extremely important because one cannot be hired or promoted until one hears of a job opening and applies for the position.

Strategies for reaching the pool of possible applicants require forethought and planning. Braddock et al. (1987) outlined several issues involved in setting up strategies. Although their area of expertise is the private sector, their strategies can be extrapolated to the academic arena. They asserted that it is easier to recruit ethnic minorities at the clerical and lower levels because the applicant pool can be accessed through newspaper advertisements, employment agencies, and walk-ins. The higher corporate positions require more aggressive recruitment methods. These methods involve contacting associations that have a high percentage of ethnic or female members, placing advertisements in periodicals or other printed material that have high percentages of the targeted readership, and using informal networks. Braddock et al. emphasized that informal networks work best. Employers who are dedicated to minority recruitment must make extra effort to gain access to the informal networks of women and minorities because the traditional informal "White ol' boy" networks have been the major culprits in excluding women and minorities from job information.

University officials are often perplexed when they cannot seem to attract minority candidates for open faculty positions, even when they appear to be using the proper recruitment strategies. In reviewing the university's current composition of faculty and students, it is usually discovered that the percentage of minorities, including women, is quite low. Braddock et al. pointed out that the composition of a firm is the best predictor of representation in the pool of recent applicants. In addition, ethnic representation in one area usually parallels the composition in other areas. Thus past commitment demonstrates that an institution is serious about promoting diversity, and the numbers act as a "priming effect" to attract more diversity. There must be prior evidence of commitment by the institution before prospective applicants will consider applying for a position. A university that has not shown evidence of treating its faculty fairly will have difficulty recruiting a newcomer because the number of professional networks among ethnic psychologists is small.

The same informal networks that help recruit faculty are the same networks that "blackball" a university. There are many major universities that have had difficulty in obtaining a "new" ethnic minority to replace the very competent "old" assistant professor who did not obtain tenure. Why should a new PhD enter a position that does not have a high probability of promotion in five to seven years? This phenomenon spirals upward because, if an institution cannot attract one targeted faculty, the priming effect is inoperative. Institutions that have demonstrated a commitment find that it is easier to bring in more faculty and students. Thus, an ad in the *Chronicle of Higher Education* or the *APA Monitor*, or a call to the ethnic psychological associations or an ethnic minority psychologist is not going to guarantee applicants.

The Connotations of Affirmative Action

Webster's Ninth New Collegiate Dictionary (1983) defines *affirmative action* (noun, originated in 1965) as "an active effort to improve the employment or educational opportunities of minority groups and women." The word *affirmative* alone means supportive, positive, or agreement. Thus one could conclude that affirmative action is a positive action. However, over the past 20 years, affirmative action has taken on a negative connotation: It has come to be synonymous with "less than qualified." Many examples demonstrate the existence of this misconception.

According to Garcia, Erskine, Hawn, and Casmay (1981), White undergraduates perceive their ethnic fellow students as less qualified academically. Ethnic students are seen as being admitted under an affirmative action policy that allows (if not promotes) a lower standard of admission. Braddock et al. (1987) reported that companies do not have high expectations for minority employees and show much concern when hiring them. The stigma of being less than qualified causes many personal and professional problems for ethnic minority individuals. Ethnic minority students and employees must live with this stigma and try to maintain their self-esteem. Stress is increased because their progress or their failure is under constant scrutiny by the institution. The effects of failures are multiplied because minorities are extremely visible. In addition, hostility may erupt from White colleagues who view the ethnic minority student or employee as the "less-than-qualified token" who "took" a position from a more qualified White student or employee.

Asians are being removed from many affirmative action lists although they continue to be discriminated against racially, economically, and politically. The argument that supports this shift in policy states that affirmative action has evolved to mean the admitting and hiring of "underrepresented groups." Because Asians are not underrepresented in many academic majors or employment categories, they no longer need to be considered a part of affirmative action policy. However, as was discussed earlier, affirmative action was designed to correct the effects of discrimination. Asians have been, and still are, discriminated against. However, when Asians began scoring higher than Whites on IQ and achievement tests, they were removed from many affirmative action lists (the federal government still includes them in the guidelines).

Job announcement terminology may also evince subtle discrimination. Job announcements that are specifically targeting ethnic minority applicants, or highlighting an institution's affirmative action activities, usually contain the phrase, "Qualified applicants are encouraged to apply." Does this mean that most ethnic applicants are not qualified? Why would an institution spell out that it wants qualified applicants? The covert message implies that many ethnic minority candidates will probably be unqualified, and affirmative action activities promote the hiring of unqualified applicants.

Thus misperceptions of affirmative action have promoted a negative attitude among Whites toward minorities—the population to which affirmative action was initially addressed. It is no wonder that ethnic minority applicants do not wish to put themselves in this situation. They are very much aware of subtle resistance and hostility.

Subtle Resistance to Affirmative Action

Defining or proving subtle resistance to affirmative action is difficult because such resistance is covert. If an employer or university does not wish to adhere to affirmative action policies, false actions can be made to resemble positive adherence. For example, an employer may recruit in an incorrect manner. As was discussed earlier, Braddock et al. (1987) demonstrated that job announcements must reach into circles where the target population can receive them—not only via printed matter but through informal networks as well. Many times the affirmative action recruitment is a charade. If an institution does not wish minorities to know of an excellent position, it will not use the networks that will elicit affirmative action candidates. The fact that no affirmative action candidate is hired is justified by stating that no one applied, or no qualified minority applicants could be found. At other times, an institution may conduct an extensive search, although a nonminority candidate already has been selected unofficially. Because the law mandates a national search, the institution obliges, but it finds reasons to explain why its preferred candidate has the desired qualifications.

Reverse discrimination is probably the most insulting issue that has emerged in the affirmative action arena. A cartoon that epitomizes a White man's perception of reverse discrimination shows a White person and a Black person trying to pick apples from a tree. The White is standing on ground level and the Black is standing in a hole in the ground, but has a ladder. The caption reads, "Why does he get a ladder?" There cannot be reverse discrimination because racism and sexism still do exist, will continue to exist for quite some time, and the remnants of past discriminatory acts still prevail. However, 15 years after the Bakke decision, many professional schools (medical and law especially) are still fearful of promoting affirmative action admission policies although the numbers of minority and female physicians are devastatingly low.

Another example of subtle resistance is hiring unqualified tokens. For many years after the affirmative action mandates, employers hired unqualified minorities knowing that they would undoubtedly fail. The result was that the company appeared to be adhering to guidelines and was able to report that the employees just "didn't work out." In a similar scenario, minorities and women who are hired by a university are asked to sit on every committee and to be the representatives of all minorities. They are scrutinized and watched for every possible mistake and have no emotional or professional support while they continue to maintain responsibility for everyday teaching duties. The burn out and attrition rate of ethnic minorities is high in environments in which there are few other ethnic minorities. The institution, however, is able to say, "We tried, but they don't seem to be able to handle it."

Tokenism

Has affirmative action worked? Former Secretary of the Interior James Watts epitomizes the American answer. When asked whether he had a diversity of advisors on a committee, Watts was quoted by the press as saying that he had "a Black, a woman, a cripple, and a Jew." America's perception of a successful affirmative action program is to have "one of each." There is no understanding of quality assurance or the need for diversity—simply quotas or tokens to placate the people or to meet federal guidelines. The main problem is the lack of motivation or appreciation for the goals of affirmative action. The Spanish term for motivation is *ganas*. Without ganas, no program can be successful. But how does one motivate people, systems, and society to care about the past, present, and future consequences of discrimination? Does the United States need to be educated about other ethnicities and cultures? Does the United States need to mandate education and tolerance?

One program that forced some people to tolerate or learn to live together was mandatory busing. Sociologists, psychologists, and many others believed that behaviors and propinquity could possibly change attitudes. Thus, the idea of forced deseg-regation was extended beyond *Brown v. the Board of Education*. Research has shown that many of the forced busing programs worked in areas where the residents already were somewhat in favor of integration; but the programs were not as successful in areas where the residents did not favor integration. Similarly, if affirmative action is viewed as a mandatory program to hire ethnic minorities, it may not be accepted. What are the alternatives? Quotas were set in the 1960s because drastic change was needed. Maybe the country should review affirmative action and amend it for the 1990s?

Racism and Benign Neglect

Is affirmative action not working because the resisters are racists and sexists? As I stated earlier, if employers wish to discriminate, they can find subtle ways to ac-complish this and still avoid the watchful eyes of the regulators. Another type of resister, who may be more dangerous than the subtle one, is the one who forgets to attend to diversity. Benign neglect is often perpetuated by liberals who think they respond to discrimination issues openly. It is a dangerous form of resistance because it is excused as an oversight rather than dealt with as a direct act of discrimination. The law, however, does not allow for oversights. It states: "Ignorance of the law is no excuse." Sexual harassment statutes also state that third party liability is enacted when the employer or supervisor knew, or should have known about the particular acts of sexual harassment that were occurring in his or her domain. Perhaps this should pertain also to covert and forgotten acts of discrimination.

Covert acts of discrimination put the victims in a position of defending themselves by having to prove discrimination. A common statement heard by many minorities and women is, "You are too sensitive; they really didn't mean that." In actuality, groups who are discriminated against are very perceptive, whereas the group perpetrating the discrimination is the one that is unaware. One study (Rollins, 1978) showed that a group of Black undergraduates were able to pick up on subtle cues of purposeful discrimination, whereas the White undergraduates were not. Ethnic minorities can also perceive racism during interviews for college. If a university is giving lip service to achieving diversity, the minority applicant more than likely will perceive the sit-uation as it really is, no matter what doctrines are advocated publicaly by the institution.

Minority groups know that discrimination exists in the real world, and recently two media broadcasts have helped prove it. For example, racist comments such as those made by Jimmy "The Greek" Snider and former Los Angeles Dodgers' executive Al Campanis are not surprising to Blacks. Non-Blacks were surprised and tried to explain the ignorant comments as mistakes. Snider's comments about genetic phys-iology were no less racist than were Campanis's comments about genetic intelligence. Both statements were racist and stereotypical. Both men were not alone in their beliefs; their comments reflect the typical thoughts of many Americans.

Suggestions for Recruitment

Psychology must begin more aggressive efforts at recruiting ethnic minorities. More scholarships, modifications of the curriculum, an increase in the number of minority faculty members, and expanded employment opportunities are needed to make psychology more attractive. Recruitment and retention of students and faculty are closely intertwined because psychology cannot repopulate its ethnic minority and female faculty without graduating students, but students are less likely to enter a field that has no faculty advisors.

Administrative Commitment

Recruitment for diversity must be approached as any administrative policy is approached. First and foremost, the department and the university must have a genuine commitment to achieving diversity. Second, short- and long-term goals must be established, and strategies must be outlined to achieve these goals. If a major university is a major university, the administration knows how to outline these tasks. Diversity is achieved in the same manner as any other university goal, that is, the administration must demonstrate its commitment by making the necessary allocation of money and personnel. Many universities, for example, recently have budgeted positions dedicated to recruitment and development of faculty.

Money also needs to be provided for increased salaries for the faculty. The academic world is in competition with the private sector. Many PhD holders with a research or clinical background can obtain more gainful employment in the private sector than in academia. Ethnic minorities and women are very marketable in the business world. One departmental chair felt that he should pay ethnic minority faculty more money because they provide professional expertise that no one else in his department is able to provide.

Tenure

New graduates with PhDs usually enter academia with tenure as a goal. If the facts indicate that obtaining tenure is unlikely, new graduates may not pursue the academic avenue. Why should a professional join an institution that disallows the possibility of advancement? The formula for obtaining tenure varies among universities, and many times within the same department, depending upon who is being considered. Presently, there are several tenure lawsuits pending concerning the denial of tenure to women and minority faculty members. Many cases previously have been settled out of court because the particular university did not wish to proceed with litigation. Every professional knows of at least one individual who feels that he or she was not granted tenure because of a differential review process.

Standardized tenure reviews are difficult because reviews are (and should be) individualized. However, if one faculty member is lauded for his or her community work or teaching evaluations, another should not be penalized for the same. Fair review processes with a diversity of "points" for specialties, competencies, and unique offerings to the university should be incorporated at all universities. The tenure process needs to be re-reviewed. Currently, it is a policy based on an "ol' boy" network, and it needs updating.

A publication record is important in the tenure review process. It is the academic "production record." But the record of ethnic minorities being published in professional journals, acting as reviewers, and serving as editors (only one ethnic minority is presently an editor of an APA journal) is not good. There are many possible reasons for this: a closed ol' boy network, research pertaining to minorities and women is not seen as legitimate, much research on ethnic groups is not conducted in the traditional APA model (e.g., no White control group), lack of publication mentors for new ethnic researchers, and so forth. Many women and minorities choose to publish in specialty journals (e.g., *Journal of Black Psychology*). Publication in these journals is seen as not being as prestigious as in other non-APA mainstream journals.

Productive and Supportive Environment

Being the sole, or one of the few, ethnic minority faculty is professionally and personally difficult. The difficulty can be seen in isolation from collaborative research and intellectual or professional stimulation. Lack of ethnic minority students puts minority faculty at a disadvantage for having research assistants and for possible joint publishing. In addition, as was discussed earlier, ethnic minority and female faculty experience burnout or overwork from being on multiple committees, acting as advisors or confidants to ethnic and female students (graduate and undergraduate), and being in the stressful position of having to demonstrate that minorities and women can succeed.

In order to reduce the personal and professional difficulties entailed in having only small numbers of minority faculty members, universities need to hire a critical mass of ethnic minorities and women. For institutions completely lacking in diversity, hiring more than one ethnic minority or woman at a time is recommended. I would like to name this the "Noah Plan." Although this plan does not guarantee that the two (or more) minority faculty will be compatible as friends or colleagues, it does increase the probability of collegiality and allows for a reduction in the work load that might have been placed on a single individual.

The final element in this recruitment equation is respect. Ethnic minority and female graduates should be treated as viable professionals. They have obtained their degrees by fulfilling all the requirements that a White male graduate has fulfilled. Their abilities are no less; their specialities no less important. An ethnic minority or female faculty member should be viewed as an asset rather than a federal mandate.

A large percentage of tenured faculty will be retiring within the next 5–10 years. Psychology has a grand opportunity to replenish the faculty with a diversity of professionals. Diversity in terms of ethnicity, sex, sexual orientation, disabilities, psychological specialties, counseling techniques, and so forth is imperative. If psychology is the study of human behavior, it must be relevant and appropriate to all humans. A commitment to accomplishing this goal and appropriate strategies must begin now.

12

THE PROBLEM OF ORGANIZATIONAL CULTURE IN ACHIEVING ETHNIC DIVERSITY IN PROFESSIONAL PSYCHOLOGY TRAINING: IMPLICATIONS FOR RECRUITMENT

Billy E. Vaughn
California School of Professional Psychology
San Diego, California

Generally, it is accepted that schools of professional psychology (SPPs) that are traditionally composed of White ethnic faculty and students need to focus on: (a) training professionals who are able to serve the underserved and (b) increasing the numbers of students in training who share social history with the underserved. There is no commonly accepted view about the means for achieving either goal. Regardless of the strategy used, an institution must consider the cultural factors that create barriers to attaining the goal.

In this chapter I discuss an organizational culture's resistance to change, particularly how organizational culture restricts the establishment of ethnic diversity in SPPs and the roles that institutional leaders and ethnic minority faculty need to assume in the establishment and maintenance of ethnic diversity in professional psychology training programs. Because the organizational culture of traditionally White ethnic SPPs is incompatible with the concept of ethnic cultural diversity, its ethnocentric nature must be replaced by culturally sensitive perspectives.

Special appreciation is given to Ms. Kendra Allen for her technical assistance. A special thanks to the leaders of member schools of NCSPP for providing the context for writing this chapter. This chapter is dedicated to Dr. George Stricker, whose leadership during the conference was outstanding and exemplary.

In the first part of the chapter I address the role of organizational culture in SPPs. The nature of organizational culture and its consequences are characterized. It is claimed that in order to effectuate multiculturalism in SPPs, organizational culture must be changed. In the second section I consider the role that leaders play, either in directing their institutions toward establishing ethnic diversification or in maintaining conditions that perpetuate ethnocentrism. I conclude the chapter with a discussion of why and how an ethnically diverse faculty is critical in bringing about institutional change.

The Organizational Culture of Schools of Professional Psychology

Culture represents the shared assumptions that constitute what members of an organization perceive and define as their activity and adaptive behavior (Schein, 1985). Culture influences how members of an organization react to institutional change. Changes that are counter to the underlying assumptions of the culture cause resistance. The resistance is primarily a function of the inherent threat of proposed changes to the institutional status quo. Although a group may be committed to change, cultural factors may impede its efforts. According to Schein (1985), cultural factors may cause resistance to institutional change by (a) influencing perceptions and behaviors, (b) unconsciously controlling behavior, and (c) potentially creating subcultures that are based on differing opinions about how to affect change.

Influence on Perceptions and Behaviors and Resistance to Institutional Change

The influence of an institution's culture on the perceptions and resulting behaviors of its members is one source of resistance to change. Perceptions are based on deeply held, longstanding assumptions about the institution's underlying philosophy, what makes it unique, and what makes it successful. In the early stages of an institution's growth, its ideology is made explicit in order to formulate ground rules for engaging as a group in clarifying objectives and operationalizing them. Over time, the ideology becomes implicit in the group's behaviors. Perceptions of appropriate behaviors, who belongs on the basis of their behaviors, and how to deal with inappropriate behaviors are instrumental in maintaining the status quo of an organization. These perceptions serve the useful purpose of identifying the boundaries of group membership. They also can act as impediments, however, if a group wishes to expand its membership to include people whose perceptions are different from those of the in-group.

Members of SPPs share many commonly held perceptions and behaviors. For example, it is generally accepted that the goal of SPPs is to train psychologists who can systematically apply disciplined knowledge in problem solving to individual assessment or community change (Peterson, 1986a). Furthermore, it is assumed that knowledge and skills should be developed in a way that allows classroom learning and practical experience to fit hand in glove. Unlike the training programs of traditional schools, which focus on research and reserve intensive practical experience for the postdoctoral period, SPPs were founded on the assumption that students and society could benefit from earlier focus on application.

Many assumptions regarding training are accepted collectively across the SPP culture, but one cannot expect that all perceptions and behaviors are universal. The theoretical basis of the various training models, for example, can be a source of controversy. Although training goals may be identical, the theoretical orientations of SPPs vary from psychodynamic to behavioral. Furthermore, there is controversy about which degree, PsyD or PhD, is more appropriate for the clinical psychologist. This dispute is intimately connected to the problem of adequately defining the scientist–practitioner training model. Both examples illustrate the cultural influence on perceptions and behaviors that underlies the formation of assumptions commonly shared by members of an institution. These assumptions are difficult to change.

Unconscious Control of Behavior and Resistance to Institutional Change

The culture of an organization tends to reside outside the conscious awareness of its members. The membership's inability to perceive how its cultural assumptions limit efforts to achieve goals contributes to resistance to change. This is evidenced by an organization's disruption when it is confronted with a demand for change that is contrary to its cultural assumptions (e.g., implementing strategies to make ethnic diversity an integral part of the organization).

Language produces an unconscious source of control over behavior. Behavior is difficult to change if language remains static. Therefore, an institution usually requires new vocabulary to help it integrate new ideas. Abstract concepts such as "good instruction," "quality control," and "competency," can mean different things to different people. A new vocabulary helps to control for a breakdown in communication that results from different interpretations of the same word. In order to facilitate discussion of ways to achieve cultural diversity in SPPs, words such as *ethnic minorities*, *underserved*, and *multicultural*, have been introduced to characterize people with a history different from that of members of the traditional culture. Vocabulary such as *competency*, *quality control*, and *resources* is used frequently in discussions concerning achieving cultural diversity because it implies agreement about shared interpretations and connotes what is not acceptable for change.

There are other ways in which an institutional culture can restrict the potential to change. For example, there is a question about the extent to which psychoanalytic training is adequate for preparing the professional psychologist to deliver service to underserved populations (B. E. Vaughn, 1988). If the culture of an SPP institution is primarily influenced by psychoanalytic views, it is conceivable that alternative training models (e.g., a cultural approach) will be met with considerable resistance. Thus an institution may be committed to change, but its training orientation restricts its ability to reshape.

Potential for Creating Subcultures and Resistance to Change

A third potential source of resistance to institutional change is the formation of subcultures. The concept of organizational culture has been extended to explain the formation of subcultures within institutions (Van Maanen & Barley, 1985) and has been considered in terms of subcultural organization in academia (e.g., Crane, 1972). Subcultural organization is a natural part of institutional growth. As the number of people within an organization increases, the likelihood of subculture formation increases. Because larger numbers of personnel tend to exist at the lower end of an institution's hierarchy, the potential for subcultural division at the lowest hierarchical level is greatest.

Subcultures are the established and sustained bonds among people who share some commonality, particularly perception and understanding of their roles in an organization. The hierarchical arrangement of institutions inherently encourages the formation of subcultures, or groups of people who share more among themselves than they do with those at other levels of the organization. Academic deans, for example, can be considered a subculture. They tend to share similar points of view about their roles in academia, often have a shared vocabulary, and appear to have more in common with each other than they do with other members of the same institution.

If an SPP has more than one training program, the different programs can be the basis of subcultural organization. Industrial/organizational students and faculty, for example, may consider themselves as having different perspectives and needs than those of students and faculty in the clinical program. There may be subdivisions within a degree program; psychodynamically oriented students may share a language that is different from those who are behaviorally oriented. When SPPs began to include ethnic minorities in significant numbers, subcultures were formed on the basis of ethnic group membership.

One type of subcultural split, common within large institutions, is based on political ideology and occurs between liberals and conservatives (Schein, 1985). Liberals tend to be newcomers who believe that making changes in some of the long-standing organizational assumptions will be beneficial for growth or refinement. The conservatives tend to be those who have been around for a long time, especially those who were a part of the founding leadership. They are more likely to promote the status quo.

Subcultural organization, usually considered a healthy part of institutional life, can be an impediment to change if the changes challenge institutional assumptions. Subcultures based on political ideology can undermine academic institutions' efforts to pursue commitments to achieve ethnic diversity. On the one hand, liberals tend to believe that ethnic minorities should be included unconditionally. They tend to understand that a multicultural environment means that people not only look different, but will speak and think differently, too. On the other hand, conservatives are likely to believe that ethnic minorities should participate only if they are not different from Whites in terms of what has traditionally been considered "good faculty" or "good students." Conservative psychologists believe that the status quo is a sufficient measure of how all should be viewed. Any variables that do not meet the conservative criteria for institutional compatibility are discounted. Although each ideological subculture imposes a different resistance to change, the conservative one is more likely to undermine efforts to achieve cultural diversity.

From an ethnocentric perspective, ethnic minorities, entering into a traditionally White ethnic SPP, will be required to demonstrate a level of conformity that is Anglocentric in nature. Ethnic minorities either will have to conform to the extent that they will no longer be able to identify with those who share their sociocultural history, or they will choose to leave the institution. It is unlikely that cultural diversity will ever be achieved as long as conservatives control institutional decisions. Liberals tend to be open to discussions about different ways to achieve diversity, especially when the advice of ethnic minority professionals is included, but it is not certain if they can accept all conditions necessary for institutional change. Bringing about change necessitates thinking in a way that both liberals and conservatives may find difficult if it requires rejection of longstanding assumptions (e.g., what constitutes a good training model).

The Role of Institutional Leaders in Effecting Change

I recommend that each SPP engage in a self-study to determine the ways in which its organizational culture creates barriers for incorporating ethnic diversity into its population and its view of training. The self-study should focus on three elements:

1. The nature of the institution's assumptions about its practice, including its social and historical development.
2. Further research to determine if and how these assumptions can implicitly undermine the institution's commitment to achieve ethnic diversity.
3. A consideration of the potential for subcultural formation within the institution in order to be able to deal effectively with the subcultures if they undermine the execution of the institution's commitment.

Achieving cultural diversity requires changes (e.g., in ideologies, values, and language) in the organization's culture that are inconsistent with the status quo. Thus, institutional leaders must assume the responsibility for guiding the effort to change the sources of ethnocentrism that create barriers to achieving diversity.

An organization inevitably faces times of transition or crisis caused by the interdependency between it and the larger institutions within which it is embedded (Siehl, 1985). The relatively recent mandate to include ethnic diversity in psychology training programs (APA, 1986a) has been a source of external pressure to psychology graduate education. Ethnic diversity was not considered an issue during the emergence of professional clinical psychology. As a result, the founders of the professional school movement necessarily created SPPs that embodied an ethnocentric culture. Presently, governing bodies, such as the APA, have become sensitive to the importance of training ethnic psychologists who reflect the ethnic diversity of the larger population. Because times have changed, it is the role of current leaders to guide their respective institutions toward making the changes that are necessary in order to meet the present challenge of achieving diversity.

Schein (1985) identified several things that managers (leaders) must be mindful of in order to overcome cultural problems faced by institutions. First, managers must be taught how to identify cultural factors and not to confuse them with values, climate, philosophy, and so forth. Second, managers need to consider how nonhuman elements of culture, such as the institution's basic sense of its mission and goals, can create obstacles to diversity. Because there is no such thing as culture-free management, managers need to understand how culture controls management, not vice versa. There is no correct culture, only different ones. The goal of a manager should be to realize the best match between cultural assumptions and environmental reality.

Achieving ethnic diversity in an historically White ethnic organization inevitably will be a source of institutional conflict. The manager must facilitate and guide the group's activities (e.g., through a self-study) with an understanding of the relation between the institution's culture and its implications for creating ethnic diversity. Adequate response to multiple subcultures (e.g., conservatives and liberals) within an institution demonstrates effective management. A much greater challenge, however, for leaders of SPPs is the management of multiple realities, based on the sociocultural differences among people, in an ethnocentric profession.

The leader's imperative, in order to meet the objective of cultural diversity, is to assign the highest priority to the hiring of ethnic minority faculty. The leader's support of ethnic minority faculty members will provide opportunities for traditional faculty to engage in productive discourse needed to promote mandated changes. In terms of carrying out a commitment to achieve ethnic diversity, it is clear that the most successful SPPs have been those with insightful leaders who have confronted ethnocentrism and implemented institutional changes in culture (e.g., California School of Professional Psychology: Los Angeles, under the leadership of Connell F. Persico and Esteban L. Olmedo).

Increasing Ethnic Minority Faculty to Defeat Institutional Ethnocentrism

Given the many obstacles to the implementation of cultural diversity in SPPs, it is not surprising that ethnic minority participation lags behind the general population's need. One way in which SPPs can attend to this discrepancy is to focus on faculty recruitment, rather than on ethnic minority student enrollment. It is clear from past research that ethnic minority students feel more institutional support when a number of faculty share their sociocultural history (Boetigger, Perry, Steiny, Vaughn, & Williams, 1988; Watts, 1987). Focusing on ethnic minority student recruitment, without sufficient faculty and curricula resources, is ineffective in attracting and retaining ethnic minority students. The essential role played by ethnic minority faculty in the recruitment of ethnic minority students cannot be overstated.

Ethnic minority faculty are critical in meeting the specific training needs of ethnic minority students because of their ability and commitment to teach courses that relate culture or ethnicity to professional practice. Ethnic faculty members assist in the recruitment and retention of ethnic minority students, teach courses that are cultural in perspective, and act as mentors for ethnic minority students. Ethnic minority faculty also serve as resources for White students who are interested in an ethnocultural training component.

In many ways, ethnic minority faculty serve as the advocates of cultural diversity. First of all, they promote minority students' needs by acting as a bridge between minority students and White faculty and administration. The ethnic minority faculty constitute a level of management that can support students and inform the administration of students' needs. They have insights into ethnic minority student needs that may go unnoticed by the White faculty.

In addition, the ethnic minority faculty serve as promoters of ethnic diversity to the institution at large. They can be instrumental in interpreting multicultural perspectives for the institutional mainstream. Minority faculty members also can help to integrate multicultural perspectives into the institutional culture.

Ethnic minority faculty value their sociocultural history and believe that traditional

SPPs are embodied within a restrictive cultural perspective. Changes in organizational culture depend on the training model's diversification of its cultural perspective. Many conservatives and some liberals believe that this means teaching about all ethnic groups. More insightful people, however, understand that sensitivity to cultural differences is a matter of defeating ethnocentric thinking rather than developing multiple perspectives.

Recently, there has been an increase in the role of ethnic minority faculty participation in professional psychology training. Many of the new faculty are still learning the culture of their SPPs. Within this group of new ethnic minority faculty, there are a few who are interested in being assimilated into their institution's status quo and are not likely to serve as leaders in ethnic minority affairs. Institutions, committed to faculty retention, will need to deal with the needs of a growing number of ethnic minority faculty who are self-actualized from their own sociocultural perspective.

Conclusion

The literature on incorporating multicultural issues into professional psychology training supports the view that the culture of traditionally White ethnic institutions creates a barrier to ethnic diversity. Most clinical psychology training programs (and, presumably, other professional psychology programs) are lacking in a multicultural approach (Bernal & Padilla, 1982) and are lacking in multicultural and multiracial perspectives, values, and implicit ideology (Chunn, Dunston, & Ross-Sheriff, 1983; Watts, 1987). An ethnically diverse training program, however, must include these elements in its curriculum in order for ethnic minority students to perceive their training as being relevant to their sociocultural experience (B. E. Vaughn, 1988; Watts, 1987).

Traditional SPPs developed from an ethnocentric perspective. Ethnic diversity was not a consideration when the language, training model, bylaws, and so forth, that served as the framework for program development were formulated. This framework has been quite successful for training White ethnic students, but it is limited from a multicultural perspective.

Ethnic minority students who attend traditional SPPs do not experience their graduate training as being sensitive to their needs. From their perspective, learning the rules not only requires taking on a perspective that is Anglocentric, but also requires a level of conformity that may interfere with their work with people with whom they share sociocultural history. In addition, ethnic minority students may be evaluated unfairly because the institutional criteria do not allow for differences in language, perception, and social history.

Institutional ethnocentrism needs to be addressed in any serious effort to achieve ethnic diversity in SPPs. Although an ethnocentric perspective may have been useful in the early stages of developing model programs for training White ethnic students, it creates a barrier when the goal is to train people of diverse ethnic histories or to train from a multicultural perspective. Studying the organizational culture of an institution is a key factor for developing an understanding of the way in which ethnocentrism creates language, perceptions, and behaviors that appear insensitive to other ethnic groups. This cannot be done effectively without ethnic minority faculty who are able to help provide the institution with such insight. Leaders of institutions who are committed to achieving ethnic diversity can use knowledge of their organization's culture to determine which factors will contribute to achieving the goal and which will create barriers. It is through their guidance and modeling of appropriate behaviors that members of their institutions can gain insight into the changes needed to become a more culturally diverse organization.

PART IV
STUDENT RECRUITMENT
AND RETENTION

13

THE COMMITMENT TO AFFIRMATIVE DIVERSITY THROUGH STUDENT RECRUITMENT AND RETENTION

W. Rodney Hammond

Wright State University
Dayton, Ohio

At its midwinter 1986–1987 conference, the National Council of Schools of Professional Psychology (NCSPP) organized the Committee on Minority Participation and Service to Underserved Populations (CMPSUP) as part of its developing commitment to focus on ethnic and racial issues. In the following year, this committee was divided into four subcommittees in order to address the following ethnic and racial training issues more specifically and more intensively: faculty recruitment and retention, student recruitment and retention, curriculum, and service delivery. The tasks of the Subcommittee on Student Recruitment and Retention were to (a) share knowledge on barriers to program entry and completion for minority students, (b) highlight successful means for making psychology training more accessible to minorities, and (c) generate resolutions on minority student recruitment and retention for NCSPP endorsement.

Two years after the inception of the CMPSUP, NCSPP designated issues in minority education and training as the theme of its midwinter 1988–1989 Puerto Rico conference. Devoting its annual conference to this issue signified NCSPP's recognition of the need for greater racial and ethnic diversity among schools of professional psychology (SPPs) and the commitment of member schools to carry out this responsibility. To assist with the implementation of effective recruitment and retention strategies, the preconference planning group presented a descriptive overview of the related issues and a set of initial recommendations.

A summary of the relevant issues underscores the complex relationships that

---

I thank Betty Yung for assistance in preparing this chapter.

influence minority student recruitment and retention, including the interaction of attitudinal, institutional, and geographic factors. These issues include the following:

1. The need for aggressive recruitment campaigns to be accompanied by equitable admissions processes and mechanisms to support the timely graduation of minority students.
2. The recognition of competition for the existing talent pool of minority students with other professions and between psychology training programs.
3. The need for multifaceted and innovative approaches to minority recruitment, including the need to assess the image of professional psychology as a career to provide a base for better informed marketing strategies.
4. The development of greater visibility among minorities at earlier levels in the career pathway, both to attract potential students to the profession and to help them prepare better for entry and successful program completion.
5. The development of traditional and nontraditional funding support for minority trainees.
6. The impact of the institutional environment on minority recruitment and retention (e.g., presence of minority role models; a visibly diverse student body; opportunities for academic study of, and clinical practice with, minority populations; and a demonstrable student support system).
7. The effects of central institutional values on the allocation of resources needed to provide a supportive atmosphere for minority trainees.
8. The need to assess and clarify goals related to the geographical focus of the training program (national, regional, state, or metropolitan) that influence the scope of recruitment efforts.

The NCSPP Puerto Rico Conference

Presentations

Each of the invited papers (chapters 14, 15, and 16 of this volume) contributed to a deeper understanding of the previously described issues, confirmed needs, and suggested solutions to identified deficits. For example, in "Minority Student Recruitment and Retention: Is There a Secret to Success?" (chapter 14), Porche-Burke reviews general barriers to the recruitment and retention of minority students, noting that practices often point to a lack of full commitment on the part of the institution. She provides a detailed description of the successful model used by the California School of Professional Psychology: Los Angeles (CSPP: Los Angeles), including the recruitment and admissions processes and the personal and academic support system made available to minority students.

McHolland, Lubin, and Forbes (chapter 15, "Problems in Minority Recruitment and Strategies for Retention") elaborate on the barriers that impede minority student participation in graduate clinical psychology training programs, including perceptions about the profession; cultural conflicts; and financial, psychological, and role constraints affecting likely candidates. They depict the interdependence of elements within the training environment that affect recruitment and retention efforts and reflect on the institutional value system and culture. They summarize survey data on the numbers of minority students, faculty, administrators, and staff within NCSPP schools and outline representative strategies used by NCSPP members to attract and support minority student inclusion.

In chapter 16, "Participation of Ethnic Minorities in Psychology: Where Do We Stand Today?" Kohout and Pion compare specific trends in ethnic minority participation in psychology to those in other disciplines. They identify trends in health service provider subfields and forecast future minority student pools by examining the numbers and educational attainments of minority students at the precollegiate and undergraduate levels. They conclude that, although there have been percentage gains in numbers of minorities completing educational programs at all levels and minority representation in psychology is greater than in other graduate science fields, there is continued underrepresentation of minorities in psychology training programs in relation to their representation in the general U.S. population and the professional work force. Kohout and Pion reinforce the perception of the need to improve recruitment and retention programs for minority trainees. Their report of decline of minority students earning bachelor's degrees in psychology verifies the need for earlier outreach in order to increase numbers of minority students in the educational pipeline and predicts that future recruitment efforts will need to be still more vigorous and creative.

Resolutions and Guidelines

The Puerto Rico conference led to the endorsement of two resolutions, signifying member schools' affirmation of intent to increase the proportion of ethnic minority trainees. These resolutions will (a) help to establish a mechanism to assist schools in developing policies and procedures for recruiting and retaining ethnically and racially diverse faculty and students and (b) provide for recognition of outstanding work in promoting cultural diversity through annual distinguished contribution awards, one to a member institution and one to an individual.

Specific guidelines were set forth to aid member schools in acting on the subscribed principles. These included (a) incorporation of principles of affirmative diversity into member schools' mission statements, (b) development of specific plans for addressing ethnic minority input within the admissions process, (c) support of ethnic minority student organizations, (d) involvement of alumni, and (e) allocation of financial and other resources to support recruitment and retention programs.

Additional Resources for Accomplishing Affirmative Diversity

By adopting *affirmative diversity* as a central value, SPPs may seek additional assistance in reinvigorating their efforts by continuing to investigate successful recruitment and retention techniques. Excellent general guidance for achieving the full participation of minorities in graduate and professional education can be found in the American Council on Education's recent publication, *Minorities on Campus: A Handbook for Enhancing Diversity* (Green, 1989). Although the contents of this publication are targeted to higher education in general, the working assumptions, principles, and recruitment and retention strategies suggested are fully applicable to psychology training programs. Of particular value is a section on conducting an internal audit, describing how to assess the status of minority participation (a first step toward developing a comprehensive plan to increase minority participation). Recruitment and retention strategies noted in the section of the handbook on graduate and professional students are comprehensive and are transferrable for use in graduate education in psychology. A checklist for assessing efforts in these areas is included, along with a list of programs that have demonstrated success.

Expertise within NCSPP member schools should be helpful in developing specific action plans. The success of CSPP: Los Angeles is noted by Porche-Burke (chapter 14, this volume). The Wright State University School of Professional Psychology is another NCSPP member that has had outstanding success in recruitment, timely program completion, and subsequent employment of minority students (Hammond, 1987). Since 1982, Wright State has awarded 214 doctoral degrees, of which 36 (16.8%) went to minority students. Current minority enrollment constitutes 24%. Factors contributing to the success of this program include the following:

1. A vigorous and multifaceted recruitment program that includes culturally specific recruitment materials directed to networks of feeder institutions, practicing psychologists, and program alumni, along with structured visitations for potential minority applicants.
2. An equitable, value-based admissions process that considers personal as well as academic characteristics of potential minority trainees and uses an ethnically diverse selection committee.
3. A culturally sensitive environment that offers coursework and practica experiences focusing on minority mental health issues and exposure to minority psychologist role models (full-time faculty and adjuncts in clinical supervision, practitioner, and teaching roles).
4. A strong student support system that offers personal and academic assistance to minority trainees, as well as opportunities to interact socially with minority faculty and staff.
5. Innovative ways to support the financial needs of minority trainees, including the application of overhead from the faculty owned and operated private practice toward stipend support for students in practicum placements, and university work–study support for practicum work in the university student counseling center.

Professional Psychology Compared With Other Health Professions

In addition to replicating the practices of specific clinical psychology training programs that have proven to be successful in minority student recruitment and retention, SPPs can benefit from the experiences of other health professions. In this regard, the example of Health Career Opportunity Program-funded (HCOP) programs may be worth reviewing. This Public Health Service program has been providing government funding for structured programs to help minority students enter and graduate from health and allied health professions since 1972, and it has invested nearly $173 million dollars in almost 400 HCOP programs since 1978 (U.S. Department of Health and Human Services, 1988). Literature describing the outcomes of such programs suggests directions that might be fruitful for clinical psychology training programs, although program characteristics vary. The recruitment and retention strategies used in typical HCOP-funded programs are shown in Table 1.

In comparison to clinical psychology, the medical professions do not have to contend with a negative stereotypical image in minority communities. They tend to experience fewer difficulties attracting minority student applications. Thus the medical professions rely on well-established feeder patterns and formal agreements with undergraduate institutions, as well as on participation in consortial type preprofessional education programs that may ultimately result in students being channelled to apply for admission to their training programs. However, barriers to entry, retention, and timely completion of medical programs seem to be greater than in psychology training programs. Entry requirements are more stringent academically, more frequently based mainly on standardized admissions tests, and rely less on personal strengths and talents that may offset academic deficiencies. As a result, the medical professions place emphasis on academic pre-preparation and earlier outreach to potential students. Curricula for such programs have an intensive discipline content focus. In addition, their study skills and academic student support programs appear to be better developed, more formalized, and better validated by research than are similar components in clinical psychology training programs.

Conclusion

The conference paper presentations, resolutions, and guidelines serve to illuminate impediments to the full and appropriate level of minority participation in professional psychology training programs. They also suggest strategies that SPPs can adopt to help them become more successful in their efforts to improve currently inequitable minority representation. However, these work products cannot affect the level of commitment and effort with which NCSPP schools approach this task.

Most SPPs seem perfectly amenable to welcoming "qualified" minorities, if they apply. Many express a fervent desire to have more minorities in their programs and profess a genuine sense of frustration at not having minorities select their schools. However, as James M. Jones noted in his keynote address (see chapter 3, this volume), there are qualitative differences between psychology training programs with high and low minority enrollments. These differences distinctly relate to the institutional valuing of, and emphasis on, minority student participation, as is reflected in allocation of resources and in specific policies and practices that facilitate program entry and completion. It is clear that if SPPs want to improve the representation of ethnic minorities in enrollment and among graduates they will have to make more than a superficial effort. Future progress must entail (a) values clarification and, in some instances, a significant change in values; (b) long-term commitment and redirection of substantial resources; and (c) organizational leadership capable of implementing those techniques and ideas likely to succeed.

As used in this chapter, the term *affirmative diversity* connotes an important principle that ideally should underlie the future efforts to include ethnic minorities among committed SPPs. It affirms the fundamental value of human diversity in society, with the belief that enhancing diversity increases rather than diminishes quality (Jones, in press). This constitutes a standard of commitment to change that goes well beyond affirmative action. It implies that successful ethnic minority student recruitment and retention will depend on an intrinsic commitment to affirmative diversity among

Table 1
Recruitment and Retention Strategies for Minorities in Health Professions Training Programs

---

Recruitment Strategies

General Strategies
- Interest groups in the discipline area
- Invitations to campus lecture series and conferences
- Pre-admission workshops and open houses
- Preliminary education programs (secondary level)
- Formal arrangements with feeder institutions
- Soliciting referrals from current students, alumni, and practitioners
- Personal contacts
- Recruitment materials especially developed for minority students
- Visits to predominantly minority institutions
- Establishment of recruitment networks (state and private health, career organizations, colleges and universities)
- Publicity campaigns (e.g., feature articles on minority practitioners in local newspapers)
- Visibility of minority faculty and staff in all recruitment activities
- Media presentations in undergraduate or high school classes
- Joint undergraduate and faculty or graduate student projects

Facilitating Entry
- Academic coursework (undergraduate review, or mini-courses in difficult subjects)
- Preparation for entrance exams
- Interviewing skills
- Clarifying admissions procedures
- Assistance with completion of financial aid forms
- Coaching on writing of autobiographical statements
- Simulated admissions exercises (with both students and selection committee)
- Advising on letters of recommendation
- Review of application materials, followed by individual guidance
- Lectures on stress management, and family role changes
- Academic skill development

Retention Strategies

Academic Supports and Study Skills
- Learning and assessment laboratories
- Test-taking and note-taking
- Practice examinations
- Self-study plans
- Individualized prescriptions
- Time management
- Library research
- Computer skills
- Writing laboratories
- Scientific writing
- Multimedia autotutorials
- Computer-assisted instruction
- Memorization skills
- Supplemental review sessions
- Analytical reading and reasoning
- Problem-solving skills
- Self-assessment of study habits
- Organization of large quantities of materials
- Improving concentration and listening

Nonacademic Supports
- "Buddy" programs
- Stress management seminars
- Family interaction seminars
- Financial management assistance
- Group or individual counseling
- Specialized support groups
- Enrichment series (e.g., minority lecture series)
- Cultural or social activities
- Social interactions with faculty
- Involvement with community support systems (alumni, practitioners)
- Conflict resolution

professional psychology training programs. Accomplishing the expected increases in the representation of ethnic minorities assuredly will be difficult for many programs. If, however, SPPs vigorously choose to fulfill the resolutions made in Puerto Rico, they will be leaders in establishing a distinct and qualitatively better future for all of psychology.

14

MINORITY STUDENT RECRUITMENT AND RETENTION: IS THERE A SECRET TO SUCCESS?

Lisa Porche-Burke

California School of Professional Psychology
Los Angeles, California

In this chapter I discuss issues related to minority student recruitment and retention and present the model that is used at the California School of Professional Psychology: Los Angeles (CSPP: Los Angeles) to address these issues. If one surveys the literature, it is easy to note the ever-present shortage of ethnic minority mental health professionals in the field of psychology (President's Commission on Mental Health, 1978) as well as the continuing underrepresentation of ethnic minority students and faculty (Bernal, Barron, & Leary, 1983). The rapidly increasing numbers of ethnic minority individuals who potentially may seek psychological services is clearly disproportionate to the numbers of ethnic minority individuals entering into and finishing doctoral programs in the field of psychology (Bernal et al., 1983). It is clear that, although ethnic minorities nearly doubled their number among doctoral recipients between 1975 and 1984, they still represent only 8.7% of the new doctorates (J.M. Jones, 1987). Furthermore, although ethnic minority students have shown interest in psychology and psychology-related experiences, their numbers in graduate school programs simply do not reflect their interest (J. M. Jones, 1987).

Why, then, does there appear to be difficulty in the recruitment and subsequent retention of minority students in graduate programs? These problems occur because most institutions are not fully committed to, and do not behave in ways that allow for, successful recruitment and retention of ethnic minority students. If institutional values do not support the development of policies and programs that are geared toward successful recruitment and retention of ethnic minority students, then, in fact, the situation that currently exists in most graduate school programs in psychology is realized fully.

When we talk about institutional values, we are in essence asking why and for what reason institutions are committed to having a diverse and mixed group of students within their educational structure. And further, we are asking what institutions plan to do to make recruitment and retention efforts for ethnic minority students successful. It may be useful at this point to discuss some of the reasons that may, in fact, explain poor recruitment and retention.

Why Recruitment Fails

The first critical step in the process of recruitment is the initial communication between the prospective applicant and the graduate program. Clearly, it will be difficult to attract the potential ethnic minority student if the program materials do not adequately describe (a) the training opportunities and facilities for working with ethnic minority groups, (b) curriculum that addresses ethnic minority issues, (c) availability of an ethnic minority student support group, and (d) other types of information that clearly indicate an interest in and commitment to issues related to ethnic minorities (Bernal et al., 1983). Furthermore, application materials should clearly indicate the program's interest in and commitment to alleviating the financial hardships that a graduate education creates. In my experience, financial concern is one of the critical reasons why ethnic minority students are not attracted to and more widely represented in most graduate programs. Without adequate financial support, the problem of cost may be perceived as insurmountable. Students who need to work full-time, in addition to managing a graduate school program and their personal lives, may perceive the price as too great and hence be deterred from the process. Therefore, application materials need to address the financial aspect and provide substantive information regarding the available financial opportunities.

It is during the college years that students begin to think about potential career opportunities. Undergraduates who have not been advised adequately about careers in psychology may be lured to other fields that do a better job of attracting them. Accordingly, recruiting efforts should be targeted to ethnic minority students during their undergraduate years. A strong selling point for a graduate program interested in recruiting ethnic minority students is a description of the ways in which its offerings would satisfy ethnic minority students' needs.

Another issue that influences recruitment negatively is the lack of planned and thoughtful recruitment procedures that are designed to be inclusive rather than exclusive. Examples include the presence of standards that are prohibitive to ethnic minorities, such as achieving a fixed score on the Graduate Record Examination or implying that, in essence, ethnic minority students are not qualified. Will an ethnic minority student, planning a future career, be attracted to a graduate program in psychology that has erected a barrier at the onset? No, the cost is simply too great to bear.

Why Students Leave

Let us assume that, in spite of inadequate recruitment procedures, some ethnic minority students enter into graduate psychology programs. Now the issue of retention becomes critical. Why, in fact, do graduate students drop out of programs? Many of the reasons why students leave graduate programs are similar, if not identical, to the ones that may have acted as deterrents originally. Financial considerations rank highest. As was discussed earlier, it is extremely difficult for students to manage a full-time doctoral program and to work full-time. Unfortunately, this is the situation in which most students find themselves.

Second, and probably as important, it is extremely difficult to exist, function, and prosper in a setting where racism and sexism go unchecked and are not dealt with in any systematic and formal way. This brings us back to the issue of institutional support and institutional values. If an institution is truly committed to making opportunities available to ethnic minority students in the field of psychology, it needs to address institutional racism and sexism. Furthermore, it must develop a training program that defines ethnic minority issues as being important and critical to the overall educational experience, and not specifically related to a student's ethnicity. A graduate psychology program must incorporate issues that are relevant to ethnic minorities into all the curriculum content areas. If it does not, why should ethnic minority students feel positive about their education and training experiences? What message does an institution convey to the ethnic minority student preparing to matriculate through a doctoral program if it cannot demonstrate any support among the faculty-at-large for the aforementioned issues and has no ethnic minority faculty to serve as role models within the institutional structure? I contend that the message is not a positive one.

Another critical issue related to successful retention of ethnic minority students is the presence of support groups. These groups provide students with a forum that helps them to deal with the myriad issues that arise as they matriculate through their respective programs. Support groups also provide a mechanism for sharing coping strategies and increasing ethnic minority faculty involvement with students as faculty members share their own graduate school experiences with students.

I contend that the secret to successful recruitment and retention lies in the presence of strong institutional support that paves the way for (a) the development of admission policies and procedures that are inclusive, (b) financial aid packages that are attractive, and (c) curriculum and training opportunities that reflect a strong interest in and commitment to ethnic minority issues. The program at CSPP: Los Angeles is one that has been successful at attracting and retaining ethnic minority students. It may be useful to examine the reasons for its success.

California School of Professional Psychology: Los Angeles

Currently, at CSPP. Los Angeles, ethnic minorities make up approximately 18% of the total student population ($n = 85$) Some of the current practices that are followed to recruit and to retain of ethnic minority students are as follows.

- Each year, CSPP: Los Angeles hosts two open houses for the purpose of recruitment. Students are invited to come and spend time with administrators, faculty, and students. During this time students are introduced to the program and given the opportunity to interact with ethnic minority faculty and students.
- Materials are presented to prospective applicants that describe the school and specifically address the school's commitment to diversity and how issues related to ethnic minorities are integrated into the curriculum and clinical field training experiences.
- Issues related to financial aid are discussed with each student and financial assistance is made possible. In awarding and determining the composition of

aid, CSPP: Los Angeles is alert to racial and ethnic group factors in expense and debt. Institutional funds (e.g., college work–study), scholarships, and teaching assistantships are used for financial support.

- There is a well-developed proficiency in ethnic minority mental health that exists under the aegis of the clinical programs. This subspecialty track offers students the option of pursuing a PhD accredited by the American Psychological Association or a PsyD. The ethnic minority mental health proficiency is designed to provide students with an in-depth educational experience that integrates ethnic minority issues in curriculum and clinical field training experiences. Students are encouraged to develop a level of self-awareness about their ethnic and cultural identity in order to maximize their own resources and subsequently their ability to work with diverse populations. There is a strong student support group for all ethnic minority students within the ethnic minority mental health proficiency that meets regularly to address students' issues and concerns.
- There is ethnic minority faculty representation on the admissions committee, ensuring the presence of an arena in which ethnic minority issues can be heard. The ethnic minority faculty admissions committee members also participate actively in the development of policies and procedures that are inclusive rather than exclusive.
- Admission requirements are flexible. The presence of a pregraduate program allows students who may not have majored in psychology to take the necessary coursework to make them eligible for matriculation in the PhD program.
- Ethnic minority students actively participate in the recruitment of other ethnic minority students. It is important for prospective applicants to see other ethnic minority students successfully matriculating through the program and to find out, first hand, that they find the educational experience rewarding.

With respect to retention issues, it is clear that effective and successful retention of ethnic minority students cannot be achieved by a narrowly defined effort. These issues must be addressed within a multifaceted framework designed to create an educational environment and experience that ensures the possibility of successful retention. Clearly, increasing the financial opportunities that will help to defray the financial burden of a graduate school education is a critical ingredient for successful retention of ethnic minority students. The freedom from financial exigency allows students to concentrate fully on the educational experience and to realize their potential in the profession. In addition, if a program puts forth the effort to provide financial opportunities for students, it makes a strong statement about its sensitivity to the needs of ethnic minority students.

The ethnic minority mental health proficiency at CSPP: Los Angeles specifically was designed to address these issues. Figure 1 shows the four aspects of the program, conceptualized as the "quad approach," that integrate curriculum, clinical field training, research, and professional development and role modeling with a specific focus on ethnic minority issues. To look at retention issues specifically, the fourth component of the program, professional development and role modeling, particularly is designed to help ensure successful retention. The specific components of this quad are as follows.

- Student support and retention dinners are held five times a year. Ethnic minority students are invited to participate in dinner discussions with professional role models from the community. Issues related to coping strategies, time manage-

Figure 1

The Four Aspects or "Quad Approach" of the Ethnic Minority Mental Health Proficiency at the California School of Professional Psychology: Los Angeles.

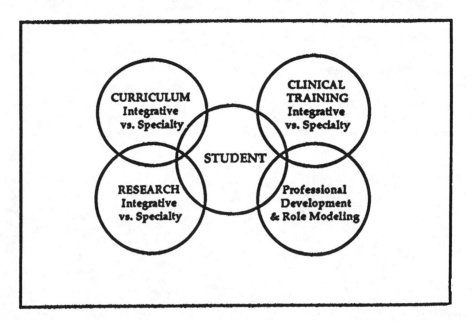

ment, and professional development are discussed, and students are given the opportunity to interact informally with ethnic minority faculty and professionals. This is a critical component of the program as it provides students with an opportunity to gain a clear perspective on what it takes to become a competent psychologist, particularly as it relates to dealing with a variety of individuals from a range of cultural backgrounds (Porche-Burke & Olmedo, 1988).

- Professional development groups is a one-credit course taken each year during students' matriculation in the program. These groups are designed to provide (a) ongoing professional development advisement for students and (b) a forum within which students discuss issues, such as racism and sexism, that affect their educational experience.

- Faculty and student advisor–advisee relationships are critical to successful retention. Each student is paired with an ethnic minority mental health faculty member who serves as the student's academic and professional development advisor. This allows for close monitoring of a student's academic and clinical field training progress during the program.

- The minority student support organization meets once a month. Members of this organization are involved in various activities of the ethnic minority mental health proficiency. For example, each year students plan and execute an annual conference that is devoted to ethnic minority issues. They are also encouraged to use this group to discuss issues or concerns that may be affecting their progress in the program.

- A peer tutorial program is organized each year by the students to assist in the preparation for comprehensive examinations. Students arrange and hold study sessions and share study materials.

- Dissertation development groups are formed for third- and fourth-year students. Students have an opportunity, on an ongoing basis, to share their research with others and receive feedback and support from both peers and faculty.

Although the aforementioned strategies are critical, none can be truly successful without the presence of strong institutional support and institutional commitment to ethnic minority issues. We need to stop paying lip service to the issues of successful recruitment and retention. Instead, as a group of educators, we must move toward implementation. The secret of successful recruitment and retention of ethnic minority students lies within us and our ability to create graduate psychology programs that are sensitive to the needs of ethnic minority students and place ethnic minority issues in a position of importance.

15

PROBLEMS IN MINORITY RECRUITMENT AND STRATEGIES FOR RETENTION

James McHolland and Marc Lubin
Illinois School of Professional Psychology
Chicago, Illinois

and

Wesley Forbes
California School of Professional Psychology
Fresno, California

The problems of minority recruitment are broad based and mirror the wider problems of American society and its professional psychology training institutions. In addressing these problems, one needs to be aware that to recruit minority applicants successfully, institutions must attend to the pervasiveness of resistance and conflict involved in the pursuit of this goal. In doing so, the face of professional psychology can be changed more effectively.

Understandably, there is a need to review the reluctance of minority populations to attend clinical doctoral programs. The review must include a discussion of the minority applicant's valid perceptions of the profession and the programs, because those perceptions may fuel the reluctance. As psychology teaches, any significant human problem is created and sustained by multiple forces. The first step in effective minority recruitment is to identify the negative forces. Then, multiple and interrelated strategies need to be developed to redress the problems that most programs experience.

Problems in Recruiting Minority Applicants

Undergraduates

One major source of applicants for psychology programs is the undergraduate pool. According to recent studies, there has been a slight decline in the number of

Blacks attending college, whereas the proportion of Hispanics and American Asians is increasing (S. V. Brown, 1988b). Academically qualified minority students are drawn increasingly to law and business schools and less to the social and behavioral sciences. Frequently these students are attracted to more familiar professions that offer immediate, visible, achievable economic rewards. Clinical psychology is a "stranger" to many minority groups and does not promise much in the way of recognition and rewards to undergraduate minorities.

Minority communities generally do not have positive images of professional psychologists. Sources of emotional and social support to minorities in American society traditionally have been associated with church, family, and cultural organizations. Because psychology has failed to establish a viable and positive presence in minority communities, the definition of its professional role image has been left to the popular culture. Aside from television and film portrayals, the mental health world is usually encountered by minority individuals when they are in severe crisis situations. Frequently these contacts are problematic and established within the more insensitive and chaotic clinic or state hospital settings. There is, therefore, a significant distrust of nonminority individuals offering help outside the expected cultural channels. When there is contact between minority groups and professional psychologists, it tends to reinforce a negative view because most psychologists, as members of the majority culture, are removed from and insensitive to the specific stresses and cultural values of a minority community.

In the academic world, the number of minority graduate faculty and the availability of these figures as role models for minority undergraduates have been very limited (DeAngelis, 1988). As a result, there has been little personal draw to the profession in the minority undergraduate's experience. Furthermore, there are few academicians on college campuses who are supportive of professional psychology, and even fewer minority psychologists who can offer direction and encouragement to minority undergraduates. Thus, the task of the minority student recruiters for professional psychology programs is twofold. First, the recruiter must make an impact on the undergraduate psychology department by specifically contacting undergraduate minority faculty and introducing and explaining the professional school concept. Second, the recruiter must educate minority undergraduates about the profession of clinical psychology, its potential to address the psychological and social needs of their communities, and its capacity to offer a worthwhile and rewarding career.

Along with an increasingly limited number of minority undergraduates interested in the social and behavioral sciences, the professional school must also compete with other graduate or professional schools in terms of offering adequate financial help throughout the student's education. Given the absence of visible psychologist models and immediate financial support, most qualified undergraduates will tend to select graduate and professional schools that offer recognition and economic security in the immediate and more distant future. The professional school, therefore, must be aware that multiple problems exist in reaching the qualified undergraduate applicant: (a) negative and stereotyped community perceptions of the role, (b) critical and limited exposure to clinical psychology in undergraduate programs, (c) general suspicion and negativism among academic undergraduate faculty, (d) absence of ethnically diverse clinical psychology role models in undergraduate programs, and (e) greater financial and economic inducements from other professional schools in business and law.

In addition, there are factors within the minority applicant's experience that may impair the pursuit of a career that appears to be in conflict with family and cultural values and expectations. It is assumed that there is frequently tension in minority and immigrant communities between the younger generation's upward mobility and greater acculturation and the parent generation's values and goals. Consequently, the specific pursuit of a career held in low esteem or that threatens to create greater emotional distance from the family or community adds to the inner conflict of the undergraduate minority student interested in clinical psychology. Enrolling in a doctoral program, which may imply potential retreat from basic family, cultural, and religious values, creates further anxiety in undergraduates struggling with creating a viable identity in a fluid and conflictual social context.

Workers With Master's Degrees

There are a number of minority individuals who have earned master's degrees in counseling, nursing, social work, and education. Moreover, minorities frequently work as psychiatric paraprofessionals, counselors, hospital aides, and in other mental health service delivery positions. These groups represent an easier population to recruit to professional schools by virtue of their already established interest and investment in a mental health career. The problem of negative or stereotyped imagery around the role of the clinical psychologist is much reduced in this population, given its familiarity and direct professional contact with the profession and the provision of psychological services. In short, this group provides a more readily available, knowledgeable, and positive applicant pool.

There are, however, significant problems in successfully recruiting such individuals to a doctoral program. Strict limitations of financial resources and the responsibilities of job or family frequently make a transition to a doctoral program quite conflictual. Usually the entire family must consider the partial loss of income from the student's reduced working hours, as well as the added fiscal responsibility of funding the education (in part or in total).

Working women with husbands and children must contend with the long-term financial and emotional stresses and sacrifices entailed by their doctoral work, including the management of child care and the marital conflict stimulated by their attendance at school. Minority women's enrollment in doctoral work may frequently threaten family equilibrium because of the reactions of spouses and family members to the actual and threatened emotional abandonment by the returning female student. In addition, minority women may have the negative experience of being in families or communities that may not be supportive of professional advancement for women. It is not difficult to understand why some minority women are reluctant to return to school.

Married minority men also face conflicts if they decide to return to school. A decrease in level of income, job status, and family prestige may seriously inhibit the decision to return to school. Moving from a position of authority to one of dependency and academic insecurity may be especially stressful for minority men with families to support.

In both these instances, there is significant loss and conflict in the decision to consider a doctoral education. Added to this anxiety is suspicion and fear of attending a facility that expects academic performance and development and requires the application of academic skills that frequently have not been practiced in years. The revival of doubt and concern regarding the delay and sacrifice involved in obtaining a distant reward (4–6 years, depending on financial and emotional resources) engenders more reluctance. Recognition that the requirements for a clinical doctoral program are more rigorous and demanding than those for bachelor's and master's degrees promotes apprehension. Such awareness creates anxiety and self-doubt in the minority applicant who, in contemplating a return to a White-dominated educational facility, may find painful academic experiences revived. Finally, some minority applicants planning to enter graduate school encounter problems with their support systems. They sense resentment and lack of support from those who may be threatened and challenged by the prospect of a friend, family member, or coworker moving ahead in his or her career development.

Perceptions About Graduate Programs

The minority applicant's perception of the specific doctoral program to which admission is being sought plays a significant part in the decision-making process. Given the nature of the minority experience in this society, the minority applicant will want to determine whether the program demonstrates an awareness of the special needs and sensitivities of the minority student and a concurrent awareness of the mental health needs of different minority populations. In essence, like all students, the minority student wants to feel assured of a welcoming and warm environment, that is, one that supports successful academic and clinical success and provides role models and learning experiences that will enhance future professional success.

Most often, the minority applicant is interested in knowing whether there is a fellowship of minority students and faculty to whom one can turn for support and understanding in this difficult undertaking. In addition, the applicant may wish to know whether nonminority faculty and students are aware of the impact of cultural differences in the understanding and treatment of individuals and groups. As a rule, such questions may be answered by the existence of a critical mass of both minority students and faculty. This presence helps to ensure that specific concerns of minority students and their future constituents will be addressed in the classroom and curriculum. A critical mass allows for a more pervasive awareness in all faculty of these issues and, ideally, greater comfort in addressing them. In addition to the much-needed role modeling that minority faculty provide for minority students, nonminority faculty also can provide mentoring and support.

The demonstrable success of current and past minority students is another critical piece of information for minority applicants. Confidence in the program's past and present commitment to the successful matriculation of minority students can make a strong impact on the minority applicant's motivation to enroll in the program. Because of their experiences as minorities in the society, minority undergraduates and workers with master's degrees will bring some doubt and mistrust to the pursuit of a doctoral degree. The knowledge that psychology doctoral programs are alert to these concerns, seriously committed to the successful doctoral experience of minority applicants, and sensitive to the needs of culturally and racially diverse groups in the society helps considerably in reducing apprehension. This means, of course, that successful recruitment depends on the presence of a committed faculty and administration.

Integrating Minority Recruitment With the Mission of the Doctoral Program

In order for the pool of applicants to be reached and encouraged to apply, it is necessary to identify potential problems in the recruitment process from the institution's vantage point. It is evident that professional psychology schools differ with respect to strategies and personnel used in the recruitment process. At some schools, specific minority faculty recruit minority applicants. Other programs draw on the resources of the admissions department, which may be staffed by minorities. Still others vest the basic recruiting responsibilities in the hands of a nonminority admissions director and the entire faculty.

The various strategies need to be assessed in terms of their impact on the particular tasks of the recruiting process. Most significant is the integrated effort of minority faculty and minority students in the development of materials and perspectives offered to prospective minority students. This effort denotes that minority faculty, students, and administrators are engaged in the recruitment presentation and process, regardless of who is selected to perform the active recruiting functions.

It is at this juncture that institutional tensions, surrounding the commitment of the program to the minority student's growth, emerge. Such tensions may be expressed by the failure to consult fully with minority faculty and administrators regarding appropriate presentation information or through the general failure of minority faculty and administrators to promote mutual collegiality in this process of commitment and program definition. Tendencies toward inadequate consultative processes or inappropriate expectations of minority staff to assume the entire responsibility for recruitment can also create a marginal recruitment effort. Minority personnel are sensitive to the us versus them equation in terms of commitment, and any recapitulation of this attitude in areas of recruitment will validate their sensitivity.

In this context, institutional ambivalence regarding full commitment to the recruiting area may be evident in ambiguous assignments, ineffective communications to and from the admissions office, inadequate follow-up on interested applicants, and admissions decisions that are not well informed regarding potential assets and liabilities of the minority applicant. It is essential that the admissions officer, minority recruiter, and minority faculty be convinced of the seriousness of the *entire* program's mission in this area. In fact, the view that the recruitment of minority students is the responsibility of only the admissions department or minority staff may well reflect a lack of full integration of the implications of this mission into the entire program.

Thus, the minority student recruitment philosophy inevitably reflects the depth of integration of the institution's mission to train all students (minority and nonminority) to provide services to minority individuals and communities. The implications of this mission inevitably stir anxiety in non-minority-dominated institutions because working relationships, policies, curriculum, and general institutional practices inevitably will change. Disturbances in the actualization of an organizational commitment to the recruitment of minorities are to be considered an indication of the institution's failure to appreciate the profound rethinking required to make an effective organizational commitment.

All institutions must recognize that successful minority recruitment demands (a) financial resources (e.g., personnel time, scholarships, marketing, and financial aid advisement); (b) available minority staff and faculty; (c) revised and sensitized curriculum; (d) ongoing institutional self-scrutiny in these areas; (e) retention personnel and careful retention processes that are committed to the mission; (f) effective communication between and within minority and nonminority faculty and administrators; and (g) the financial, personnel, and programmatic support of boards of directors or trustees. In essence, the problems of minority recruitment reside in a total ecology that embraces the potential minority applicant and his or her family and community, the profession of clinical psychology and its mission, the national economy and availability of adequate institutional financial resources, and the overall commitment of the full institution to the task of educating minority psychologists to help serve, and to inform those who serve, the extensive network of racially and ethnically diverse communities that make up American society.

Strategies for Retaining Minorities

Nearly any ethnic minority student or faculty member will tell you that environmental change and environmental support are requisites for successful recruitment, retention, and graduation of ethnically diverse students. The purpose of this section is to provide specific meaning to the concepts of "environmental change" and "environmental support." Both general and specific strategies are identified.

We sought to learn how these concepts were understood and operationalized through use of the Minority Retention Practices Survey, which was completed by 32 of 34 member schools of the National Council of Schools of Professional Psychology (NCSPP) in the fall of 1988 (see Appendix A at the end of this chapter). The results of the survey provide relevant definition to the major concepts of environmental change and environmental support and offer specific change and retention strategies tested by member schools. First, we outline these strategies, then we present a plan that comprehensively addresses the complementary concepts of environmental change and support.

Effecting Environmental Change

Environmental change often means the recruitment of a core of ethnic minority students, faculty, administration, or staff. Otherwise, a sea of White faces with White value systems will be present to greet any potential minority students. According to the 1988 Minority Retention Practices Survey, in all NCSPP member schools, 10.2% of students were minorities, with a range of 0% to 80%. The Caribbean Center for Advanced Studies serves a largely Hispanic population. When this large group of minority students is deleted from the statistics, the average number of ethnic minority students drops to 7.7% per program. Twelve programs were below the mean. Seven schools had an ethnic minority student population ranging from 12% to 24%. According to data presented in the *APA Monitor*, "racial and ethnic minorities (in 1987–1988) represent about 11 percent of the full time students enrolled in doctoral programs" (cited in DeAngelis, 1988). The NCSPP member school average for 1988 was below that figure.

The minority faculty for all member schools averaged 13.9%, with a range of 0% to 98%. Again, if the Caribbean Center were not counted, the average minority faculty per program would drop to 10.8%. Fourteen programs were below the mean, with 7 reporting no minority faculty. Thirteen programs, however, reported a range of

13% to 33.3% of core minority faculty. The DeAngelis report concluded that minority representation among faculty was about 5%. The NCSPP member school average was double that figure. When adjunct faculty were considered, the average percentage of minority faculty was 9.1%, with a range of 0% to 80%. If the Caribbean Center were not considered, the average dropped to 6.8%, with 17 programs below the mean and 8 programs reporting no employment of adjunct minority faculty. Although it is beyond the scope of this chapter, S. V. Brown's (1988a) research report and recommendations on increasing minority faculty is essential reading for any program serious about this issue.

The average percentage of ethnic minorities employed in high-level administration positions for all programs was 6.6%. If the Caribbean Center were discounted, the average percentage drops to 3.6%. Aside from the Caribbean Center, only six programs reported *any* ethnic minority people filling top administrative posts, with a range of 14% to 30%.

Of all the categories considered, staff positions had the highest percentage of ethnic minorities; the average was 20.4%, with a range of 0% to 95%. When the Caribbean Center was not considered, the percentage dropped to 18%, with a range of 0% to 71%. Fourteen programs had no ethnic minorities hired in staff positions. In 12 programs, the range of employed minorities in staff positions was 26% to 71%. When individual surveys were examined, those programs with a high percentage of minority students also seemed to have a high percentage of core minority faculty. However, the presence of a high percentage of core minority faculty, in itself, was not always associated with a high percentage of minority students. Programs with a minority student enrollment ranging from 15% to 24% had ethnic minorities in at least three of the four following groups: core faculty, adjunct faculty, top administration, or staff personnel. The two programs with the highest ethnic minority student enrollment (24% and 18%) employed ethnic minorities in all four groups, and the percentage of ethnic minority faculty was at least 20%.

Additional research could help to define precisely what constitutes a critical mass of minority students, faculty, and administration in order for a program to be seen as having achieved sufficient environmental change to be effective in retaining students. Nonetheless, it is apparent that, in the absence of any minority faculty or staff, it would be difficult to sustain the impression that the program was at all interested in the training of minority psychologists. The ways in which environmental change is created and environmental support provided to minority students, faculty, and staff is somewhat beyond the scope of this chapter. However, certain survey items address the issue of environmental change and are discussed in this chapter. Earlier in the chapter, problems in the recruitment of minority students were considered. At the least, it would seem that a program would have to *want* to recruit minorities before it would accept minorities into its program. Member schools were asked, "Do you actively recruit minority students?" Twenty-nine answered yes, two answered no, and one program failed to respond to the question.

Whether it is appropriate to establish a minimum quota of minority students has been considered widely. Some have found quotas to be objectionable. Some minorities, however, believe that a quota represents a real commitment to minority recruitment, because it holds the institution accountable. In the 1988 NCSPP survey, eight programs indicated that they had a quota, 19 did not, and 5 did not answer the question. Of the schools surveyed, one of the two programs most successful in recruiting minorities used a quota system.

In order to sensitize all students to ethnic minority issues, some of the schools surveyed included required courses in the curricula. Twenty-three programs required at least one course in minority issues; 9 programs did not. Three of the latter also enjoyed successful minority enrollment. Several programs required the integration of ethnic issues into all courses. Other specific strategies that have been used for achieving and demonstrating environmental change are as follows (the names of the schools using the strategies are cited because they have materials that may prove helpful to other programs).

- A letter to minority mental health centers and minority undergraduate psychology majors—University of Denver.
- An open house for prospective minority students, including a specific statement of commitment to minority students—the Illinois School of Professional Psychology: Chicago (ISPP).
- A resource manual for Black psychology students that is made available to all Black students—New York Association of Black Psychologists (NYABPsi) and Association of Black Psychologists (available from NYABPsi, P.O. Box 1764, New York, NY 10027, at $3 per copy. A comparable resource manual for other ethnic groups presumably could be developed).
- External newsletter articles on minority events.
- Ethnic and racial sensitizing experiences for faculty, administration, staff, and students—California School of Professional Psychology: San Diego (CSPP: San Diego), ISPP: Chicago, and NCSPP Conference on Ethnic Sensitizing. Also see chapter 2, this volume, and Appendix B, this chapter.
- The Black and Hispanic Caucus—Adelphi University, The Derner Institute.
- External consultants used to assist a program in focusing on ethnic and multicultural issues—CSPP: San Diego, CSPP: Berkeley, and ISPP.
- Program catalog information relating to the number of ethnic minority students and faculty—CSPP: Los Angeles.
- Recruitment brochure on ethnic minority mental health—CSPP, all branches.
- An ethnic minority mental health track in the doctoral program—CSPP: Los Angeles.
- A roster of minority persons who have graduated from member schools for use in the recruitment of faculty and administrators—currently being developed by ISPP, in cooperation with NCSPP.

Environmental Support of Minorities

The services that are provided to minority students after their enrollment in the graduate program are defined as environmental support. Several specific questions in the 1988 NCSPP survey were intended to elicit information about the nature of programs' environmental support. Most often, minority students received the same orientation as all students. Only three programs provided both a separate orientation for minority students and an orientation for all entering students. Minority faculty advisors were provided in nine programs. In eight of these nine programs, the percentage of enrolled minority students exceeded the mean. Some programs did not automatically provide minority advisors, but if a student expressed a preference, a minority advisor could be assigned.

Institutional financial aid for minority students was provided frequently. Forty-one percent (41.2%) of all minority students in member school programs received financial aid from their respective programs. The percentage of students receiving financial support ranged from 0% (six programs) to 100% (six programs). Programs with the highest minority enrollment, with one exception, provided a minimum of 40% of their minority students with institutional financial aid. The program with the highest minority enrollment provided financial support to all its students; the second ranking program provided financial assistance to 24%.

The specific nature of the financial support was defined in a NCSPP survey reported in February 1988 by the Committee on Minority Representation and Service to Underserved Populations. Fellowships, tuition grants, assistantships, work study, and student loans were offered to minority and nonminority students. One half of the schools responding to that survey agreed that "in awarding aid to minority students, we are alert to racial, ethnic group differences in resource expense and debt profiles in determining the composition of financial aid."

In addition to financial aid, the nature and extent of other minority student supports was explored by the survey (e.g., minority student support groups, peer tutorial programs, writing skills programs, financial advising, and minority student organizations). Twenty-four programs indicated that they provided at least one type of student support, whereas eight programs did not provide any. One half of the programs ($n = 16$) made support groups available to minority students; one half ($n = 16$) did not. Programs describing successful minority support groups were Wright State, the Caribbean Center, and ISPP. Six programs offered a peer tutorial program, but 24 did not. Nine programs offered a writing skills program, including both programs with the highest minority enrollment (i.e., Wright State and CSPP: Los Angeles). One half of the programs ($n = 16$) provided financial advising, including the 2 with the highest minority enrollment; 14 provided none. Twelve programs had a minority student organization, including Wright State and CSPP: Los Angeles, but 18 did not.

Additional student supports provided by various programs included the following:

- Regular student–faculty get togethers (CSPP: Los Angeles).
- Peer advisement (CSPP: Los Angeles, and University of Denver).
- Quarterly support dinners (CSPP: Los Angeles).
- Black professional development seminar (Wright State).
- Minority practicum training sites (Wright State and ISPP).
- Ethnic minority alumni group (Rutgers).
- A council on minority and multicultural affairs (CSPP: Berkeley).
- In-house assistantships (University of Denver).
- Outside, paid placements (University of Denver and Wright State).
- The Ethnic Minority Institute (CSPP: Fresno and Pacific Graduate School of Psychology).
- Ethnic minority full tuition, housing, and stipend (ISPP—two new awards per year).
- The Conference on Ethnic Issues (Fuller Theological Seminary and Chicago School of Professional Psychology).
- One percent of systemwide tuition revenue reserved for minority scholarships (CSPP).

Ethnic Minority Institute: A Proposal

The Ethnic Minority Institute plan at CSPP: Fresno incorporates structural institutional change and ongoing support for ethnic minority students. I present it as a
model for other schools to consider. During the past two decades, researchers and
practitioners, representing a variety of interests and perspectives, have criticized the
paradigms of American psychology as being ethnocentric and as representing Anglo-
American male values and worldviews (Caplan & Nelson, 1973; Lorion, 1978; Nobles,
1976; President's Commission on Mental Health, 1979; Sampson, 1977; Tyler, Sussewell, & Williams-McCoy, 1985). This paradigm has gravely affected the preparation and
training of psychologists and perpetuated their incapacity to provide services to ethnically diverse clients. Collectively, these criticisms highlight the need for a paradigmatic
shift. According to Tyler et al. (1985):

1.   Psychological paradigms must incorporate the importance of culture, race, and
      ethnicity in defining constructs, concepts, and parameters.
2.   Psychological paradigms must fully acknowledge clients as "knowing individuals
      who shape their worlds and destinies through conceptual frameworks (which
      they develop about the world), and their lives" (p. 311).
3.   Psychological paradigms must acknowledge the role of the system and indi-
      vidual interactions in formulations about how people function and organize
      their lives.

CSPP was founded to address a need for well-trained clinicians to provide mental
health services to the general public (O'Neil, 1987). Although the model of training
has been very successful in preparing students to provide services to the majority
culture, less attention has been paid to the needs of minority populations. The changing demographics of the state and nation, that is, the increase in the numbers and
types of minority populations, points to the need to better prepare students to serve
the expanding group of ethnically diverse clients.

At the 1986 CSPP Board of Trustees retreat in Napa, CA, administration, faculty,
and trustees developed an agenda for CSPP through the year 2000. There was a strong
sentiment to make social advocacy a stated goal for the school and to change the
focus from private practice to social practice, addressing the needs of the underserved
and ethnic minority populations. CSPP took a risk by moving away from the traditional
academic community and seeking alliance with the providers of mental health services
to California's quickly changing population. Although not without problems, the risk,
by and large, has proven successful. Today, CSPP is regarded as a leader in the mental
health profession (O'Neil, 1987).

CSPP combines clinical training with high-quality research and theory. Research
focuses on the psychological factors associated with many of the social problems of
America (e.g., chronic mental illness, homelessness, acquired immune deficiency
syndrome, and alcoholism). This research is helping to determine the shape of the
psychology profession in the next century (O'Neil, 1987).

The trustees, administration, faculty, and students of CSPP are committed to
addressing the needs of the underserved. They recognize that there are a number of
deficits and problems in CSPP's systemwide program that need to be corrected. A
recent report from the Task Force on Quality of Student Life (Boettiger et al., 1988)
reviewed minority and multicultural issues:

It is clearly a time of dramatically growing awareness of the importance of minority and multicultural training in professional psychology, and particularly appropriate that leadership be assumed in California, where demographically, minority issues are expected to become majority issues by the turn of the century. In listening to minority students, faculty, and staff on our four campuses, we were struck again by the commonality of issues and, in this instance, by four markedly different situations. One of our campuses has been a nationally recognized pioneer in this realm for several years. A second has begun to make significant strides during the past two years in minority faculty, staff, and student recruitment, and recognition of the needs for curricular change and its own community education and service opportunities. Two of our campuses (for a variety of complex reasons) have very few minority faculty or students, and, as yet, little in the way of developing programs in these areas; their minority students, predictably, feel isolated, alienated and underserved. (p. 11)[1]

If greater leadership in these areas is to be assumed, much work needs to be done. According to minority faculty and students, CSPP is characterized in Black and Hispanic communities as expensive, middle-class White, traditional (because of its psychodynamic and psychoanalytic orientation), and not sufficiently sensitive to diverse cultures. The goal, as stated by one of CSPP's minority female faculty members, is still far away.

CSPP should become known *as a place, standing in the public eye, for fine training and sensitivity to minority and multicultural issues. We need to develop better relations with the wider community, improve placement opportunities, tutoring and mentoring, develop our own programs, and educate our own faculty—change our own communities, raise the money and cover the ground to recruit the students who can't, or won't, otherwise come to us. (Boettiger et al., 1988, p. 12)*

As CSPP continues its quest to improve the quality of life for all people, it must expand its efforts to serve the underserved. CSPP: Fresno, with 65 diverse ethnic minorities in its community, is ideally located to pursue this quest. The community comprises (a) both established and newly arrived Asians; (b) the vast and growing Hispanic population, with its hard-to-reach migrant farm workers; (c) the Native Americans living in rural communities; (d) the Black community, which is difficult to penetrate and which views psychologists as insensitive to their plight and part of a system that wants to keep them down; and (e) the rural farmers who are plagued with stress because of the pending loss of their farms and who know no other way of life.

In order to meet the challenge of advancing the value of life for all people and increasing efforts to serving the underserved, CSPP: Fresno intends to establish the Ethnic Minority Institute (EMI). EMI will provide special minority issue education and training at CSPP: Fresno and will be duplicable by other schools and universities that are interested in training psychologists and other human service providers. EMI will be composed of the Campus Committee (EMIC), the Community Advisory Board, and the EMI Initiative Team. The team will consist of the Associate Dean for Professional Affairs, the Director of Training, the Director of Development, and the Director of Research. The team will work in conjunction with the campus community committees toward fulfilling its goals and objectives.

In approaching the problems of the underserved, EMI aims to develop an ethnic minority proficiency that will provide special instruction and clinical research ex-

---

[1]From *Task Force on the Quality of Student Life: Report and Recommendations* (p. 11) by J. Boettiger et al., 1988, San Francisco: California School of Professional Psychology. Copyright 1988 by J. Boettiger. Reprinted by permission.

periences on minority issues. It is the intent of the EMI to add to, rather than replace or change, the existing program. Whenever appropriate, EMI will work cooperatively with the ongoing CSPP: Fresno proficiencies of neuropsychology, behavioral medicine, and child and family in addressing ethnic minority issues. Analogous to the other proficiencies, the ethnic minority proficiency will incorporate the general clinical program as the basic training foundation, but it will provide more specialized training and experiences in ethnic minority issues in its courses.

EMI will be a part of the CSPP: Fresno program, responsible for expanding and providing another vehicle of training for students interested in working with ethnic minorities. EMI will have the task of researching and developing a specialty course of training for those students interested in working with ethnic minorities. In addition, EMI will provide elective courses for the general student population, in-service training for the faculty, and courses and workshops for other service providers through CSPP: Fresno's continuing education program.

Goals and Objectives

Phase 1

1. To establish a campus committee (EMIC) to develop policy and to monitor and assist the development of ethnic minority initiatives on the CSPP: Fresno campus.
2. To establish a Fresno community advisory board to develop linkages and to share in assessing the needs of the EMIC to support contract and grant development.
3. To develop a mentoring and support program to aid in the retention of ethnic minority students and faculty.
4. To establish an EMI Proficiency, which will work cooperatively with the existing program proficiencies (i.e., behavioral medicine, child and family, and neuropsychology), in order to address ethnic minority issues.
5. To establish an EMI student association to provide a support system to address social and personal issues.
6. To develop an in-service training program for administrators, faculty, staff, and students to aid people in developing more sensitivity to ethnic minority issues.

Phase 2

1. To participate in the recruitment of ethnic minority faculty and students to bring more diversity and ethnic and racial balance to the Fresno campus.
2. To develop and pursue ongoing fundraising initiatives to support the EMI program scholarship and initiative.
3. To assist in curriculum development to integrate ethnic minority issues into the core curriculum when appropriate, and to develop new course offerings for the ethnic minority proficiency and the continuing education program.

Phase 3

1. To develop a satellite of the CSPP Psychological Service Center (PSC) that provides programs and services that are sensitive and relevant to the ethnic minority communities and addresses the following:

a. reduction of the incidence of mislabeling of socially, economically, and culturally deprived clients;

b. assurance that cultural difference from the dominant culture norms are considered both in diagnostic assessments and treatment;

c. provision of counseling on feminist issues for men and women;

d. provision of bilingual counseling for Hispanic clients;

e. an increase in the availability and use of services to "high-risk," multiproblem families;

f. provision of innovative counseling methods that will include as well as transcend multicultural issues;

g. research, expansion, and development of its holistic approach, which provides a more comprehensive treatment service designed to meet the special needs of its clients;

h. provision of psychological assessments and treatment of emotional problems;

i. provision of individual, group, and family therapy, plus marriage and vocational counseling, based on psychological assessment;

j. provision of preventive treatment to aid in reducing delinquent acts, and contact with the criminal justice system by "high-risk," multiproblem clients;

k. utilization of the services of other social service agencies in order to provide a comprehensive treatment plan for the client; and

l. research and evaluation of the effectiveness of approaches, methods, and treatment modalities employed in order to evaluate EMI's performance in reaching its stated objectives.

Appendix A
Minority Retention Practices Survey
September, 1988

NCSPP is interested in learning how your program retains minority students. Please take 8–10 minutes to complete this survey and return it in the enclosed envelope to Jim McHolland by October 30th. The results will be shared at our Puerto Rico meeting.

Please answer in relation to your program to school.

1.   What percentage of your students are minorities?   _____ %

2.   What percentage of your core faculty are minorities?   _____ %

3.   What percentage of adjunct faculty are minorities?   _____ %

4.   What percentage of top administration are minorities?   _____ %

5.   What percentage of staff personnel are minorities?   _____ %

6.   Do you actively recruit minority students?   __ yes; __ no;

7.   Do you seek a minimal quota of minority students?   __ yes; __ no;

8.   Minority students are given __ a separate orientation; __ same orientation; __ the same orientation all students receive.

9.   Are minority students provided a minority faculty advisor?   __ yes __ no

10. How many (what percent) minority students receive *Institutional* financial aid?   _____ %

11. Does your program require any courses regarding ethnic/minority issues?   __ yes; __ no; __ number

12. Is a person designated in charge of minority recruitment, retention or advising?   __ yes; __ no;

               Name of person: _____

13. Do you offer any of the following as minority student supports:

     a.   Minority student support group   __ yes; __ no
     b.   Peer tutorial program   __ yes; __ no
     c.   Writing skills program   __ yes; __ no
     d.   Financial advising   __ yes; __ no
     e.   Minority student organization   __ yes; __ no

14. Please list briefly any other supports you provide ethnic-racial minority students.

     Name of the person completing survey: _____

     Name of School: _____

Appendix B
Ethnic Sensitizing Experience and Plant Statements

Committee on Ethnic Minority Representation
National Council of Schools of Professional Psychology

Dear Committee Member:

Please find below a list of potential plant statements developed for the group simulation. You will recall that the committee agreed to develop a workshop in the form of a simulation for the Atlanta meeting. The goal of the simulation is to serve as a group experience through which representatives of member schools can explore their own attitudes and beliefs about recruitment and retention of ethnic minority students and faculty. We agreed to develop plant statements that would serve as stimuli in a fishbowl exercise. Please read each potential item carefully, given their purpose. Comment on these by July 7th, so that I can develop them into simulation cards. That is, edit, add, delete, etc. I think we will need at least twelve items. Six for each of the two areas of interest (faculty and students).

Plant Statements

Recruitment of students

CARD 1: A minimum GRE score should be used for all student applicants, regardless of ethnicity.

CARD 2: It is important to determine if ethnic minority applicants have adequate conceptual skills.

CARD 3: It is important that ethnic minority applicants have good writing skills before they are admitted.

CARD 4: Each ethnic minority applicant should automatically receive an interview.

CARD 5: Ethnic minority applicants should not be penalized for poor GRE scores.

CARD 6: Quota systems are necessary to ensure ethnic minority participation in professional schools.

CARD 7: Some ethnic minority applicants should be admitted even if they may need remediation.

CARD 8: Ethnic minority applicants should not be treated any differently than any other applicants.

CARD 9: White ethnic faculty are not adequately prepared to evaluate ethnic minority faculty applicants.

CARD 10: No matter how well-developed your program, you will continue to be overwhelmed by the number of ethnic minority students who will struggle through the program.

Faculty recruitment

CARD 1: More ethnic minority academic administrators are needed before significant numbers of ethnic minority students will be attracted to a professional school.

CARD 2: Ethnic minority faculty should be articulate.

CARD 3: Ethnic minority faculty have to work two to three times harder than White ethnics to obtain a raise or tenure.

CARD 4: White ethnic faculty are not adequately prepared to evaluate ethnic minority faculty applicants.

CARD 5: Ethnic minority faculty tend to have difficulty teaching White ethnic students.

CARD 6: Most ethnic minority faculty candidates tend to be overly weak in important areas needed to train students.

16

PARTICIPATION OF ETHNIC MINORITIES IN PSYCHOLOGY: WHERE DO WE STAND TODAY?

Jessica Kohout
American Psychological Association
Washington, DC

and

Georgine Pion
Vanderbilt University
Nashville, Tennessee

Increasing the participation of ethnic minorities in psychology continues to be a major concern for the discipline and its training programs (Guthrie, 1976; Howard et al., 1986; Russo et al., 1981). Although psychology has fared reasonably well, as compared to many other scientific fields, in terms of attracting ethnic minorities to its ranks, the numbers and percentages of non-White doctoral psychologists still are relatively small. For example, in 1987, of the 56,400 doctoral psychologists, approximately 1,300 were Black, 900 were Asians, and 100 were Native Americans (National Science Foundation, 1988b). An estimated 1,000 were Hispanic.

Since the early 1970s, a number of strategies have been developed to address this problem. Colleges and universities, along with federal and state governments, have launched major initiatives to attract and to retain ethnic minorities. Some examples are the program at the University of South Carolina for recruiting and retaining

---

The opinions expressed in this chapter are those of the authors and do not reflect those of the organizations with which the authors are affiliated. Throughout this chapter, the term *doctoral psychologist* refers to those individuals who are employed in psychology and who hold a PhD. Although we recognize that there are other legitimate degrees in the field (e.g., PsyD), the majority of available, national-level data are collected on individuals who hold a PhD. Given that PhDs comprise more than 95% of all doctoral psychologists, the inability to include other doctoral degrees should not substantially affect the conclusions of this chapter.

Black students of any major, Arizona State University's program to recruit Hispanic women, the Department of Education's Strengthening Developing Institutions Program funded by Title III of the Higher Education Amendments of 1965, and the National Institute of Health's Minority Access to Research Careers Program. Many of these programs have been quite successful in increasing the educational attainment of ethnic minorities at all degree levels and in a variety of fields (e.g., Garrison & Brown, 1985; U.S. Congress, Office of Technology Assessment, 1989). Over the next decade or so, several demographic, educational, and economic trends will influence the future success of these programs. In order for undergraduate and graduate psychology programs to attract and retain Blacks, Hispanics, Asians, and Native Americans, however, an increased awareness of these trends, along with psychology's past progress toward increasing minority participation is essential.

The primary purpose of this chapter is twofold. First, we provide a brief retrospective glance at ethnic minority participation in psychology during the last decade so as to review the discipline's performance to date. Second, we summarize ethnic minority participation at all stages of the formal educational pipeline, beginning with completion of high school and ending with graduation from a doctoral program. This is intended to help identify the major points at which attrition from the educational system occurs.

It is important to understand the size and characteristics of the ethnic minority pool from which doctoral psychology programs can recruit students. Improving the representation of ethnic minorities in psychology, given that the doctorate is the entry-level degree for most career roles in the field, cannot be confined solely to efforts at the graduate level. As we shall see, by the time of application for admission to a graduate program, a significant number of talented and potentially qualified individuals has already been lost.

As was noted by the Government–University–Industry Roundtable (1987) sponsored by the National Academy of Sciences: "Every educational and developmental stage is a potential point of intervention, and a comprehensive approach to nurturing science and engineering talent must address the whole pipeline" (p. v). This statement holds no less true for psychology. The rates at which ethnic minorities complete high school, enroll in college, obtain a bachelor's degree in psychology, and finally obtain a doctorate must all be matters of concern for ensuring the continued health and vitality of the discipline.

Current Representation of Ethnic Minorities in Psychology

As is shown in Table 1, compared to their representation in both the U.S. population and the work force, ethnic minorities as a whole remain underrepresented in professional and scientific occupations. At the same time, however, distinctions emerge among the various ethnic minority groups. For example, Blacks and Hispanics continue to be significantly underrepresented among all employed professionals (6.7% and 3.3%, respectively), as do Native Americans (0.1%). Their rates of participation decrease even further when one considers only the population of doctoral scientists and engineers. In contrast, Asians are much more likely to have earned a doctorate and be working in a science or engineering field (8.6%), and their level of involvement actually exceeds that of Asians in all professional careers and occupations.

The picture for psychology, although slightly different, is not much more en-

Table 1

Percentages of Ethnic Minorities Represented in the U.S. Population, Labor Force, and Professional and Scientific Careers (1980–1986)

Group Represented in	Whites	Blacks	Hispanics	Asians	Native Americans
U.S. population (1980)	83.4	11.7	6.4	1.6	0.7
U.S. population (1986)	84.7	12.1	7.9	—	—
Total U.S. labor force (1986)	86.4	10.7	6.9	—	—
Professional and related occupations (1980)	86.9	6.7	3.3	3.0	0.1
Doctoral scientists and engineers (1985)[a]	88.7	1.4	1.5	8.6	0.1
Doctoral psychologists (1985)[b]	94.6	2.2	1.4	1.9	0.1

[a] Includes PhDs employed in the physical sciences, mathematical sciences, computer and information sciences, environmental sciences, life sciences, psychology, social sciences, and engineering fields.

[b] Includes PhDs.

Note. Data on the U.S. population in 1980 are from *General Social and Economic Characteristics, U.S. Summary Census of Population, 1980* by U.S. Department of Commerce, 1983, Washington, DC: U.S. Government Printing Office. Data on U.S. population in 1986 are from *Current Population Reports* (Series No. P-60, p. 25, Table 13) by U.S. Bureau of the Census, 1987, Washington, DC: U.S. Government Printing Office. Data on the 1986 U.S. labor force are from *Employment and Earnings, 34*(1), by the U.S. Department of Labor, Bureau of Labor Statistics, 1987, Washington DC: U.S. Government Printing Office.

Data on professional and related occupations are from *Women and Minorities in Science and Engineering* by the National Science Foundation, 1988d, Washington, DC: Author. Data on doctoral scientists and engineers and for doctoral psychologists are from *Doctoral Scientists and Engineers: A Decade of Change* (NSF Publication No. 88-302) by the National Science Foundation, 1988a, Washington, DC: Author.

couraging. In 1985, the percentage of doctoral psychologists who were ethnic minorities was 5.1%—about the same as it was 10 years earlier (National Science Foundation, 1988a). Data from several statewide surveys aimed at describing the characteristics of the population of licensed psychologists within each state indicate similar underrepresentation (e.g., Haley, 1984; Hammond, 1988; Neutzler, 1986; Office of Comprehensive Health Planning, 1989).

Table 2 indicates that, within psychology, the bulk (63.4%) of both White and ethnic minority psychologists has been concentrated in the health service provider subfields of psychology. In 1983, the highest percentage of ethnic minorities was in the heterogeneous group of "other" fields of psychology, the second highest percentage was in educational psychology, and the lowest occurred for industrial/organizational psychology and experimental, comparative, and physiological psychology. Compared with science and engineering overall, psychology also has a mixed track record in terms of ethnic minority participation (see Table 1). In 1985, 2.2% of all doctoral psychologists were Black—a proportion somewhat higher than the 1.4% for

Table 2
Ethnic Minority Status of Doctoral Psychologists in Selected
Subfields: 1983

Subfield	Ethnic Minorities[a]		Whites	
	N	%	N	%
Clinical, counseling, and school	1,540	4.7	30,899	95.3
Developmental	110	5.0	2,090	95.0
Educational	237	7.5	2,920	92.5
Experimental, comparative, and physiological	95	3.7	2,466	96.3
Industrial organizational	94	3.2	2,850	96.8
Social and personality	107	5.5	1,851	94.5
Other in psychology[b]	246	11.5	1,901	88.5
Total	2,429	4.7	48,770	95.3

[a] Includes Asians, Blacks, Hispanics, and Native Americans.

[b] Includes psychometrics, engineering psychology, environmental psychology, and health psychology.

Note. Data are dervied from "Census of Psychological Personnel: 1983" by J. Stapp, A.M. Tucker, and G.R. VandenBos, 1985, *American Psychologist, 40*, 1317–1351. Copyright 1985 by the American Psychological Association. Reprinted by permission.

all science and engineering fields. Both the percentages of Hispanics and Native Americans were similar to those for all science and engineering fields combined. In contrast, Asians were significantly less represented in psychology—1.4% versus 8.6% for science and engineering as a whole.

Other data attest to psychology's lower success in attracting Asians and Native Americans as compared to Blacks and Hispanics. From 1975 to 1985, the proportion of all Black doctoral scientists and engineers who were psychologists increased from 16% to 21.1%, and the estimated number tripled from 400 to 1,200 (National Science Foundation, 1988a). In fact, psychologists were the largest *single* disciplinary group among Blacks, followed by biological scientists (14%). Among Hispanic doctoral scientists and engineers, the percentage and number who were psychologists also rose dramatically—from 200 (10%) in 1975 to 1,000 (16.9%) 10 years later.

In contrast, psychology has made much less progress in terms of increasing involvement by Asians and Native Americans. In 1975, Asian psychologists totalled about 300, comprising 2.2% of all Asian doctoral scientists and engineers. Although this number had more than doubled to an estimated 800 by 1985, the percentage remained the same, given that the number of Asian doctorate holders in other science and engineering fields had increased at almost the same rate. Thus, the discipline has not managed to achieve any significant gain in terms of recruiting new Asian psychologists to its ranks. The situation is no more optimistic for Native Americans. Although psychology has been a popular career choice of Native American doctorates

Table 3

U.S. Doctoral Recipients in All Science and Engineering Fields and in Psychology by Race or Ethnicity: 1977–1987

Field and Race or Ethnicity	1977		1979		1981		1983		1985		1987	
	N	%	N	%	N	%	N	%	N	%	N	%
All science/engineering fields												
Native American	29	0.2	28	0.2	26	0.2	28	0.2	40	0.3	55	0.3
Asian	738	5.4	865	6.5	814	6.0	771	5.7	799	6.1	946	6.8
Black	303	2.2	309	2.3	316	2.3	305	2.2	331	2.5	335	2.4
Hispanic	186	1.4	220	1.6	230	1.7	262	1.9	280	2.1	359	2.6
White	12,464	90.8	11,882	89.3	12,166	89.8	12,201	89.9	11,723	88.9	12,269	87.8
Total	13,720	100.0	13,304	100.0	13,552	100.0	13,567	100.0	13,173	100.0	13,964	100.0
Psychology												
Native American	9	0.3	10	0.4	9	0.3	9	0.3	10	0.3	16	0.6
Asian	33	1.2	36	1.3	41	1.3	44	1.5	44	1.6	47	1.7
Black	95	3.5	115	4.2	113	3.7	112	3.7	105	3.8	92	3.4
Hispanic	40	1.5	49	1.8	66	2.1	93	3.1	69	2.5	95	3.5
White	2,541	93.5	2,550	92.4	2,849	92.5	2,767	91.5	2,563	91.8	2,464	90.8
Total	2,718	100.0	2,760	100.0	3,078	100.0	3,025	100.0	2,791	100.0	2,714	100.0

Note. Data for 1977–1985 are from *Science and Engineering Doctorates: 1960–86* (NSF 88-309) by the National Science Foundation, 1988c, Washington, DC: Author. Data for 1987 are from *Summary Report 1987: Doctorate Recipients from United States Universities* by S.L. Coyle and D.H. Thurgood, 1988, Washington, DC: National Academy Press.

(20% of all Native Americans with doctoral degrees in science and engineering are working in psychology), the number remains woefully small. In 1985, there were only about 100 Native American psychologists.

Psychology's progress (or lack thereof) in recruiting and retaining ethnic minorities also is illustrated by trends in doctoral production over the last decade, as is seen in Table 3. Although the total number of PhDs awarded in psychology each year has remained relatively stable, the number of doctorates earned by ethnic minorities rose from 177 in 1975 to 250 in 1987. Thus, by 1987, the percentage of new doctoral recipients who were ethnic minorities had inched up to 8.5%, as compared to 6.5% 10 years earlier.

However, not all minority groups experienced increases. Although the total population of Black psychologists has increased markedly, the number and percentage of Blacks earning PhDs have remained relatively stable during this time period. Slight increases occurred for both the number and percentage of new doctoral recipients who were Asians, and the number of new PhDs awarded to Native Americans has continued to be woefully small. Growth has occurred in the production of new doctorates among Hispanics. The number of Hispanics earning doctorates in psychology more than doubled between 1977 and 1987, with an accompanying increase in the percentage from 1.5% to 3.5%. Nevertheless, the overwhelming majority of new psychologists (90.8%) in 1987 were White, and this percentage is still slightly higher than that for science and engineering as a whole.

Table 4 reveals that, once again, differences in ethnic minority participation occurred across the various subfields. Comparing total PhD production in 1978–1982 with that in 1983–1987, it can be seen that the largest increase in doctorates among ethnic minorities occurred in the health service provider subfields. At the same time, however, the *percentage* of ethnic minorities in clinical, counseling, and school psy-

Table 4

Ethnic Minority Status of New Doctoral Recipients in Psychology:
1978–1982 and 1983–1987

| | 1978–1982 | | | | 1983–1987 | | | |
| | Ethnic Minorities[a] | | Whites | | Ethnic Minorities | | Whites | |
Subfield	N	%	N	%	N	%	N	%
Clinical, counseling, and school	572	7.7	6,833	92.3	747	5.1	13,871	94.9
Developmental	62	6.4	910	93.6	60	6.6	854	93.4
Educational	60	8.6	638	91.4	40	6.5	575	93.5
Experimental, comparative, and physiological	154	7.8	1,800	92.2	55	4.6	1,128	95.4
Industrial/organizational	19	5.1	357	94.9	30	6.1	460	93.9
Social and personality	105	9.6	985	90.4	180	19.6	738	80.4
Other in psychology[b]	174	9.8	1,599	90.2	187	8.9	1,901	91.0

[a] Includes Asians, Blacks, Hispanics, and Native Americans.

[b] Includes psychometrics, engineering psychology, environmental psychology, and health psychology.

Note. Data for 1978–1986 are from *Science and Engineering Doctorates: 1960–86* (NSF 88-309) by the National Science Foundation, 1988c, Washington, DC: Author. Data for 1987 are from *Summary Report 1987: Doctorate Recipients from United States Universities* by S.L. Coyle and D.H. Thurgood, 1988, Washington, DC: National Academy Press.

chology dropped; these fields also were quite successful in attracting White students, and there was a burgeoning of Whites earning PhDs in these subfields. The situation was somewhat different for personality and social psychology, for which both the absolute number and percentage of ethnic minorities increased, in contrast to a sharp decline in the number of White doctoral recipients. Growth also was evidenced in the number of ethnic minorities earning PhDs in industrial/organizational psychology, but the number awarded each year remains quite small. Conversely, educational, experimental, comparative, and physiological psychology have suffered major losses in doctoral production, and these reductions particularly have occurred for minorities.

As the previously cited statistics indicate, psychology doctoral programs cannot afford to slacken their efforts in training ethnic minorities. The question then becomes "How can this best be done?" A first step in addressing this issue is to examine the scope of the problem, that is, the size and nature of the pool from which potential graduate students may be drawn over the next decade. In doing this, several components of the educational pipeline must be considered: (a) completion of high school, (b) attendance at and graduation from college, and (c) entry into graduate school.

Ethnic Minority Participation in the Educational Pipeline

Completion of High School

There has been a decline in the number of high school graduates since 1981 (Wilson & Carter, 1988). This decline primarily can be attributed to a decreasing number of White graduates. During this same time period, the number of Black high school graduates increased by 25% (from 2,238,000 in 1976 to 2,801,000 in 1986), and the number of Hispanics grew as well (862,000 vs. 1,506,000). Data on completion rates for Native Americans and Asians were unavailable.

Given that the steady increase in ethnic minorities is also reflected in projections of the 18-year-old population in the United States (i.e., by the year 2000, more than 25% of the college-age population will be Black or Hispanic), it is important to look at the proportions of the 18- to 24-year-old population that have graduated from high school. In general, high school completion rates have increased during the last decade. However, the magnitude of the increase for each ethnic minority group differs (Wilson & Carter, 1988). In 1976, 80.1% of all Whites aged 18 to 24 completed high school, as compared to 82.1% in 1986. For Hispanics, the group with the lowest completion rate, there was some improvement (55.6% in 1976 vs. 59.9% in 1986). The completion rate for Blacks increased markedly, rising from 67.5% in 1976 to 76.4% 10 years later. Nonetheless, ethnic minorities, a group that will account for more and more of the U.S. population, are much less likely than Whites to complete high school.

As such, even at this early stage (4–6 years before possible entry into graduate school), the shrinking of the ethnic minority pool of individuals who might one day be interested in and qualify for admission to graduate programs has already begun. Although both the increasing numbers of Black and Hispanic high school graduates and the gains made during the last decade in the percentages that complete high school are encouraging, there is considerable room for improvement. For example, although the number of Hispanic youths is rising, large high school dropout rates for these individuals (40% in 1986) persist, and there remains a considerable loss of talent in terms of further educational involvement for these individuals. In addition, the number of Black 18-year-olds recently has declined, which could portend a steady reduction in the number of Blacks graduating from high school (U.S. Congress, Office of Technology Assessment, 1988). If this trend continues and high school completion rates for Black students do not improve, fewer and fewer Blacks will be eligible for college, let alone the pursuit of graduate study.

Enrollment in College

Table 5 presents data on undergraduate enrollments in U.S. colleges and universities between 1976 and 1986. As can be seen, the number of enrollments has risen by 19.1% during the past 10 years, primarily fueled by increases in the number of women and older students (Ottinger, 1989). Whites have accounted for the majority of undergraduate enrollments (82.2% in 1976 vs. 80.2% in 1986). Blacks remain the single largest ethnic minority group, followed by Hispanics, Asians, and Native Americans.

Although undergraduate enrollments have increased for all ethnic minority groups over the past decade, the majority of growth has been centered in the Asian and Hispanic populations, which grew by 136% and 55%, respectively. In 1986, Asian undergraduate students accounted for 3.7% of all undergraduate enrollments—up from 1.8% in 1976. The proportion of Hispanic students also rose from 4.9% to 6.4%. Enrollment of Native Americans in higher education did increase, but the percentage remained the same (only 0.7%), so that this group still constituted a very small proportion of undergraduate students.

Table 5
Undergraduate Enrollments in the United States by Race or Ethnicity: 1976–1986

Race or Ethnicity	1976 N	1976 %	1978 N	1978 %	1980 N	1980 %	1982 N	1982 %	1984 N	1984 %	1986 N	1986 %
Native American	61,416	0.7	61,418	0.7	67,875	0.7	67,040	0.7	64,014	0.7	75,605	0.7
Asian	154,947	1.8	181,014	2.1	217,382	2.4	254,670	2.8	288,308	3.2	365,623	3.7
Black	866,315	10.3	887,899	10.4	927,311	10.1	883,525	9.7	832,008	9.2	901,403	9.0
Hispanic	409,664	4.9	459,253	5.4	509,906	5.6	541,711	5.9	532,751	5.9	634,937	6.4
White	6,891,093	82.2	6,940,185	81.3	7,427,407	81.2	7,360,638	80.8	7,280,952	80.9	8,008,399	80.2
Total	8,383,435	100.0	8,529,769	100.0	9,149,881	100.0	9,107,584	100.0	8,998,033	100.0	9,985,967	100.0

Note. Data are from unpublished tables by the U.S. Department of Education, Office for Civil Rights, Washington, DC.

The smallest increase was evidenced in terms of Black enrollment, which inched upward by only 4.1%. In fact, the percentage of undergraduates who were Black declined slightly, given the more rapid expansion in enrollments of other ethnic minority groups. Furthermore, college participation rates for Blacks have eroded, and fewer and fewer Blacks are enrolling in college (Wilson & Carter, 1988). This is particularly true for Black men, for whom the number who apply to and enroll in college has declined 7% since 1976 (Ottinger, 1989).

These trends are significant inasmuch as the number of college students who major in psychology or a social science and who earn a bachelor's degree—the source of most students in graduate psychology programs—can be adversely affected by declining enrollments. Furthermore, there appears to be little indication that psychology is becoming increasingly attractive to undergraduate students. In 1985, psychology was named as the choice of study by between 3% to 4% each of Whites, Blacks, Hispanics, and Native Americans, and these percentages have not changed radically since the late 1970s (Cooperative Institutional Research Program, 1987). Asians, a group that is not well represented among psychologists, were least likely to name psychology as their intended field of interest (2%), preferring instead to major in engineering and other scientific fields.

Completion of College

The pool of bachelor's degree holders in psychology is the primary supplier of doctorates in the discipline. Consequently, as the pool becomes smaller and smaller, the difficulty of recruiting graduate students increases, particularly in terms of attracting ethnic minorities. Table 6 shows that, since 1975, the number of bachelor's degrees awarded in psychology has been declining. Although the number of bachelor's degrees in all science and engineering fields decreased slightly (0.4%), the erosion in psychology, along with the social sciences, has been much more severe. Between 1975–1976 and 1984–1985, the number of bachelor's degrees awarded in psychology declined by 24.5%.

Although reductions in the number of awarded bachelor's degrees in psychology occurred for almost all ethnic minority groups, it was particularly characteristic of Whites. The number of bachelor's degrees awarded to White students decreased by 25.5%, dropping from 43,795 in 1975–1976 to 32,610 in 1984–1985. In addition, the number of degrees awarded to Blacks and Hispanics declined by 21.9% and 22.7%, respectively. Bachelor's degrees earned by Native Americans decreased by 11.5%. In contrast, the number of degrees awarded to Asians grew by almost 30%, rising from 614 in 1975–1976 to 795 10 years later.

These trends, in light of the increases previously discussed in undergraduate enrollments for ethnic minorities, must be viewed in the context of college completion rates. Data from the High School and Beyond study indicate that, by 1986, 71% of Black high school graduates, 66% of Hispanic high school graduates, and 65% of Native American graduates who entered postsecondary education by 1982 had left *without* a bachelor's degree (National Center for Education Statistics, 1988b). The comparable percentages for Asians and Whites were 47% and 55%. Thus, recruiting ethnic minorities into undergraduate degree programs is only part of the solution to increasing participation levels; a similar commitment must be made to ensure that they stay in school and graduate with a degree.

Table 6
Bachelor's and Master's Degrees Awarded for Science, Engineering, and Psychology in the U.S.: 1975–1976 to 1984–1985

Degree Level, Field, and Race or Ethnicity	1975–1976		1978–1979		1980–1981		1982–1983		1984–1985	
	N	%	N	%	N	%	N	%	N	%
Bachelor's degrees										
All Science and Engineering Fields										
Native American	3,498	0.4	3,404	0.4	3,593	0.4	3,361	0.4	3,889	0.4
Asian	11,323	1.2	15,471	1.7	18,794	2.1	20,956	2.3	24,228	2.7
Black	59,187	6.5	60,185	6.6	60,673	6.7	57,129	6.3	54,964	6.0
Hispanic	26,220	2.9	29,652	3.2	21,832	2.4	28,929	3.2	26,067	2.9
White	811,772	89.0	799,740	88.0	807,319	88.5	794,573	87.8	798,713	87.9
Total	912,000	100.0	908,452	100.0	912,211	100.0	904,948	100.0	907,861	100.0
Psychology										
Native American	192	0.4	177	0.4	196	0.4	150	0.4	170	0.5
Asian	614	1.2	778	1.8	842	2.1	819	2.1	795	2.1
Black	3,219	6.5	3,214	7.6	3,303	8.1	2,995	7.7	2,515	6.7
Hispanic	1,666	3.4	1,734	4.1	1,808	4.4	1,470	3.8	1,287	3.4
White	43,795	88.4	36,598	86.1	34,679	84.9	33,106	85.9	32,610	87.2
Total	49,486	100.0	42,501	100.0	40,828	100.0	38,540	100.0	37,377	100.0
Master's degrees										
All Science and Engineering Fields										
Native American	795	0.2	999	0.4	1,034	0.4	920	0.4	1,256	0.5
Asian	4,037	1.4	5,495	1.9	6,282	2.3	7,186	2.8	7,782	3.1
Black	20,351	6.9	19,393	6.9	17,133	6.3	15,099	5.9	13,939	5.5
Hispanic	6,356	2.2	5,544	1.9	6,461	2.4	6,815	2.7	6,864	2.7
White	262,851	89.3	249,051	88.8	241,216	88.6	222,329	88.1	223,628	88.2
Total	294,390	100.0	280,482	100.0	272,126	100.0	252,349	100.0	253,469	100.0
Psychology										
Native American	14	0.2	20	0.3	32	0.4	41	0.5	37	0.4
Asian	89	1.2	87	1.1	77	0.9	88	1.1	129	1.6
Black	416	5.5	476	6.1	424	5.5	469	6.2	426	5.3
Hispanic	206	2.7	176	2.2	179	2.3	262	3.4	273	3.4
White	6,888	90.5	7,078	90.3	7,016	90.8	6,758	88.7	7,218	89.3
Total	7,613	100.0	7,837	100.0	7,728	100.0	7,618	100.0	8,083	100.0

Note. For bachelor's and master's degrees (1975–1976) and bachelor's degrees (1980–1981, 1982–1983, and 1984–1985), data are from *Data on Earned Degrees Conferred by Institutions of Higher Education by Race/Ethnicity and Sex* by U.S. Department of Education, Office for Civil Rights, 1988, Washington, DC. For bachelor's and master's degrees (1978–1979), data are from *Digest of Education Statistics* by the National Center for Education Statistics, Office of Educational Research and Improvement, 1982, Washington, DC: U.S. Government Printing Office. For master's degrees (1980–1981 and 1982–1983), data are from *Digest of Education Statistics* by the National Center for Education Statistics, Office of Educational Research and Improvement, 1985–1986, Washington, DC: U.S. Government Printing Office.

The exact reasons for these differential completion rates are not entirely clear. Part of the explanation is that those least likely to earn a bachelor's degree within 6 years of first enrolling in college are those students who postpone entry to college, attend 2-year colleges, or attend college on a part-time basis (Wilson & Carter, 1988). These characteristics are particularly true of ethnic minorities. For example, one half of all Blacks in higher education begin by attending 2-year colleges (U.S. Congress, Office of Technology Assessment, 1988). In 1986, 43.1% of all Black undergraduate students, 55.3% of all Hispanics, and 56.7% of all Native Americans were enrolled in 2-year colleges. The corresponding percentages for Asians and Whites were, in most cases, much lower (41.5% and 36%, respectively) and thus help to contribute to higher college completion rates for these two groups.

Other reasons that have been offered for lower college completion rates for ethnic minorities include the failure of institutions to provide adequate financial support; the lack of helpful faculty, students, and staff who are ethnic minorities; and the absence of family interest and support for pursuing a degree (G. E. Thomas, 1986; U.S. Congress, Office of Technology Assessment, 1989).

Entry Into Graduate/Professional School

Between 1980 and 1986, total graduate enrollments in higher education have increased from 1.34 million to 1.43 million. As can be seen in Table 7, graduate enrollments in all science and engineering fields grew by 26.3%, rising from almost 257,000 in 1980 to about 324,000 in 1986. During this time, ethnic minority representation also increased from 11% to 13% of all graduate enrollments in science and engineering fields. Once again, much of this increase can be attributed to marked growth in the number of Hispanic and Asian graduate students.

Despite the declining number of bachelor's degrees awarded in psychology, enrollments in graduate psychology programs increased substantially, rising by 38.7%. The percentage of ethnic minorities remained relatively stable during this time, hovering around 12%. This proportion is slightly lower than that for all science and engineering enrollments. Blacks remain the single largest ethnic minority group with 5.3% of all psychology graduate enrollments, followed by Hispanics (4.8%), Asians (1.9%), and Native Americans (0.4%).

Compared with science and engineering as a whole, there are larger percentages of Blacks and Hispanics in graduate psychology than in all science and engineering fields (see Table 7). In contrast, Asians remain less represented in psychology graduate programs. In both psychology and science and engineering overall, Native Americans constitute an extremely small minority of graduate enrollments.

This differential growth in participation by individual ethnic minority groups in psychology also can be seen by looking at the distributions of ethnic minority graduate students across the various scientific and engineering fields. For Blacks, Hispanics, and Native Americans, psychology programs ranked second in terms of graduate enrollments; the social sciences claimed more students. In contrast, psychology placed fourth among the fields with the highest numbers of White graduate students and sixth for Asians (National Science Foundation, 1988d).

The data presented in Table 7 depict all graduate enrollments—both full- and part-time. Since 1980, the growth in psychology graduate enrollments has primarily been in terms of part-time enrollments. Between 1980 and 1986, part-time enrollments increased 3.7%, as compared to a 1.9% increase in full-time enrollments. Furthermore, there has been an increasing tendency among all ethnic minority groups to pursue graduate studies on a part-time basis. Full-time enrollments for Whites, Blacks, and Hispanics grew by less than 25%, whereas enrollments for Asians rose by 68%. Increases in part-time enrollments were much higher for all ethnic minority groups. Part-time enrollments for Whites increased 82% between 1980 and 1986, whereas part-time enrollments for Blacks, Hispanics, and Asians increased by more than 100% (National Science Foundation, 1987). This tendency toward part-time pursuit of graduate degrees has several implications, including the lengthening of time required to earn a degree and become ready to join the work force and even the reduced likelihood of completing the degree.

Table 7
Graduate Enrollments in the U.S. for all Science and Engineering Fields and Psychology: 1980–1986

Field and Race or Ethnicity	1980		1981		1982		1983		1984		1985		1986	
	N	%	N	%	N	%	N	%	N	%	N	%	N	%
All science and engineering fields														
White	228,655	89.0	219,415	89.1	261,581	88.7	276,835	88.1	278,216	87.3	277,787	87.1	282,154	86.9
Black	11,627	4.5	11,144	4.5	13,325	4.5	14,468	4.6	14,870	4.7	14,567	4.6	14,394	4.4
Hispanic	7,412	2.9	7,282	2.9	9,326	3.2	11,169	3.5	12,062	3.8	11,415	3.6	11,552	3.6
Asian	8,224	3.2	7,787	3.2	9,335	3.2	10,657	3.4	12,327	3.9	14,165	4.4	15,184	4.7
Native American	915	0.4	747	0.3	1,176	0.4	1,219	0.4	1,164	0.3	1,031	0.3	1,055	0.3
Total	256,833	100.0	246,375	100.0	294,743	100.0	314,348	100.0	318,639	100.0	318,965	100.0	324,339	100.0
Psychology														
White	24,736	88.2	23,497	88.1	30,321	89.1	32,702	88.1	33,229	85.5	34,064	87.9	34,087	87.6
Black	1,418	5.1	1,450	5.4	1,643	4.8	1,916	5.2	2,200	5.7	2,075	5.4	2,047	5.3
Hispanic	1,298	4.6	1,231	4.6	1,471	4.3	1,830	4.9	2,596	6.7	1,749	4.5	1,869	4.8
Asian	372	1.3	406	1.5	441	1.3	532	1.4	699	1.8	683	1.7	750	1.9
Native American	233	0.8	93	0.3	139	0.4	135	0.4	133	0.3	158	0.4	149	0.4
Total	28,057	100.0	26,677	100.0	34,015	100.0	37,115	100.0	38,857	100.0	38,729	100.0	38,902	100.0

Note. Enrollments are for all institutions and include estimates for master's-granting institutions surveyed on a sample basis beginning in 1984. Both full- and part-time students are included; students responding "other," "no report," or "foreign" are excluded.

Data are from *Early Release of Summary Statistics on Academic Science and Engineering Resources: October 1987* (Table 13) by National Science Foundation, 1987, Washington, DC: Author.

Discussion

The trends noted in this chapter suggest that there is still a great deal of work to be done if psychology is to attract and retain qualified ethnic minorities successfully. At this time, ethnic minority representation remains low, although differences appear for individual groups. Compared with other science and engineering fields, psychology has been more successful in recruiting Blacks and Hispanics to the field than it has with Asians and Native Americans.

During the next decade or so, psychology needs to work hard to improve ethnic minority participation rates, particularly given current demographic and educational trends. An increasing percentage of the college-age population will be members of ethnic minority groups, enrollments by ethnic minorities in undergraduate programs are on the upswing, but the number of bachelor's degrees in psychology is declining steadily. As such, efforts, focused on the undergraduate level, need to be mounted to enhance the attractiveness of psychology—both as a profession and as a scientific endeavor.

Doctoral training programs can contribute to these activities in many ways. For example, faculty, students, and alumni can participate in outreach efforts geared at improving the transition of ethnic minorities from 2-year colleges, a primary locus of higher education for minority individuals, to 4-year institutions and, ideally, to psychology programs in these settings. Activities also need to be devoted to exciting high school and undergraduate students about psychology and the many different types of opportunities it offers (e.g., as faculty member, practitioner, organizational consultant, etc.).

Considerable efforts also need to be made in improving the availability of financial support to ethnic minorities (e.g., G. E. Thomas, 1986). Over the past decade, there have been substantial changes in how graduate psychology students support their training, with the trend toward an increased reliance on employment, family contributions, and loans. The increased level of indebtedness often faced by new doctoral recipients has lessened the attractiveness of psychology as a career. The lack of financial aid or insufficient levels of support dissuade ethnic minorities in particular from (a) pursuit of graduate study, (b) successful completion of the degree, and (c) completion of the doctorate in the minimum amount of time.

As is indicated by previous research (e.g., Astin, 1982), training programs, along with their host institutions, need to devote special attention to developing culturally diverse educational environments in which ethnic minority students (a) have access to faculty who can serve as mentors or advisers; (b) have available role models among the faculty, staff, and students; and (c) can locate easily other resources within the institution or program for meeting individual, specialized needs (e.g., tutoring or emotional support).

PART V
CURRICULUM

17

ETHNIC DIVERSITY AND CURRICULUM

Elizabeth Davis-Russell

California School of Professional Psychology
Los Angeles, California

When thinking and planning for the inclusion of ethnic minorities in professional psychology, one must include ethnic minority issues in the curriculum. Both chapters in this part stress such inclusion and provide the rationale for it. They cite a moral imperative, especially in light of the changing demographics of the United States. Tracing the history of organized psychology's attention to issues of diversity, they point out the lag between that first attention and any action. This lack of action can be attributed in part to the perpetuation of two myths that I discuss in chapter 18, "Incorporating Ethnic Minority Issues into the Curriculum: Myths and Realities." In chapter 19, "Ethnic and Cultural Diversity and the Professional Psychology Training Curriculum," Troy points out that, given a favorable political environment, now is the time to include ethnic minority issues into the curriculum.

In chapter 19, Troy raises two important issues. These are the centrality of diversity and its universality of exposure, or the extent to which diversity "is truly viewed as an issue for all." Although he does not explore these issues in depth, he points out two problems that can occur. First, cultural diversity might well be centrally treated, but trivially so with respect to the majority culture. Second, exposure to issues of diversity may be required of all students, but the focus is at the periphery.

Although I state it differently, I consider these problems in my discussion of the disadvantages of the area-of-concentration and the separate-course models. Whereas the area-of-concentration model makes central the issues of diversity, its inaccessibility to large numbers of the majority culture leaves the majority culture virtually untouched, primarily because it is the converts (ethnic minorities) who choose these areas of proficiency. The separate-course model, although universally exposed by being required for all students, treats diversity at the periphery.

Troy proposes "conceptualizing the curricular building blocks as discrete competencies" as a way of removing the threat to diversity being dealt with centrally, whereas "invoking a notion of the core curriculum as the aggregate of sets of formal competencies for the professional entry level" reduces the threat to the universality of diversity. If all courses of the core curriculum are structured according to the integration model discussed in chapter 18, the effect anticipated by Troy will occur;

that is, the threats to both centrality and universality will be virtually eliminated. I say virtually because, as Troy points out, "the entrenched ideas of those faculty, administrators, and students who are antipathetic to the centrality of diversity within the curriculum" pose a threat.

Both chapters show the importance of professional competencies, although from different vantage points. I articulate proposed minimum competencies for the culturally competent clinical psychologist, whereas Troy's focus is more universal. He sees courses as particular manifestations of the competencies. If the focus is on professional competencies, then coursework and field training can be integrated, thereby preserving the interrelationship among competencies.

For any training program to become successful in its mission to make ethnic diversity both central and universal, administration and faculty endorsement and involvement are critical. To help professional schools of psychology accomplish this goal, delegates to the midwinter 1988–1989 Puerto Rico conference of the National Council of the Schools of Professional Psychology (NCSPP) proposed (a) that NCSPP conduct workshops and provide resources on curriculum development for its membership and (b) that the member schools provide didactic and consciousness-raising activities that will provide the faculties with the opportunity to develop skills, knowledge, and attitudes to become both culturally sensitive and skilled.

18

INCORPORATING ETHNIC MINORITY ISSUES INTO THE CURRICULUM: MYTHS AND REALITIES

Elizabeth Davis-Russell

California School of Professional Psychology
Los Angeles, California

The social sciences in general, and psychology in particular, have taken an etic approach to the study of the relation between human behavior and social systems. Such an approach, according to Gordon (1985), has a long tradition of searching for principles that are multicultural, multiethnic, nonspecific to sex, and with multicontextual applications. Because there are commonalities among all members of the human race, scientists in the etic tradition have sought to demonstrate that all human experiences are subject to the same processes. However, some social scientists have begun to question this overemphasis on a search for universals, which some see as "at least, premature, if not mistaken, [because it has] inhibited rather than enhanced the encirclement of social science knowledge" (Gordon, 1985, p. 117). Adoption of the assumptions that are inherent in this approach has led to the promulgation of a number of myths regarding the study of ethnic minorities. In this chapter I discuss two of these myths and examine the realities that underlie them.

Two Myths About the Study of Ethnic Minorities

Current Research and Practice Are Adequate and Appropriate for Minority Groups

Psychology's overemphasis on the search for universals has led to the belief that "current research strategies and approaches as well as mental health practices are adequate and appropriate in application to various minority groups" (D. W. Sue et al., 1982, p. 45). Many scientists, several of whom are ethnic minorities, provide convincing documentation that refutes this myth. The social sciences have a long history of searching for the relations between human behavior, experience, and

171

systems. Nonetheless, according to Gordon (1985), they have neglected to study the unique impact that culture, ethnicity, and sex have on human behavior and the social systems that are expressive of behavior. Others, such as Bryde (1971), D. W. Sue and S. Sue (1972), A. Thomas and Sillen (1972), Williams (1970), Smith (1973), Padilla and Ruiz (1973), and Samuda (1975), also lend credence to the argument that challenges this myth.

This tendency of the social sciences to exclude ethnic minorities systematically in their theoretical conceptualizations has resulted in a narrowing of their knowledge base. This, in turn, has resulted in a failure to create a realistic understanding of ethnic minorities in America (D. W. Sue et al., 1982). Nowhere is this more evident than in the study of Black Americans. According to Gordon (1985), when one attempts a serious examination of the literature it becomes unmistakably clear that the approach has been

> *to understand the life experiences of socially diverse groups through a narrow cultro/ ethnocentric perspective, and against an equally narrow cultro/ethnocentric standard. Thus, the issue of cultural and ethnic diversity has been incompletely or inadequately assessed and has insufficiently influenced knowledge production. (p. 118)*

Core propositions such as objectivity, empiricism, and positivism, which form the bases of social science theorizing, are being demonstrated as culture bound, thereby calling into question their explanatory usefulness. Theories have situational and temporal utility. In addition, Gordon (1985) argued that implicit in the work of Scriven and Von Wright is

> *the notion that the relative magnitude or strength of a social variable may be more a function of the stimulus characteristics that are attributed or adhere to the variable than to the variable itself. Obviously, the attributional character of the stimulus is also a cultural product. (p. 119)*

Looking at these formulations, which have their bases in research that challenges the assumptions of universality, Gordon (1985) determined that

> *we are led to conclude that variables have different characteristics, different meanings, and different impacts for persons whose life experiences are different, and whose attributions may be idiosyncratic to their positions in life. For example, gender, culture, ethnicity, and social class are increasingly understood to influence the mechanisms by which the behaviors are developed and consequently the theories by which they are explained. (p. 120)*

Summarizing the arguments articulated thus far, it must be concluded that, because of the diversity in the experiences and characteristics of humans, any study of behavior conducted by psychologists must occur within the cultural and experiential contexts in which the behaviors are developed, expressed, and investigated (Gordon, 1985).

Another argument leveled against the myth that research and practice for minorities are adequate is the observation that theoretical propositions and laws are not value free (D. W. Sue et al., 1982; Gordon, 1985). Gordon (1985) stated:

> *Explication of human behavior is dependent on the investigator's interpretation of the origins of behavior, the values placed on the behavior and the behaving persons, as well as on the interpretation of the behavior itself. The questions and problems of interest to the investigator generally reflect the theoretical bias of the investigator. (p. 121)*

Given an investigator's ethnocentrism, these personal, professional, and societal value systems can be biased against ethnic minorities. This problem is compounded by clinical psychology's bias toward the study of pathology. The result is that ethnic minorities' behaviors, taken out of the experiential and cultural contexts in which they are developed, expressed, and investigated, are seen too often as pathological. This tendency, especially with the study of American Blacks, results in the development of deficiency models. The earliest of these was the genetic deficiency model, which was resurrected in the writings of Shuey (1966), Jensen (1969), Herrnstein (cited in Atkinson et al., 1983), and Shockley (cited in Atkinson et al., 1979). In an effort to counteract the negative effects of the genetic deficiency model, many well-intentioned social scientists translated cultural difference to mean cultural deficiency. As D. W. Sue et al. (1982) pointed out, this shifted the locus of the deficiency to the life-styles or values of ethnic minorities and created a disturbing assumption that "cultural deprivation is synonymously equated with deviation from, and superiority of White middle class values" (p. 259).

Another argument offered against the universalist position is that "racial and ethnic factors may act as impediments to counseling and psychotherapy" (Atkinson et al., 1983, p. 259). Both patients' and therapists' perceptions of the ethnic differences between them make trusting and establishing rapport more difficult. Yamamoto, James, and Palley (1968) pointed out that such factors may be related to early termination of therapy, which is characteristic of a large percentage of ethnic minority clients. This early termination rate was also found by others in their studies of ethnic minorities (S. Sue, Allen, & Conaway, 1978; S. Sue & McKinney, 1975; S. Sue, McKinney, Allen, & J. Hall, 1974).

Ethnic Cultural Issues Are Relevant Only to a Small Segment of the Population

The second myth that has plagued psychology over the years asserts that "ethnic cultural issues are only the province of a select few individuals who are considered experts in the field because it applies to a small segment of the population" (D. W. Sue et al., 1982, p. 45). A number of authors, concerned about this tendency to relegate ethnic minority issues to ethnic minority groups and to a few devotees, have advised against perpetuating such a practice (Brislin, 1983). Ridley (1985) cautioned about "the need to integrate accurate ethnic and cultural content into the mainstream of psychology curricula. Failure to do so, undermines psychological scholarship . . . given the unfortunate misrepresentation of significant portions of the populations" (p. 615). Ethnic minorities today do indeed constitute significant portions of the population. If the increase in minority populations in the California public schools is indicative of the future, the numbers of ethnic minorities in some states will become the majority populations. The excuse that minorities are only "a small segment of the population" is no longer acceptable.

The majority population is also disadvantaged by this exclusion. According to Espin (1979):

> If counselors can acquire a greater understanding of their own ethnicity and its overt and covert influences on their personalities and interpersonal styles, they will be better able to recognize the ways in which ethnic background influence different individual behavior, peer interaction, values and life goals of counselors. (p. 1)

If these issues continue to be relegated to ethnic minority populations, majority clinical psychology trainees are deprived of the opportunities to explore their full identities. One's sense of identity is inclusive of one's race, ethnicity, sex, age, socioeconomic status, and religion—all variables that traditional psychology has tended to ignore.

The fact that the United States is a multiracial, pluralistic society can no longer be disregarded. To ascribe to a philosophy that dictates a blending of pluralism denies a reality that begs recognition. America's pluralism does not threaten its existence, it enriches it. The same can be said of psychology. As Ridley (1985) said, "Professional psychology cannot retain its integrity by representing only the interests of the dominant culture" (p. 612).

The Realities of Pluralism

The Present Curricula and the Competencies

The American Psychological Association (APA), through its Council of Representatives, recognizing the reality of America's pluralism, and psychology's responsibility, issued the following resolution in 1979:

> *It is the sense of APA Council that APA accreditation reflect our concern that all psychology departments and schools should assure their students receive preparation to function in a multi-cultural, multi-racial society. This implies having systematic exposure to and contact with a diversity of students, teachers, and patients or clients, such as, for example, by special arrangement for interchange or contact with other institutions on a regular and organized basis. (p. 5)*

In January 1981, the Education and Training Committee of APA's Division 17 issued a position paper in which it articulated minimal cross-cultural counseling competencies to be incorporated into training programs. By February 1989, those competencies, or their substitutes, had made their way into a miniscule number of programs. They are being reiterated here with the anticipation that many more counseling and clinical psychology training programs will begin to incorporate them into the curriculum.

The competencies are arranged in three broad categories: beliefs and attitudes, knowledge, and skills. Existing clinical psychology training programs tend to be biased in favor of imparting general knowledge and developing skills in research and clinical practice. They do not fare well, however, in designing and implementing systematic ways of developing beliefs and attitudes. In dealing with ethnic minority issues, systematically developed beliefs and attitudes are critical because of the biased attitudes and beliefs that have prevailed throughout the history of ethnic minorities in America. The beliefs and attitudes competencies include the following:

1. Awareness of, and sensitivity to, one's own cultural heritage; valuing and respecting differences.
2. Awareness of how one's biases may affect ethnic minority clients.
3. Comfort with racial differences.
4. Awareness of, and sensitivity to, factors that necessitate referring clients to therapists from a similar race or culture.

A variety of experiences that enable the clinical psychology graduate student to interact with ethnic minorities can be invaluable in promoting these competencies. Experiential courses are tools that have been demonstrated to be effective at some institutions. These, coupled with daily interactions with ethnic minority graduate students, faculty and administrators, and field placement supervisors, serve as highly effective means of inculcating beliefs and attitudes consistent with the above competencies. The knowledge competencies include the following:

1. Knowledge of the sociopolitical system and its impact on ethnic minorities.
2. Knowledge of specific ethnic minority populations.
3. Knowledge of the generic characteristics of psychotherapy.
4. Knowledge of the barriers that prevent use of mental health services by ethnic minorities.

These competencies can be built into courses with a didactic focus. The skills competencies include the following:

1. Ability to generate a wide variety of verbal and nonverbal responses.
2. Ability to send and receive both verbal and nonverbal messages accurately and appropriately.
3. Ability to use institutional intervention skills on behalf of the client.

Structure and Design Options Available

Those who have embraced the value of incorporating ethnic minority issues into the curriculum have wrestled with how best to do so. Relevant training models and alternative methods of counseling have been suggested for ethnic minority populations (Copeland, 1979; Gunnings & Simpkins, 1972; D. W. Sue, 1973; E. Woods, 1977). Copeland (1982), operating on the premise that traditional counseling theories and practices were developed to meet the needs of White middle-class clients and are ineffective with ethnic minority clients, proposed methods by which materials relevant to ethnic minority populations can be successfully integrated into traditional programs. Although her proposal specifically targeted counselor education programs, there is wide applicability to graduate programs in clinical psychology. It is because of this applicability that I discuss the four models reviewed by Copeland.

Separate-course model. This model involves the addition of one course to the existing curriculum, and as such it may show wide variation in the goals, design, and content. As Copeland (1982) pointed out:

Some courses provide a historical perspective (i.e., ethnic studies approach), others focus on the study of appropriate theoretical models, others are more active oriented in nature and assume the form of encounter or sensitivity groups, and still others are comprehensive in nature, addressing each of the aforementioned topics. (p. 189)

A number of approaches have been taken regarding the target population of the separate-course model. In some places, the course's focus has been on a single, ethnic minority population, for example, Blacks in Dayton, OH, because that population represents the largest minority group in the area. In other areas, such as Southern California, where the representation of four ethnic minority groups (Blacks, Asian Americans, Hispanics, and Native Americans) is large, some institutions, using the separate-course model, have developed a course inclusive of the four ethnic minority groups. Examples of such courses are Minority Mental Health at the California School of Professional Psychology: Los Angeles and Cultural Issues in Psychology at the Chicago School of Professional Psychology.

The separate-course model is put to a disadvantage if it is taught in a single semester because this time frame does not permit intensive study of any one group. The problem can be addressed if one adopts the area-of-concentration model. However, if the decision is made to adopt the separate-course model, some necessary steps must be taken in order to make this selection effective. The course must not be viewed as ancillary but must be required of all students.

In addition, there must be the identification of a faculty member who has expertise in the area and the development of clearly defined course objectives (Copeland, 1982). The faculty member may be an adjunct or visiting faculty member if the institution does not have anyone on its present faculty with the expertise to teach the course. A disadvantage of having an adjunct or visiting faculty member teach the course is that it absolves the *total* faculty of any responsibility, involvement, and commitment, thereby perhaps perpetuating the myth that ethnic minority issues are the province and responsibility of a select few. This model may appear attractive to many institutions, because it ensures coverage of ethnic minority content without requiring a total program evaluation (Copeland, 1982).

Area-of-concentration model. This model is designed for training students whose goal is working with specific ethnic minority populations. The curriculum comprises the basic clinical psychology curriculum, with the addition of an interrelated core of courses in ethnic minority issues, permitting more in-depth study of ethnic minority populations. This provides students with exposure to more diversity and with the opportunity to study the similarities and differences in approaches (Copeland, 1982). Practica, prepracticum skills building, and internships, in settings with ethnic minority populations and with supervision from professionals with the expertise, provide direct experience for students to practice with ethnic minority populations. Dissertations written about the area-of-concentration model add to the sorely needed research and discourse in ethnic minority mental health.

Some disadvantages of the area-of-concentration model become apparent. Because the number of students who elect to develop proficiencies in working with ethnic minority populations is smaller than those who actually work with those populations, all students may not be reached who need to be reached. Because the model requires a core of courses in addition to the basic clinical psychology curriculum, it may extend the length of training. And last, given APA's sentiments regarding specialization at the predoctoral level, this model could be interpreted as advocating specialization.

Interdisciplinary model. According to the interdisciplinary model, students take courses outside the clinical psychology curriculum. These courses could include anthropology, sociology, economics, political science, and ethnic studies (Copeland, 1982). The interdisciplinary model eliminates the concern that clinical psychology programs do not have the expertise and other resources to provide such a variety of courses. The exposure to the other disciplines broadens the base of the student's experience (Copeland, 1982). Such a model within a university setting relies heavily on interdepartmental cooperation, but has the chance of reducing redundancy in course offerings and fully utilizes the university's resources (Copeland, 1982). In freestanding schools, the interdisciplinary model requires contracting with outside faculty to teach the needed courses. In both settings, unless the courses outside the program are requirements, only a select few students would elect to take them.

Integration model. The major weakness of the three models previously discussed is their dependence on students electing to take the courses. The integration model not only addresses this weakness, but is highly desirable in other ways. For example, a potential danger inherent in the separate-course and interdisciplinary models is the tendency to conclude that competency in ethnic minority issues is being achieved because of the addition of a course or courses. Such a conclusion can be misleading, especially to students. The integration model eliminates the road to this false conclusion.

Although highly desirable, the integration model is the most difficult to implement. "Adapting the model ... involves more than just the superficial addition of course content to include one unit on ethnic and racial minorities" (Copeland, 1982, p. 191), a practice that may occur with the other models. For an existing clinical psychology program, the adoption of the integration model means the redesigning of courses and field experience, thereby involving the commitment and time of administration, faculty, students, and field coordinators and supervisors. Lack of administration and faculty support can spell doom for the planning and implementation of this model. According to Copeland (1982), implementation of the model provides several positive outcomes:

1. The program elicits cooperation and input from all individuals involved.
2. Faculty, students, practicing professionals, and potential client populations take an active role in program evaluation. (These groups should have the opportunity to interact on a continuing basis in the sites that serve diverse groups. If this does not occur, the task may be insurmountable.)
3. A review of course offerings, along with comments from those in the field, provides useful information to assess what modifications are needed.

Outcome

Whichever model an institution selects to implement, success entails careful planning and evaluation. The unwavering support and commitment of the administration, as well as necessary resources, are critical. In addition, trainees must have access to ethnic minority populations at all levels. This includes ethnic minority trainees with whom to study and interact on a daily basis, ethnic minority faculty and administrators, professionals in field training sites as supervisors, and ethnic minority clients with whom to work.

Methods of evaluating changes in students' beliefs and attitudes as well as their knowledge and skills must be built into the chosen model. Sharing what works must be a vital part of this process. To date, much of the information that has been generated on ethnic minority issues has remained in ethnic minority publications. Mainstream psychology publications need to become more receptive to ethnic minority issues and disseminate them in order to reach a wider audience.

19

ETHNIC AND CULTURAL DIVERSITY AND THE PROFESSIONAL PSYCHOLOGY TRAINING CURRICULUM

Warwick G. Troy
California School of Professional Psychology
Los Angeles, California

It is inevitable, in a book containing successive chapters on a single theme, that redundancies and overlaps occur. This chapter—focusing as it does on ways in which the curricula of schools of professional psychology may approach issues of diversity and ethnocultural pluralism—necessarily touches on, without fully treating, points made in other presentations. Although the magnitude of the redundancy may be relatively unplanned, the fact of overlap in the series is deliberate. Certain moral and ethical aspects of the human condition are irreducible threads in any consideration of the professional psychology training curriculum. These include (a) the legitimacy of social diversity, (b) inequalities in accessibility to needed care and support, (c) the normative stance of the professional psychology training curriculum, (d) the organizational values reflected in administrative decisions concerning minority training, and (e) the kind and degree of support for pluralism as manifest in the training curriculum, and the expression of such support in recruitment, student selection, and faculty performance criteria. These themes are discussed in other chapters in this book as authors strive to provide syntheses of noncynical and nonreactive approaches that might be taken to deal with the powerful realities of institutional racism in the United States and in the academic institution.

In this light, one would hope that, in the United States of the late 1980s, it would be considered axiomatic for psychological and other human services to be directly and significantly informed by knowledge of and respect for the cultural differences among groups. The collective presence of the National Council of Schools of Professional Psychology (NCSPP), at its midwinter 1988–1989 Puerto Rico conference, is testimony to the conviction that this rhetorical observation has minimal widespread acceptance. It is the purpose of this chapter, therefore, to identify and illuminate a limited number of challenges that confront the professional psychology training curriculum as it attempts to produce psychological service providers who are capable of conducting themselves professionally and personally in ways that truly assist those in need, and in ways that reflect knowledge of and respect for the ethnocultural diversity that is one of the great manifest realities of the United States.

The Normative Rationale of Embracing Diversity

The normative framework of this chapter is exemplified in the following assumptions:

1. Issues of diversity are immanent in the wider scope of pluralism in the United States.
2. Formal incorporation of issues of diversity into the professional psychology training program is an axiomatic good and an obligation, and such incorporation enriches the majority culture.
3. Issues of ethnic and cultural pluralism and diversity pervade the entire professional psychology training curriculum and are central to it.
4. Systematic treatment of these issues in the training curriculum, research, professional (field) training, and professional socialization is mandated by issues of equity and accessibility with respect to traditionally underserved groups, the vast majority of whom are ethnic minorities.

Diversity and the Role of Organized Psychology

One could summarize the history of organized psychology's incorporation of the centrality and universality of ethnic and cultural diversity into training programs as "little and late." Although views on the centrality of cultural and ethnic diversity had found some early expression in the work of individual ethnic minority psychologists, it was the 1973 Vail Conference on Levels and Patterns of Professional Training in Psychology (Korman, 1976) that first provided the crucible for a collective expression of this centrality within organized psychology. Unfortunately, the collective expression of centrality of cultural and ethnic diversity voiced at Vail was slow in gaining acceptance by mainstream professional psychologists. The passionately voiced recommendations of Task Group 9 (Professional Training and Minority Groups) of this conference were not tangibly supported in subsequent years by governance groups within the American Psychological Association (APA). Indeed, some expression of the centrality of ethnic and cultural diversity in professional psychology training did not find endorsement until more than 13 years later at the Mission Bay conference—the NCSPP midwinter 1986–1987 meeting (Bourg et al., 1987), itself an anomaly within organized psychology!

It must be conceded that since Vail, APA's own accreditation guidelines have been modified to address cultural diversity, but they do not speak to its centrality in the professional psychology training curriculum. More recently, the National Conference on Graduate Education and Psychology (American Psychological Association, 1987) endorsed diversity in a less ambiguous and less self-conscious way than its historical antecedents. It is significant that this conference included the full scope of graduate education and training. Early in 1988, APA's Committee on Graduate Education and Training authorized a subcommittee to flesh out, in functional ways, the conference recommendation on diversity and student and faculty recruitment and retention. Finally, Division 17 (Counseling Psychology), in its 1987 Conference on the Future of Counseling Psychology in Atlanta, rather cautiously committed itself to exploring a formal place for diversity in counseling psychology training programs (B. R. Fretz, personal communication, April 1987).

Diversity as a Moral Imperative

What may one conclude from this outline of organized psychology's treatment of diversity? If one focuses on the accretion of successive expressions of clear endorsement, the result is a catalog of modest achievements. If one examines the result from the viewpoint of efficacy, what passes for achievement may be seen as little more than the expression of pious hopes, and cynical ones at that.

Although this interpretation is a true reflection of reality, there is a signal accomplishment for those psychologists who have worked for so long to have ethnic and cultural diversity appropriately and centrally treated within the professional psychology training curriculum. It is simply that the issue can no longer be evaded. Although the historical role that organized psychology has played in relation to diversity and the needs of the underserved has been shameful, the issue itself is no longer in doubt. What remains in question, however, are the acceptance of the *centrality* of this issue and the extent to which the exposure of students to the issue is *universal* within the training curriculum.

Context of Curriculum Design and Program Implementation

There are two important and problematic aspects of the role of diversity within the training curriculum. One is its centrality in the curriculum. The other is its universality, or the extent to which it is truly viewed as an issue for all. Thus, in one program diversity might well be centrally treated, but trivially so with respect to the majority culture. Alternatively, exposure to issues of diversity may be required of all students, but the focus is at the periphery. There exist two related mechanisms—actually constructs—by which these two challenges may directly and effectively be addressed: (a) formal professional competencies and (b) the core curriculum. These mechanisms, used in tandem judiciously, provide significant corrective action both to threats to the centrality of diversity, and to its universality of exposure.

Centrality and Universality

Significantly, NCSPP has already displayed clear leadership within organized psychology in regard to centrality and universality. The Mission Bay conference resolutions adopted in December of 1986 speak directly to the need to base professional psychology training on a set of six discrete professional competencies that, at the basic (journeyman) level, should also "serve as a professional psychology core curriculum" (Bent & N. Jones, 1987, p. 36). Thus envisioned, these competencies—which comprise knowledge, attitude, and skill components—and not traditional content areas, are the building blocks of the core curriculum.

Knowledge, attitude, and skill components are all clearly involved in the variety and complexity of issues concerned with the curricular treatment of ethnocultural diversity, and they can be translated into discrete, structural entities within the curriculum. The work of one of NCSPP's current standing committees, the Program Development Committee, will conceivably be useful as a resource for the mechanics of curriculum construction. The hard work, however, must inevitably be done at the level of the individual training program. Appropriate ways of incorporating issues of diversity (with knowledge, attitude, and skill components) within the training curriculum are facilitated by conceptualizing the curricular building blocks as discrete competencies. This largely removes the threat that diversity will not be dealt with centrally. Furthermore, by invoking a notion of the core curriculum as the aggregate of sets of formal competencies for the professional entry level, the likelihood of obligatory exposure for all students is enhanced.

Organizational Threats to Program Development and Implementation

Thus far, it has been shown that (a) there is a moral imperative for the treatment of ethnocultural diversity within the curriculum; (b) there exists a favorable political environment for such action; and (c) certain mechanisms are available that, if judiciously and consistently used, can reduce many of the threats to both the centrality and universality of diversity within the training curriculum. Particular threats to a positive outcome bear on the motivation and energy of program developers to engage in and to sustain what is, in essence, a planned organizational intervention designed to disseminate an innovation: the acceptance of issues of diversity as central and universal to the training curriculum. One source of threats is the entrenched ideas of those faculty members, administrators, and students who are antipathetic to the centrality of diversity within the curriculum. Other potential sources, perhaps paradoxically, include "sanctioners" such as state licensing and other regulatory entities, regional accreditation authorities, APA governance groups, and the specialty accreditation within APA itself. These organizations are threats because of their failure to demand change.

The approach to organizational assessment and strategic intervention planning that is required to ensure the appropriate diffusion of an innovation has been exhaustively treated in the organizational change development literature. Suffice it to say that one cannot overemphasize the role of key, senior administrators in helping establish, with conviction and force, the organizational structure and decision-making procedures appropriate to ensure positive change. Without significant manifest and sustained support from the leadership of schools of professional psychology, the threats to an adequate treatment of diversity—threats arising from the inhospitable value stances of other administrators, faculty, and students—may easily prevail. These threats may appear either in the early, formative stages of program development or in later stages, when the energy and resources so crucial to the maintenance of organizational change cannot be sustained.

Strategies to ensure the success of the diffusion must be based on a thorough assessment of the resources and ideologies of the institution and program in question. Without such an appraisal, the in-house sanctioners vital to the success of the venture may not be identified or, if identified, may not be sustained. These in-house sanctioners may eventually be drawn from the ranks of those with views initially inhospitable to the kind of program herein envisioned.

Looking Inward

Those program developers who would seek to have diversity both centralized and universal within the curriculum need to acknowledge and work directly with the diversity that is immanent in the academic and professional community. Open, collegial, and examined discourse on contentious issues must prevail and must be seen to prevail. The role of senior administrators in facilitating and modeling this kind of community self-appraisal is as important as their role as trenchant advocates for the place of diversity, in all its complexity, in the education and training of professional psychologists.

For program development of the kind discussed here to flourish, a critical mass of advocates—particularly faculty—must be present. The identification and nurturance of such a critical mass is the initial and singular challenge for school administrators. Although administrators may, to a large extent, control resources and, to a smaller extent, sanctions and rewards, Draconian imposition of the administrative standpoint will surely ultimately fail, despite the perception of short-term gains.

An informed faculty's considered endorsement of the centrality and universality of diversity in the curriculum must be the ultimate goal of campus leadership. Once arrived at, however painful and protracted the process may have been, the prime responsibility of administrative leadership is its stewardship of that goal through strategic and fair manipulation of resources, sanctions, and rewards. Innovations inevitably confront the forces of entropy. Effective administrative leadership recognizes this, reidentifies objectives, and provides the support necessary to sustain the gains whose achievement has consumed scarce resources. Maintenance of organizational change is as difficult as its implementation, and it requires continued vigilance.

Selecting a Model

Having examined the context of curriculum development, having noted the role of professional competencies in the professional core training curriculum, having apprised possible threats to implementation and maintenance, and having taken into account resource and other constraints, the program developer is faced with the task of selecting the kind of curricular formats that best embody the normative rationale. This choice having been made, the issue of content remains.

Types of Curriculum Structures

It is necessary to consider the question of the form and content of a curriculum that places diversity centrally and requires universal exposure. Immediately the problem arises that, almost without exception, formal courses are the building blocks of a program. One must deal with the reality that using discrete courses to build curricula is enormously convenient. Content is, presumably, appropriate; formats are understood, units can easily be assigned, and courses have a clear beginning and end. All members of the academic community (and external sanctioners) are familiar with the course-work model.

This tradition, then, leads the program developer to think exclusively in terms of the construction of courses. Conversely, it has been argued earlier that the appropriate structural elements of curriculum (program elements) ought to be the professional competencies, organized at a basic level in the form of a core curriculum. This dilemma is resolved if one considers traditional course work as subordinate to the formal competencies. In other words, courses are viewed as particular manifestations of the competencies. This is reflected in the following example.

One of the six key competency areas for the generic professional training curriculum, as identified at the NCSPP Mission Bay conference, is called *relationship*. This general competency area is construed as a set of many separate competencies, all bearing on knowledge of, values inherent in, and skills relevant to the role of the generic professional psychologist as a caregiver and change agent who must effectively work with the enormous diversity of characteristics among individuals and groups of individuals. The general term, *relationship*, for this class of competencies refers to concepts such as interpersonal sensitivity; acceptance of, comfort in, and respect for notions of individual and group differences; knowledge of sociocultural differences and their genesis and manifestation in American society; knowledge of and developed skills for combating institutional racism; knowledge of and sensitivity to the general and unique needs of the traditionally underserved; and knowledge of how health policy affects accessibility to care. Each of the elements in this list may be considered a competency of knowledge, value, or skill. How are these many and varied competencies, which bear directly on the theme of diversity, best incorporated into the curriculum?

Courses, Competencies, and the Core Curriculum

In attempts to incorporate competencies in the curriculum, one thinks immediately of a course. But a course in what? Five years ago, California School of Professional Psychology: Los Angeles (CSPP: Los Angeles), developed a nonfield didactic practicum called Principles of Service Planning and Delivery. All first-year clinical students are required to take it. It is regarded as a key, foundation course intended to introduce students early to the ever-changing variety of organized care settings; to prepare them for field-based practica in their second year; to demonstrate (through supervised visits to a variety of agencies) the different ways in which organized care settings use scarce resources to meet service demands; and to introduce students to the essential inequities with respect to public and private funded care and to differences in accessibility to care for traditionally underserved people. Students meet with agency administrators to discuss the agency's problems and programs. In the process, the students learn something that surprises them: Most of them will be engaged in agency administration earlier rather than later.

This "dipracticum," as it is called, is required of all students (universal). All must take it early (foundational). It is linked with another (traditional) mandatory course in clinical interviewing (central), and students' performance is carefully evaluated by faculty members who accompany student groups to agencies (role modeling). Requirements of the dipracticum also include attendance at a faculty-led integrative seminar, during which students' reactions to the experiences are shared and learnings consolidated.

In describing this curricular offering, several points must be considered: (a) The dipraticum provides exposure to, rather than mastery of, a great number of professional competencies, with value, skill, and knowledge components represented. (b) The dipracticum is foundational within the core curriculum to the extent that it anticipates certain other key courses (second-year, field-based practicum and fourth-year seminar in professional roles). (c) It provides for the formal modeling of appropriate professional behaviors by faculty and other professionals. (d) It emphasizes the essential artificiality of the distinction between academic course work, on the one hand, and field work, on the other. (e) The dipracticum emphasizes knowledge-oriented and, particularly, value-oriented competencies far more than skill-oriented competencies. (f) The dipracticum emphasizes the interconnectedness of the six broad competency areas by examining program development, program evaluation, administrative, therapeutic, and consultative modes of service delivery. (g) It focuses to a large extent, although not exclusively, on the manifold issues of diversity. (h) It was designed to provide a forum wherein the beginning graduate student could examine, and receive comment on, her or his own professional growth in the area of values.

In curriculum development, the central focus should be on the professional competencies. Instead, one is accustomed to turning to courses to handle the content and format questions. Although there is nothing wrong with that, per se, it does present two dangers. First, the coverage of central issues, such as diversity, tends to be incomplete if entrusted solely to a course. Second, the essential interrelationships among competencies tend not to be preserved well if treatment of complex curriculum issues is restricted to courses. The assumption at CSPP: Los Angeles is that course work is neither a necessary nor a sufficient modality to deal with complex issues in the training curriculum. Furthermore, even if it were, one is still left with the question of how one constructs curricula using competencies.

Using the discussion of the dipracticum as a general guide, the following may be concluded about courses, competencies, and the core curriculum.

1. The basic curriculum is defined as an irreducible *core* of discrete professional competencies, organized for convenience into various instructional formats in which appropriate competencies are introduced and developed, and the performance of students with respect to these competencies is formally and continuously evaluated.

2. It is perfectly legitimate to use a course (or courses) to treat curricular issues involving sets of competencies if course objectives are clearly delineated and expressed in the form of competencies.

3. The total set of value-, knowledge-, and skill-based competencies required for adequate treatment should be mapped out and assigned to various year levels of the curriculum to be packaged, variously, into courses, seminars, field work, subcourse modules, workshops, and so on.

4. This packaging of the set of competencies has two significant advantages: It keeps the focus of the curricular treatment of the issue clearly on the set of competencies to be mastered over successive years of the curriculum, and it contributes to the belief that treatment of a complex aspect of the curriculum extends beyond a single course, to other courses and instructional formats, as the student progresses through the training curriculum.

5. Each training program should do its utmost in its development of the curriculum not to impose the inherent artificiality of course-work boundaries. Instructional formats are not sacrosanct and represent convenient ways of packaging and dealing with the competencies to be acquired.

6. There are no functional differences between field work and academic course work, no differences between academic and practical work, and no differences between academic and professional aspects of the curriculum. These are different kinds of packages, with each providing a different and valuable focus for dealing with the acquisition and eventual mastery of professional competencies at the basic level.

7. In conceptualizing the core curriculum, each training program needs to map out precisely the linkages between the various instructional packages (whether dipracticum, field practicum, internship, pro-seminar, module, workshop, etc.). These various instructional formats frequently and legitimately overlap in the competencies they treat: They may, for example, treat the same competencies in different ways.

8. The process of acquisition and mastery at beginning professional level is evolutionary. At the beginning, the emphasis is on value and knowledge-related competencies. With the successive years, levels change and skill-related competencies begin to emerge. The instructional formats are graded vehicles in this curricular progression.

Key Elements of a Model Training Curriculum

I conclude this chapter with a summary of key elements of the clinical training curriculum at CSPP: Los Angeles with respect to its treatment of diversity. The summary is presented to illuminate some of the key curricular issues addressed in this chapter, and not to depict a model of excellence. It represents solely developments within a single training program, and it emphasizes what yet needs to be done rather than any present accomplishments.

Within the clinical psychology training curriculum at CSPP: Los Angeles, diversity is treated both generically and specifically. The treatment is generic in that concepts of diversity are explicitly dealt with in certain mandatory courses at each year level. These courses, which are required of all clinical psychology students, regardless of their areas of subspecialty, are as follows:

Year 1: Dipracticum in Principles of Service Planning and Delivery
Clinical Interviewing
Professional Development Group
Year 2: Ethnic Minority Mental Health
Professional Development Group
Field Practicum
Year 3: Internship
Professional Development Group
Year 4: Internship
Professional Roles

It is of concern to the program that this generic treatment of diversity by no means includes all core courses. For example, a year-long course in assessment does not currently expose all students to diversity issues in assessment, ascertainment, and appraisal, although some instructional groups are, in fact, systematically exposed to such concepts.

The curriculum also provides for specific (nonuniversal) coverage of diversity. This specific treatment tends to be structural: It is handled by means of a formal clinical psychology subspecialty (proficiency) in Ethnic Minority Mental Health (EMMH). This EMMH proficiency, or track, provides for (a) limited track-specific course work (with the emphasis on the final 2 years of the program), (b) track-specific, field-based practica and internship, (c) track-specific research activity for PhD students, and (d) track-specific instructional groups with the core (generic) curriculum. EMMH track-specific course work is generally available to students from other subspecialty areas. At CSPP: Los Angeles, each student is required to affiliate with one of the four subspecialties: EMMH, Health Psychology, Community–Clinical, and Individual and Family.

In addition to the content-specific curricular offerings just described, the EMMH track (including faculty, students, and administrative personnel) identifies itself in the form of a fully articulated program of resource sharing and personal and academic support. Thus, academic advisement and professional role modeling for EMMH students is directly handled in the track-specific Professional Development Groups. In addition, professional role modeling is sustained through individual faculty supervision of student field work, dissertation development groups, special workshops and training modules, and track-specific course work focusing on diversity. EMMH student professional development is fostered through minority student support organizations, a peer tutorial program, and student support and retention dinners.

At the core of the EMMH track are (a) a sophisticated minority student and faculty recruitment program, (b) ongoing support and mentoring activities for both minority students and faculty, (c) formal linkages with minority professionals in the psychological community, and (d) maintenance of linkages with agencies and agency administrators serving predominantly ethnic minority clients. Finally, there is manifest and overriding *administrative* support at CSPP: Los Angeles for the treatment of diversity within the generic curriculum and for the EMMH faculty and students.

It is this final element, administrative support, that is viewed as being most critical to the ultimate survival of the program. Those with the ultimate authority must be explicitly committed to ensuring the centrality and universality of issues of cultural diversity and must be willing to allocate adequate resources to the mission. Without this kind of backing, the future of diversity within the professional psychology training curriculum is dim indeed, and hope for centrality and universality is inevitably dashed.

Postscript: In 1986, I observed to Lisa Porche-Burke, Coordinator of the EMMH track at CSPP: Los Angeles, that the track really will have come of age when a nonminority student seeks and is granted affiliation with the track. This occurred, in fact, early in 1988. Currently, three nonminority students are enrolled in the subspecialty.

PART VI
SERVING UNDERSERVED
POPULATIONS

20

UNDERSERVED PEOPLES: AN INTRODUCTION

Eduardo Duran

Pacific Graduate School of Psychology
Menlo Park, California

Service providers usually are concerned with populations. Initially, this chapter had the title "Underserved Populations: An Introduction." Somehow, the word *populations* had a dehumanizing ring to it. *Populations* was changed to *peoples* because the later word seemed to bring the issues closer to all. It was in this humanizing spirit that the midwinter 1988–1989 Puerto Rico conference of the National Council of Schools of Professional Psychology (NCSPP) approached the age-long task of integrating peoples of diverse types within the discipline of psychology. The Puerto Rico experience was difficult. Nevertheless, it provided hope that a new beginning was at hand. There were overtones of old 1960s cliches. Yet, most conferees felt that the small steps taken in Puerto Rico will make a long-term, if not a permanent, systemic change in psychology.

Schools of professional psychology (SPPs) have traditionally subscribed to the intention of making psychology more ethnically diverse. However, after several years of intention, ethnic diversity is far from becoming a reality. Most programs have a few teachers and students who represent people of color. Most of the conference participants agreed that, as institutions, firmer commitments must be made and fulfilled if psychology is to be diverse. Not only is it important to have diverse people in places of power within the institution, but also it is important that curricula reflect ethnic diversity. None of the institutions has a program that encompasses the best of all worlds, that is, an ethnically balanced administration, faculty, student body, and curriculum.

In order to address the needs of underserved peoples, it is imperative that training programs in SPPs incorporate an ethnically diverse perspective. Institutions cannot continue the paternalistic approach, common in most schools today. The old solution to the issue of diversity was simplistic and inadequate. Fallaciously, many SPPs added a course to the curriculum that supposedly dealt with cross-cultural issues and assumed that such a course was adequate for training students to serve the underserved.

The chapters in this part are particularly important because they present a realistic analysis of the complex issues involved in serving the underserved and make recommendations for ethnic diversification. An overall review of the literature is presented in chapter 21, "Mental Health Services for the Culturally Different," by VandeCreek and Merrill. In this chapter, the authors discuss the problems and challenges of cross-cultural work, as well as the limitations of traditional theory and practice. They give a realistic and straightforward discussion of outcome literature that highlights the ongoing issue of therapist–client matching, intracultural differences, assessment and diagnosis, and the limitations of prior research. The authors summarize the chapter by presenting a valuable discussion on psychotherapy strategies, including an in-depth analysis of the literature. Chapter 21 is a worthwhile resource for institutions that do not have a comprehensive cross-cultural curriculum consistent with the needs of ethnically diverse communities. This chapter enables institutions to know, at the very least, where to start when it comes to understanding service delivery within a cross-cultural context.

In "The Therapeutic Equation and Cross-Cultural Psychology," chapter 22, Jackson focuses on the actual therapeutic encounter. She delineates some of the issues that emerge in the process of psychotherapy and offers solutions based on her analysis of the literature. She approaches the therapeutic encounter as an equation that, in order to be solved, requires an appreciation of all of its elements.

In chapter 23, "Third and Fourth World Concerns: Toward a Liberation Psychology," Guillory, Villanueva, and I take a critical step out of the psychological arena by offering an analysis of the cross-cultural problem through a discussion based on socio-political theory. This is accomplished by tracing the cross-cultural problem in a historical context. The solution that emerged from this analysis is that communities of color must be self-determined, or they must be allowed to structure the form and content of the clinical and research psychology that they believe is best for them.

When analyzed within the context of all conference papers that dealt with crucial aspects of diversity, the chapters presented in this section provide a realistic overview of the problem, as well as point the way to solutions. The Puerto Rico experience taught participants that ethnic diversity is necessary and that establishing it is difficult, because change itself is difficult. The conferees began to understand that diversity is a positive idea for *all* ethnicities, that is, everyone is enriched by working toward a more diverse discipline. Importantly, the membership decided that *ethnic diversity* is the correct terminology, not *minority*.

The conference resolutions derived from the section on underserved peoples were basic and pragmatic. It was recommended that all SPPs implement training that is relevant to people of color. In order to make certain that quality is, indeed, being offered to the public, a resolution was put forth to open a dialogue with the American Association of State Psychology Boards to ensure that psychology licensing examinations adequately reflect the well-being of ethnically diverse peoples. The current licensing process does not guarantee quality clinical services or research for people of color. The protection of the public is of critical concern.

The issue of licensing is particularly difficult to assess and to change because it is an established status quo system. The need for changes in this system is best illustrated by a recent occurrence in the state of California. A Native American psychologist was failed on the oral part of the licensing examination. The reason, according to the committee, was "an overidentification with Indian culture affects judgment." All opinions, including the most conservative, have stated that the committee's decision was a clear act of racism and epitomized White supremacist thinking. Other events of a similar nature indicate that, if psychology is to be relevant, fundamental changes in the licensing structure need to be made. If ethnic diversity is implemented only within educational institutions, and not at the licensing level, systemic and continual institutional racism will be perpetuated.

The conferees at the NCSPP midwinter 1988–1989 Puerto Rico conference attempted to analyze critically the White, middle-class worldview, currently held by most SPPs, in the training of clinicians and researchers. Effort was made to raise consciousness through the presentation of conference papers that openly and honestly discussed the literature and history of service delivery. Analyses of the past and the present situation provided the foundation for future change.

One of the greatest achievements at Puerto Rico was NCSPP's commitment to ethnic diversity. After difficult discussion, the conference participants agreed that membership in NCSPP would be contingent on commitment to have ethnic diversity as part of school policy. There are still other hurdles to jump, such as changing NCSPP bylaws in order to give ethnic representatives, who may not be administrators, voting rights. However, the outlook for approaching problems and working toward solutions is promising. It is this spirit of humanizing psychology that pervaded the Puerto Rico experience that perhaps I will remember best. I hope that the work started in Puerto Rico will continue until all goals have been surpassed.

21

MENTAL HEALTH SERVICES FOR THE CULTURALLY DIFFERENT

Leon VandeCreek and
Wendy Merrill
Indiana University of Pennsylvania
Indiana, Pennsylvania

The bonds of culture are invisible and the walls are glass. We may think that we are free. However, we cannot leave the trap until we know we are in it. (Ferguson, 1980, p. 105)

The Problem of Biased Mental Health Services

Three out of every 10 Anglo-Americans who begin counseling or psychotherapy drop out of treatment before achieving a satisfactory resolution of the difficulties that led them to seek help. This attrition rate might cause providers of mental health services to wonder whether they need to consider different psychotherapeutic strategies. In the treatment of people from ethnic groups outside the Anglo-American majority, however, the necessity for change in psychotherapeutic modalities is glaringly apparent and demands immediate consideration. One half of the culturally different people who might benefit from counseling services generally do not come back after a third counseling session (S. Sue, 1977). Six out of 10 Asian Americans and Pacific Islanders who could use mental health services do not bother to seek out such help (Yamamoto et al., 1982), and the same may be true for Black Americans (Pedersen, 1988). In 1977, the President's Commission on Mental Health's Special Populations Task Force (1978) concluded that culturally different individuals "are clearly underserved or inappropriately served by the current mental health system in this country" (p. 73).

According to Pedersen (1986), minorities underutilize mental health services because counseling and psychotherapy, as currently practiced, are culturally biased. Counselors and psychotherapists look through the lenses of their own cultural values when considering clients' problems, failing to take into account the ways in which the worlds of minority people differ from their own. In a survey conducted by Acosta (1980), the most frequently cited reasons for premature counseling terminations by Mexican American and Black American clients were "a negative attitude toward therapists and perceiving therapy as of no benefit" (p. 441).

Some authorities, S. Sue (1988), for example, have questioned whether or not it is true that minorities receive inadequate mental health services. It is possible that some potential minority clients view their problems as medical or spiritual, rather than mental or emotional, and look to physicians or clergy for help. When faced with other kinds of problems, minority group members may turn to neighbors and family members for help. Conversely, some evidence suggests that minority groups overutilize some types of mental health services, such as hospitalization. Clearly, more research and study are needed in order to understand minorities' mental health needs and the barriers to mental health services that minorities face.

Who Are the Culturally Different?

The term *culturally different* is often used for people who may be identified as different on the basis of overt physical characteristics, such as skin color or facial features; social and economic status; or ethnic heritage. It is more accurate to think of culture as consisting mostly of *internalized* values and beliefs, or emotional and mental qualities. Culturally different individuals do not necessarily have overt physical characteristics or identifiable ethnic heritages that distinguish them from the dominant cultural group. The culturally different individual is defined as one who has internalized values and beliefs about the world that are different from those of the dominant culture. The assumption that every member of a racial group is culturally different from the middle-class White majority is as mistaken as the assumption that every minority individual is the same as the majority. Either assumption can lead to discrimination and prejudiced or inappropriate treatment.

The characteristics of a culture also include shared communication styles, traditions, myths, and structures of family and society (J. Katz, 1985). Within this framework, the stress of any life event is viewed and responded to in culturally patterned ways (Smith, 1985). From this perspective, it is apparent that the delivery of effective mental health services to culturally different people requires an understanding of their cultural framework.

It is important to remember that culture is "not an accidental collection of customs and habits thrown together by chance," [but is better seen as a] "logically integrated, functional, sense-making whole" (Foster, 1969, p. 88). The melting pot idealism of America, however, has in part led to a "colorblindness" and "cultureblindness" that denies or, at least, ignores the unique worldview and ethnic identity of the culturally different. When this practice is extended to mental health services, well-meaning counselors may overlook the unique life stressors of culturally different populations that critically interact with the problems for which help is sought. For example, depression may be complicated by a sense of isolation experienced by culturally different patients if they are treated as outsiders by counselors who are from the dominant cultural group.

No one, mental health professionals included, can be immune to the effects of culture. Mental health professionals who are not aware of their own cultural assumptions and biases may misunderstand their clients and unwittingly choose treatment strategies that are ineffective and reinforce cultural stereotypes. Wrenn (1985) referred to such counselors as "culturally encapsulated." This encapsulation may be seen, in part, as a by-product of the basic assumptions of traditional theories and practices of psychotherapy and counseling.

Limitations of Traditional Theories and Practices

The revered idea that the mental health professions are to remain morally, politically, and ethically neutral may represent a noble aspiration, but it certainly does not correspond to reality (D. W. Sue, 1981). The values and norms of White, Anglo-European, and male-centered culture are imbedded in mental health theory, research, and practice (Guthrie, 1976). Reflections of mental health professionals' political, social, and economic values are regarded as healthy or normal.

J. Katz (1985) suggested that the counselor's cultural values, unconsciously internalized, serve as the criteria for judging clients, but the accuracy of the criteria is never judged. For mental health professionals, this means that the values on which traditional psychotherapy and counseling theory are based have become the yardstick by which mental health is measured. The accuracy of this yardstick, however, is generally unquestioned.

Because *normal* is defined by traditional criteria, it is impossible for culturally different groups to achieve the standard of normal mental health. For example, a mentally healthy Black American who identifies strongly with his or her own cultural heritage will not be seen as meeting the criteria for normality because the measures are based on White, middle-class values. For culturally different groups, this bias has resulted in inaccurate models of *normal* and *abnormal* mental health functioning. The unfortunate consequence of models built from the perspective of traditional theory is a view of culturally different individuals that implies deviance, deficiency, or inferiority.

When counselors remain unaware of their own cultural contexts, efforts to aid culturally different clients reflect the counselor's beliefs and biases. Consciously motivated or not, such biased perspectives implicitly deny the possibility of co-equality of cultures. One culture is presumed to be superior to the other, thereby assigning inferior status to individuals of the "subordinate" culture.

Research on Treatment Outcomes

Clearly, there are numerous aspects of culture and counseling that influence the course and effectiveness of the mental health services available to the culturally different individual. To date, research efforts have focused on two general areas: (a) the necessity of a racial or ethnic match between the client and the therapist and (b) the importance of recognizing the differences that exist between individuals within a single culture.

Matching Therapists and Clients

Most of the research on cross-cultural counseling has been devoted to the debate over the necessity or appropriateness of a therapist–client match in cultural identity. Both proponents and opponents cite the well-documented literature in social psychology that indicates the importance of similarity in the social influence process. There is disagreement, however, as to whether similarity is a matter of attitude (the counselor being able to understand and empathize with the viewpoint of a culturally different individual) or of group membership (the counselor being of the same ethnic or racial group as the client).

In a critical review of the research on the similarity between therapists and clients in the counseling of four different ethnic groups (Native Americans, Asian Americans, Blacks, and Hispanics), Atkinson (1983) concluded that, although there was a *preference* for ethnically similar counselors by Blacks, little evidence exists for the superior *effectiveness* of ethnically similar dyads in any of the cultural groups studied. In a review of research literature, S. Sue (1988) concurred with this analysis. He suggested that the ability to adopt a similarity in attitude, not ethnic match, is the important variable in effective counseling of culturally different people.

Intracultural Differences

Although the research on therapist–client matching suggests that therapy with culturally different dyads is both feasible and potentially effective, it is an error to conclude that cultural variables play no role in the counseling process. Culturally different individuals vary in the degree to which they are influenced by their native culture and by the dominant culture. Unfortunately, most early cultural counseling research incorrectly assumed that all individuals within a culture were homogeneous. This unfounded assumption of cultural homogeneity cast doubt on the research, and worse, it promoted the transference of cultural stereotypes into the counseling process.

If, for example, a therapist unwittingly accepts the stereotype that all Blacks are submissive, he or she inadvertently may consider only treatment options that are consistent with the stereotype. The therapist may use only relaxation training for anxiety experienced during interpersonal conflicts, thereby omitting other treatments, such as assertiveness training, that may be helpful to the client. The therapist, failing to recognize submissiveness as an adaptive attempt to manage the stress of trying to fit in with the expectations of the culturally dominant group, perceives and treats submissiveness as a cultural or inherent personality characteristic of the Black minority client.

Some recent research has focused on the differences between individuals within a particular subculture. Cross (1971) proposed the idea that Blacks go through distinct stages of development in awareness of their own culture and identification with it. Using this theory, Parham and Helms (1981) explored the possibility that individuals in different stages of racial identity might express different preferences for counselors. They found that Blacks, at the "reencounter stage" of racial identity (characterized by rejection and devaluation of Black culture), expressed a preference for White counselors, whereas those at later stages preferred Black counselors.

Expanding on this research, Pomales, Claiborn, and LaFromboise (1986) found that the cultural sensitivity of the counselor, as defined by acknowledgment of and interest in the role of culture or race in the client's problems, made a difference in the way the client rated the counselor's expertness or competence, depending on the client's stage of racial identity. This effect was particularly pronounced with Blacks who were classified as being at the "encounter stage" (characterized by strong awareness and concern about Black culture). If such findings are representative of individual differences within ethnic groups, then a wide range of individual interests and reactions to counseling are to be expected. Culturally aware counselors must be sensitive to these intracultural differences if they are to provide effective services.

Limitations of Prior Research

The research on the effects of cultural differences in counseling and therapy is open to serious criticism. Cross-cultural research typically has been of two types, analogue and clinical–archival. Analogue research involves a simulation of the counseling process, that is, studying people who, in some way, act "as if" they were clients. In some situations, this kind of research is preferable because of ethical considerations or because of the researcher's wish to have more control over the nature of the counseling situation to be studied. However, it is a leap of faith to presume that the study of individuals in "as if" conditions will result in the same findings as those that result from real counseling conditions.

Clinical–archival research is the review of mental health facility treatment records to determine how they differ on factors such as length or type of treatment. Several shortcomings of archival studies are apparent. For example, one cannot be sure that all patients at a facility received the same treatment, or even about what treatment was delivered. Typically no information exists about the quality of the service or about the client's perceptions of the appropriateness of the treatment. Finally, as was noted earlier, research based on service utilization rates does not tap into mental health needs or barriers to service, as they are perceived by members of culturally different groups.

In addition to these flaws, many studies have used inadequate measures of change in clients. Furthermore, as S. Sue (1988) noted, researchers have applied very different interpretations to nearly identical research findings. Observing that the interpretation of the findings tends to depend on the ethnicity of the researcher, Abramowitz and Murray (1983) proposed that such research amounts to the testing of "heartpotheses" (studies with covert political purposes), rather than of hypotheses, and this is why the interpretations are so discrepant.

In spite of these difficulties, researchers continue to try to resolve some of the ongoing controversies about counseling the culturally different individual. Although more research is needed in order to identify the critical elements involved in cross-cultural counseling, some of the themes that have emerged have been useful in guiding the development of training programs for counselors working with culturally different patients.

Special Issues in Assessment and Therapy

Assessment and Diagnosis

Some research suggests that culturally different patients are overrepresented in the more serious diagnostic categories. Consistently, studies have shown at least 65% higher rates for schizophrenic diagnoses in Black compared with White populations (Lefley & Pedersen, 1986). In contrast, Blacks have much lower rates for depression, which some consider to be a less severe diagnosis (C. Bell & Mehta, 1980). Similar trends have been found in other cultural groups (Lefley & Pedersen, 1986).

Assessment of culturally different individuals requires the adoption of a transactional perspective in which behavior is regarded as a product of multiple components, including culture. Accuracy of assessment and diagnosis requires the consideration of (a) the influences of culture on perception and cognition, (b) interpersonal interactions, and (c) cultural variations in behaviors regarded as normal or abnormal. Yet, as Spiegel and Papajohn (1986) noted, cultural differences are largely disregarded as significant data in diagnosis and treatment. Without taking these factors into account, it becomes exceedingly difficult to differentiate between personality abnormalities and cultural idiosyncrasies.

For example, traditional theory and practice in counseling and psychotherapy regard the verbal self-disclosure of the client as vital to the therapy process and as a diagnostic indicator of mental health. However, historically, disclosure has not always been in the best interest of culturally different individuals. This is particularly true for Blacks. The unaware therapist is likely to regard the Black client's reluctance to disclose as a symptom of pathology and fail to recognize it as "healthy cultural paranoia" (Ridley, 1984) toward a counselor who is a member of a historically op-pressive and exploitive cultural group.

Psychotherapy Strategies

Ultimately, the culturally sensitive counselor must shift from a unicultural ori-entation toward a multicultural frame of reference (Pedersen, Sartorius, & Marsella, 1984). Counselors who are aware explicitly of their own cultural assumptions and values are better able to conceptualize and implement therapeutic strategies with culturally different people, thereby preventing the treatment from being uninten-tionally driven by cultural assumptions. If therapy is to be sensitive to cross-cultural issues, strategies must include several factors.

First, there must be an understanding of the inherent difficulty of distinguishing between psychopathology and cultural practices. Second, there needs to be a means for establishing good client–counselor interaction despite some cultural norms of social distance that might interfere with developing a close working relationship. Third, there must be sensitivity to cultural variations in family or interpersonal re-lations. Finally, the therapeutic goals must be consistent with the acculturation conflicts that are being experienced by the individual (Spiegel & Papajohn, 1986).

The worldview of the culturally different client may give rise to special issues that hinder the establishment of a productive therapeutic relationship and the setting and implementation of treatment goals. For example, in traditional counseling and psychotherapy, there is a tendency to presuppose that individuals can master and control their environment. However, this may not be true for some culturally different individuals because they have little direct control over the psychosocial stressors of oppression and discrimination. The sensitive mental health professional will not place the responsibility for oppressive environmental elements on the individual.

Furthermore, if the therapist has a naive belief in the possibility of total cultural assimilation, it may result in increased distress and misorientation for the culturally different individual by ignoring or stripping away the client's cultural identity. It is both impossible and undesirable, for example, to attempt to create a White, Black individual in therapy! The cross-cultural counselor or therapist faces a complex par-adox: To insist that there are differences between cultural groups seems racist and culturally naive, but to insist that there are no differences is equally racist and naive.

S. Sue and Zane (1987) emphasized the importance of the counselor's credibility in the treatment of the culturally different. Counselors do not need to be experts on every culture, but they need to demonstrate their openness to explore what they do not know about that client's culture. Essentially, counselors cannot know what is abnormal until they know what is normal for an individual.

Culturally different clients also may hold unique expectations about therapy. By understanding these expectations, sensitive counselors can avoid the error of relying on their own implicit assumptions about treatment. Although in some cases language may prove to be a formidable barrier to counseling, Maruyama (1978) argued that communication breakdowns are more likely to result from different structures of reasoning in different worldviews than from differences in languages.

The setting in which the mental health service is offered may be a barrier to the culturally different individual. Mental health facilities that are located in medical settings or in suburban clinics may not be accessible. Such settings also may project a White, middle-class atmosphere that is offensive to some minorities. In addition, help-seeking patterns of some cultural groups may emphasize reliance on internal resources such as family, religious groups, or neighborhoods (Pedersen, 1986) and may stigmatize assistance-seeking outside the culturally designated system. If this is true, efforts to address the problem simply by improving the therapist's skill will not be sufficient.

Conclusion

Competent cross-cultural counseling demands (a) multiskilled training of therapists and counselors, (b) changes in the basic conceptual framework of traditional psychotherapy and counseling, and (c) modifications of the mental health system by which the counseling is implemented. Culturally different individuals are underrepresented as clinical and counseling professionals and as academicians in training programs. Similarly, publications and presentations on the culturally different are also underrepresented in professional journals and organizations. These facts serve to perpetuate a unicultural focus in models of psychotherapy and in methods of service delivery.

Clearly, it is an illusion to hope that therapists can achieve complete transcendence of their cultures. Comprehension of other cultures is always limited. Recognition that one's view can never be completely multicultural, however, does not free counselors from striving to acquire competencies that will permit, at the least, relative objectivity.

Training programs in cross-culture counseling should aim for a multiskills, multilevel approach. Such programs should include mental health directors and planners, as well as practitioners, as vital participants. Important areas of concern include (a) increasing awareness of one's own culture; (b) assimilating knowledge about different cultural practices, values, and alternative views of healthy functioning; and (c) acquiring an understanding of factors common to various cultures to make it possible to view problems from a larger cultural perspective.

Training must provide an understanding of the unique stressors faced by culturally different populations and the strain encountered in the process of adapting to life in a different culture. Opportunities to engage in experiential, supervised activities with individuals from different cultures is an essential part of the training process. Such programs should increase the flexibility with which the mental health professional can operate when treating culturally different clients.

22

THE THERAPEUTIC EQUATION AND CROSS-CULTURAL PSYCHOLOGY

Jacqueline Skillern Jackson
Pacific Graduate School of Psychology
Menlo Park, California

The Therapeutic Equation

The therapeutic equation for the provision of psychological services can be expressed as follows:

distressed client + therapist + therapeutic interaction = positive change

Imagine this scenario. A distressed client has a series of interactions with a therapist during which various strategies and techniques are explored and implemented, and these, in turn, optimally result in distress resolution, reduction, or management. The distressed client brings to the interaction a set of treatment issues and personal issues that affect therapy. The therapist, likewise, brings a set of issues that can affect therapy. This occurs against a backdrop of treatment issues to be addressed and used as an impetus for change.

Counselor training, for the most part, has focused on the academic and clinical preparation of therapists: to assess the manifestations of distress (symptoms), to determine the pathology the distress may represent (diagnosis), and to develop and apply effective techniques for relieving distress (treatment). Therapists who work with clients who are prototypes for traditional assessment, diagnostic, and treatment models are relatively successful clinicians in the therapeutic arena. However, when applying those models to clients and cultures that are significantly different from the prototype, success rates are called into serious question. Historically, attempts to apply traditional psychotherapy to ethnic, racial, and cultural minorities have often resulted in feelings of frustration and failure on the part of both the therapist and the client.

Clients have responded to their frustration by either not seeking psychological services or by responding in therapy sessions in an emotional survival mode. Survival mode behaviors reflect one's attempt at self-protection when perceiving physical or psychological danger in the environment. In the therapeutic interaction, the presence of these behaviors significantly reduces, if not prevents, a successful experience.

Researchers have identified some of the most obvious survival mode behaviors: perceiving the therapist as the enemy, distrust of the therapeutic process and the therapist, minimum communication, lack of willingness to self-disclose (identified as a significant problem in mixed race counseling), high drop-out rates, and hypervigilance (Baekeland & Lundwall, 1975; Harrison, 1975; Ridley, 1984). Therapists have responded to their frustration by avoiding culturally diverse clients when possible, or often viewing the survival mode behaviors as supporting evidence of more severe pathology or deviance.

Thus, a negative therapeutic experience between traditionally trained therapists and minority clients has several negative outcomes. Therapists find themselves frustrated by the relative ineffectiveness of tools that they have been trained to use. Minority clients do not seek psychological services or find therapy, at best, to be helpful marginally. In an attempt to understand this equation as it relates to providing psychological services to minorities, I examine the components in the therapeutic equation and how they are affected by a cross-cultural overlay. Suggestions for improved counselor preparation are included.

Clients

There is a tendency on the part of therapists to view clients entering therapy as vessels or containers of treatment issues. Too little thought appears to be given to the components of the clients, that is, their makeup, capacities, individual, and collective experiences. Yet, these characteristics have a significant impact on the interactions in therapy sessions. Historically, approaches to client issues have focused on assessment of the client's personal functioning capabilities and styles, as well as the resources (usually external or institutional support) available to facilitate distress resolution.

Client issues, particularly for minorities, reflect a structure within which the therapeutic experience must fit positively if the outcome is to be successful. These include worldviews held by the client, personality variables, stress and stressor definitions, the client's ability to recognize stress, the mediators affecting that ability, and problem-solving approaches and strategies. Several client issues identified by Ponterotto (1988) as particularly important with minority clients are the client's expectations in therapy; the client's attitudes toward counseling; intracultural differences; and the psychosocial variables within and outside the culture that have an impact on therapy, such as learning styles, communication styles, social practices, oppression, discrimination, and poverty.

Survival skills are an invaluable, yet often overlooked, resource when considering client issues. History has shown that most minority populations, subject to abominable conditions and treatment, have survived and flourished. Thus, while assessing the negative factors contributing to the presenting problems, it would be useful also to examine a client's survival skills, methods, strategies, and resources because they provide insight into thought and behavior processes available for use in the resolution of the presenting problems. A word of caution should be included at this point. While highlighting client issues as an avenue for developing and understanding models of behavior that are more culturally relevant, it is equally important not to overgeneralize about minority populations. Just as there are differences between ethnic groups, there are differences within groups, and one must be careful not to construct the same limiting views with new names.

Counselors

Counselor issues include the values, beliefs, attitudes, feelings, and stereotypes that a counselor brings to the therapeutic interaction. These issues act as mediating factors in interactions with minorities. Part of the professional, ethical, and moral responsibility of the therapist, in addition to addressing client and treatment concerns, is to take inventory of personal issues that could have a negative influence on the therapeutic process. Although this kind of inventory is sometimes done relative to treatment or some client issues, race, ethnicity, and culture seldom make the inventory list. Therapist issues that have surfaced in the cross-cultural counseling literature over the past 10 years include the impact of similarity of counselor and client on the counselor's comfort in working with certain clients (Wright & Hutton, 1977), the high percentage of minorities who terminate counseling after one session (D. W. Sue, 1977), and the possible relationship of high no show rates among minorities with their perceived acceptance by and comfort with the nonminority counselor (M. J. Miller, 1983).

Color or ethnicity is one of the most salient features about individuals and, thus, is not easily overlooked. P. Bell and Evans (1981) outlined several ways in which counselors appear to handle the ethnicity or race of their clients. They may, indeed, feel comfortable working with minority populations ("culturally liberated counselors"); they may attempt to ignore the issue of color and deny any feelings of discomfort ("color-blind counselors"); they may feel uncomfortable, because of a lack of knowledge, and convey that discomfort to clients ("culturally ignorant counselors"); they may provide services to minority clients while trying consciously to hide negative feelings, recognizing them as inappropriate ("covert prejudiced counselors"); or, least frequently, they make no attempt to hide negative feelings from clients ("overt racist counselors"). In recent years, color blindness has been the modal response among therapists. Although color blindness may have been a necessary step in order to move traditional thinking from a cultural deficit model to a cultural difference model, it has long since outlived its usefulness.

In any case, all but the culturally liberated counselors are consciously or subconsciously siphoning off energy, in order to control or ignore their assumptions, stereotypes, and attitudes about minority populations, that could better be used to establish positive therapeutic relationships. The exception is overtly prejudiced counselors who seldom make any attempt to address or change positions vis-à-vis minorities. With adequate academic, clinical, and experiential training, culturally ignorant and color-blind counselors can become liberated.

For covertly prejudiced counselors, the process may be more complicated, requiring personal psychotherapy for resolution to occur. Overtly prejudiced counselors, and possibly covertly prejudiced counselors, depending on their motivation, pose the ethical question of whether they could ever work with minority populations without being detrimental to their clients, either consciously or through attitudinal leakage. In order to move toward cultural liberation, therapist issues to be addressed include examining stereotypes, attitudes, beliefs, and feelings about minorities; being open to the possibility of redefining mental health and pathology from a minority perspective; personal preparedness and willingness to work with diverse populations; and comfort with different worldviews and philosophies.

Treatment

Historically, the treatment component of the equation has been the focus of academic, clinical, and research energy in the field of psychology. Counselor training and education have emphasized preparing therapists to identify, assess, formulate, and address treatment issues. Successful mastery of this component, in traditional schools of thought, has required the acceptance and internalization of a framework of psychology that is based on Western, White philosophies, values, and beliefs. The framework includes theoretical explanations of human behavior and development, definitions of normal and pathological behavior, diagnosis and assessment of pathology, and treatment strategies and techniques.

Treatment issues, although the most focused on and written about component of the equation, are most susceptible to being rendered invalid when applied to ethnic and culturally diverse populations. The current framework of this component reflects the culture of its authors, not its consumers. The framework was written by, for, and about nonminorities. Therefore, when attempting to apply it to minority populations, the gaps have been painfully apparent.

Traditional theoretical explanations of human development and behavior are valid only for studied populations or fairly close prototypes. When indiscriminately applied to significantly different populations, their validity must be immediately called into question. Invalid theories and constructs used to explain behaviors, thoughts, and beliefs increase the risk of inaccurate definitions of normalcy and pathology, inappropriate diagnostic tests and techniques and, consequently, ineffective treatment strategies.

To make this component responsive to the needs of minorities, frameworks must be developed that are more reflective of the values, philosophies, and worldviews of non-White people. Although it would be cumbersome to duplicate the entire framework for each minority population, it is imperative to incorporate other philosophies, thereby reducing the inflexibility of current constructs. Treatment issues, including definitions, assessment, diagnosis, interventions, and prevention, must be approached from a culturally relevant perspective.

For the therapeutic equation to be useful in addressing the needs of minority clients, each component must be as responsive as possible to race, ethnicity, and culture. The most effective way to address counselor, client, and treatment issues from a multicultural perspective is through research. Literature of the past 10 years, increasing significantly in the last 5 years, has focused on crucial therapist training components and recommended areas of focus for research.

Therapist Education and Training

Ponterotto and Casas (1987) examined the extent of cross-cultural training in counselor education programs reported in the literature between 1976 and 1986. On the basis of their review, Ponterotto and Casas (1987) concluded that: (a) less than 1% of counselor education programs had any requirements for the study of diverse populations; (b) 4.2% of the programs had culturally sensitive materials in a seminar format; (c) 2.8% had courses offering didactic and experiential exposure to racial and ethnic issues; and (d) out of 95 programs surveyed, 33% had required courses or practice in cross-cultural counseling. Although change from 1% to 33% in 10 years undeniably represents progress, the fact remains that only one third of the training programs in this country are addressing the issue of cross-cultural psychology in a systematic manner.

Ponterotto and Casas (1987) further identified the top five training programs in the country, as determined by 20 leaders in the field of multicultural counseling, and examined the content of their programs. They found that all five had faculty members committed to cultural issues in counseling, four of the five programs required at least one course on multicultural issues in counseling, there was an attempt to infuse multicultural issues into all program curricula, and there was racial–ethnic student and faculty representation in the programs.

Traditional therapist training, which does not include specific training in minority therapy, places the burden on the therapist to extrapolate the training components that he or she assumes will apply to minority populations. This is insufficient training to produce mental health providers who are competent and effective with minority clients. Programs are needed that will allow students to develop multicultural skills both personally and professionally, thus ensuring their abilities to work with minority as well as nonminority populations. Three primary areas of multicultural preparation needed in counselor training programs are academic course work, clinical and practicum training, and personal growth and development opportunities.

Academic Course Work

Academic preparation for multicultural work should focus on (a) increasing basic knowledge of various minority cultures; (b) interaction patterns and styles within and between minority cultures and nonminority cultures; (c) similarities and differences between cultures; (d) sociological issues affecting minority populations (e.g., poverty, oppression, and racism); (e) how stressors are identified, recognized, manifested, and resolved in various cultures; and (f) the pivotal interactions and behaviors that can be determining factors in the success or failure of interactions with members outside the culture. Knowledge of, and familiarity with, healthy behavior in minority cultures is also necessary, as it provides a basis for assessing and diagnosing pathology and determining appropriate treatment and prevention goals.

Copeland (1982) outlined four possible models of course work organization for counselor training programs: the separate-course model, the area-of-concentration model, the interdisciplinary model, and the integration model. The separate-course model consists of adding one course to an existing curriculum. The content area of the course focuses on a theoretical base from which to study minority populations and historical and cultural issues relevant to minority populations, and it helps students to develop the cognitive and affective skills that are necessary to work with minorities. The area-of-concentration model allows for more in-depth work and is designed for students wishing to specialize in working with minorities. It consists of a core of courses in cross-cultural counseling, skills training, and practicum and internship placement in multicultural settings.

The interdisciplinary model interfaces with related areas, allowing students to take courses in sociology, anthropology, political science, and ethnic studies. In the integration model, all courses taught in the standard curriculum include culturally relevant material. Course development, planning, assignments, and practicum experiences reflect cross-cultural content. The model of choice for incorporating multicultural training into counselor education curriculum depends on a number of factors, including school commitment, economic feasibility, staff, and available expertise. Minimally, every counselor training program should at least be implementing the separate-course model.

Clinical Training and Personal Development

In addition to academic information about minority populations, students must have the opportunity to develop and practice clinical skills (strategies, techniques, and tools). This is best done in a clinical training format that includes practicum, internships, and on-campus counseling clinics. Supervised training in multicultural settings allows prospective therapists to interact with minority clients in closely monitored situations in which immediate feedback and support are available. The experiences allow students to develop both clinical skills and comfort with diverse populations.

Opportunities for personal growth and development must accompany academic and clinical training that prepares counselors for multicultural work. Students enter training programs with a variety of experiences relative to minorities and cross-cultural issues. Some may be totally ignorant, some may have negative (covert or overt) constructs regarding minorities, and others may need fine tuning. Students need an opportunity to interact personally with minorities, ask questions, and explore issues on both a theoretical and personal basis. Beale (1986) proposed a structured cross-cultural dyadic component to counselor training. In his model, minority and non-minority students are paired and given the opportunity to interact around specific questions. To be effective, this would be done best as part of a course.

Cross-Cultural Research Issues

Ponterotto (1988) conducted a content analysis of all research concerning racial and ethnic minority issues that appeared in the *Journal of Counseling Psychology* between 1976 and 1986. He found that of the 934 articles and brief reports published, 53 (5.7%) focused on racial and ethnic minority variables. Although this is only one journal, the low percentage is indicative of the absence of cross-cultural research and publication and raises questions as to why there is an absence of research and what needs to be done to fill the void.

The issue of why there is little cross-cultural research was addressed by Clark (1987) in his report of research conducted by Segall in 1986. Clark stated that cultural variables do not play a major role in the research foundation of most mainstream psychologists. In fact, cultural variables are considered nuisances and are addressed primarily by holding them constant or by working within a single culture. He asserted that, even when they cannot be ignored, as in the psychological assessment of a minority person, cultural variables often are minimized.

As the importance of racial, ethnic, and cultural considerations began to emerge in the 1970s, cross-cultural researchers focused on the impact of race and ethnicity on therapeutic satisfaction and outcome. Articles and research were criticized on methodological and conceptual issues. The results were interpreted as either conclusive for competing positions, or simply as inconclusive, thereby shedding little light on cross-cultural issues.

Within the last 5 years, research in cross-cultural psychology has increased, with an emphasis on conceptual and methodological reexamination. Clark (1987) suggested that research, instead of viewing culture as an independent variable, should focus on identifying culture-related variables. What is more important than examining intercultural differences is to look at specific variables mediating patterns of similarities and differences. Research should not be limited to examining psychological variables, but it also should study related variables such as sex, socioeconomic status, generational issues, and education levels.

S. Sue (1988) supported this conceptual move by stating that ethnicity per se tells very little about the attitudes, behaviors, values, and experiences of an individual. He suggested that it is more important to study the meaning of ethnicity than ethnicity itself. Casas (1984) suggested that research should address not only intergroup differences but intragroup variations among minority populations. Conceptually, research is moving from race and ethnicity per se to the meaning, components, and interactions likely to be represented under the umbrella of, or inextricably connected to, race, ethnicity, or culture.

Methodological issues of cross-cultural research have been discussed most recently by Ponterotto (1988). He suggested that research must broaden to include methodologies used in other areas such as cultural anthropology, sociology, ethnopsychiatry, and political science. He recommended research methods such as field techniques, ethnographic reports, longitudinal observations, oral histories, and $n = 1$ studies. He stated that such methodologies may provide valuable information that cannot be acquired through traditional statistical methods.

As conceptual models of emphasis emerge and methodological strategies to explore them are employed, the field of cross-cultural psychology will continue to be refined. A prime place to work on conceptual and methodological issues of cross-cultural psychology is in counselor education and training programs. Research is an integral part of most graduate programs and, thus, provides opportunities to participate in the development of cross-cultural psychology. Training programs must commit to encouraging and supporting cross-cultural research among students and faculty. The validity and importance of cross-cultural issues must be highlighted in training programs and research.

Conclusion

The therapeutic equation describes one of the primary functions of psychology—the provision of mental health services through psychotherapy. Each component of the equation contains a set of variables capable of negatively or positively influencing the therapeutic interaction and ultimately the outcome of treatment. The impact of cultural diversity on the equation has, for the most part, been ignored or minimally addressed. As has been discussed in this chapter, the introduction of race and ethnicity into the client component of the equation causes several significant changes.

Initially, the presence of race and ethnicity activates a set of culturally specific issues in each component of the equation. These issues must be appropriately responded to for the equation to remain in balance and result in positive therapeutic outcomes. If the responses are inappropriate (ignoring them, denying their importance, or inadequately addressing the issues raised), the therapeutic equation is at risk for failure. A second shift that occurs in the equation concerns the relative importance of each component to a successful outcome. In traditional approaches to psychology, the treatment component has been the most heavily weighted in the equation. When race and ethnicity are introduced, client and counselor issues emerge as the primary areas of concern. Success in handling these issues is necessary in order to set the stage to address treatment issues effectively.

Historically, counselor education and training have focused on treatment issues, whereas counselor and client issues have been relegated to the "also ran" categories. Course work and clinical training have been aimed primarily at developing counselor competence and treatment issues (i.e., assessment, diagnosis, intervention, and prevention). Effective work with minority clients requires equal competence in addressing counselor and client issues. To accomplish this, schools must develop and implement programs that provide students with academic course work, clinical experience, and opportunities for personal growth. The inclusion of culturally relevant material in each component of counselor education and training is imperative to produce therapists who are sensitive to multicultural issues.

The field of multicultural counseling is constantly being reexamined and refined. Through research, concepts and theories are maturing, as are methodologies that are less limiting without compromising validity. Graduate training programs offer students and faculty opportunities to engage in research that can contribute to the growing body of knowledge of multicultural counseling.

The possibility of delivering adequate mental health services to minority populations increases as the field of psychology moves toward including multicultural issues as an integral part. Inclusion can be facilitated by incorporating multicultural awareness, sensitivity, and competence at the entry levels to the field (counselor training programs), and encouraging participation in the continued development of multicultural psychology through research.

23

THIRD AND FOURTH WORLD CONCERNS: TOWARD A LIBERATION PSYCHOLOGY

Eduardo Duran
Pacific Graduate School of Psychology
Menlo Park, California

Bonnie Guillory
University of California
Berkeley, California

and

Michael Villanueva
Pacific Graduate School of Psychology
Palo Alto, California

We chose the title of this chapter in order to focus concern on the ways in which psychology currently is dispensed in cross-cultural settings and to designate the future direction that we hope psychology will follow. The people of the world can be divided into four groups according to their worldviews. The First World is made up of people who sustain a Western worldview. No one disputes the fact that most psychology (clinical and research) is based on a Western (Euro-American) worldview and philosophical ideology, sociopolitically entrenched in a capitalistic and individualistic system of cognition. (Traditionally, the First World has been used to denote people from developed countries such as the United States and Western Europe.) The Second World consists of people from developed Communist countries. (Psychology, as practiced and researched in Second World countries, is not discussed in this chapter.)

The Third World comprises people from developing countries. The Fourth World is composed of indigenous people living on their traditional lands under the occupation of a colonialistic government. Fourth World people, for example, include Native Americans, Australian Aborigines, and Palestinians. People of color and people from the Third and Fourth Worlds are woven into the fabric of American society. At present, what is of critical importance to psychology is how practice, research, and training affect these people—the underserved groups that are the focus of this chapter.

Sociopolitical Outcomes of Professional Practices

In any system where there is an unequal distribution of resources and power, systems of domination exist that act symbolically or instrumentally to reinforce that domination. Because psychology does not exist in a vacuum, it is important to examine some sociopolitical issues that directly affect the profession. The fact that American society is racist is indisputable. In this chapter, racism is defined as the principle of social domination, by which a group that is seen as biologically inferior is exploited economically and oppressed socially and psychically (Blauner, 1969).

The devastating psychological effects of colonization on indigenous people has been well documented by Fannon (1963) and Memmi (1965)—voices for oppressed people and recognized leaders in understanding psychological oppression. According to Fannon (1963), oppressed people are plagued with self-hatred and identity problems because of negation of their humanity by the colonizer. Many times, the colonized may resort to assimilation as a way of escape from oppression. The colonizer, however, does not accept the assimilated as equal (Memmi, 1965).

Psychology has been a very useful tool in the effort to control oppressed people. The profession openly assists oppressive systems to continue to perpetuate supremacy. This is particularly evident in professional practices such as testing, research, diagnosis, treatment, and training.

Testing

The whole assessment movement has its roots deeply entrenched in the biological deterministic world view of the past century (Gould, 1981). The inability of therapists to relate to different world views is compounded by a plethora of assessment instruments that are irrelevant and, at times, result in institutional racism. Gould (1981) traced the evolution of testing as a method to support White supremacy. To this day, this view continues to be fueled by proponents of genetic inferiority. The history of psychology and its continued use against people of color in this country are immoral. Yet, these practices always have been considered inside the boundaries of "ethical" observance.

Only a few decades ago, testing was used to justify massive sterilization of men and women of color. Early pioneers in testing paved the way for the justification of racism based on testing (Terman, 1916). The violence, justified through the use of psychological testing, continues to exist as the U.S. educational system currently channels children of color into vocational and dead-end educational tracks. Some of the leading forces in psychometrics, such as Jensen (1969), continue to expound ideologies (Gould, 1981) that support activities performed under the guise of legitimate empirical science.

Research and Diagnosis

The very tools that are available to research psychologists are contaminated with the ideology of White supremacy. Statistics, which are used to validate and generalize the science, have deep historical roots in the attempt to discriminate against people of color (Gould, 1981). There is historical evidence that traces the development of statistical techniques as a process to find the g factor of intelligence that confirms the preconceived racial genetic inferiority theory to which its founders were committed (Gould, 1981).

The use of testing and the formulation of diagnostic categories have played a major role in the justification of harsh diagnoses for people of color (Gross, Knatterude, & Donner, 1969; Malgady, Rogler, & Constantino, 1987). Once diagnosed, patients are medicated or shocked (Morgan, 1985) to a point approaching psychological genocide, thereby extinguishing any hope to engage with a First World lifestyle. Psychology has become a tool that has had great impact in social control situations. Paradoxically, First World psychologists deem similar practices, actuated by psychologists in so-called totalitarian countries, as immoral.

Treatment

One problem in the delivery system is its inability to move from a linear Western cosmology toward different worldviews held by people of color. Providing service per se is not sufficient, because irrelevant service equates with no service. The literature indicates that psychological services and approaches reflect a middle- and upper-class bias (Pine, 1972). The research and clinical literature on the delivery of mental health services to ethnic minority populations consistently reports inadequacies in provision of services. In summarizing the work of its Asian and Pacific-American, Black American, Hispanic American, and Native American/Alaska-Native subpanels, the Special Populations Task Force of the President's Council Commission on Mental Health (President's Council, 1978) concluded that ethnic minorities "are clearly underserved or inappropriately served by the current mental health system in this country" (p. 72).

In places where ethnic minorities have sought treatment, regardless of utilization rates, all ethnic minorities had significantly higher drop-out rates than Whites (S. Sue & Zane, 1987). Furthermore, S. Sue and Zane (1987) stated that "without belaboring the point, we believe that there is ample evidence that ethnic minorities are not faring well in our mental health system" (p. 37). Many factors contribute to making the mental health system inadequate for ethnic minorities. However, "the single most important explanation for the problems in service delivery involves the inability of therapists to provide culturally responsive forms of treatment" (S. Sue & Zane, p. 37). Most therapists are unable to devise culturally appropriate forms of treatment; therefore, minorities find services foreign and unhelpful (S. Sue & Zane, 1987).

Training

Since the 1960s, there have been many policy statements concerning equality of services for all populations in this country. Yet equality of services has not been achieved. The recent setbacks of the accomplishments of the civil rights movement have made discrimination, via institutional racism, more widespread and acceptable. Many schools of professional psychology (SPPs) voice concern about underserved people and people of color. The reality is, however, that institutional policies make it very difficult for ethnic people to enter and successfully complete psychology training programs. At present, the percentages of ethnic students completing training programs is less than their representation in the general population. This is indicative of ongoing institutional racism.

Institutional explanations for this disproportion are varied, imaginative, and well thought out. The reality, however, is that the SPPs are failing and excuses or reasons for the failure are of little or no consolation to the people who remain underserved. SPPs must make a firm commitment to ameliorate the situation by assigning a high priority to the inclusion of people of color. The time for straddling the fence must come to a close. As institutions, SPPs must be either part of the solution or part of the problem.

Some contend that the historical implications are grave and appear to predispose the profession to some sort of pessimistic future. Yet, if history is openly confronted, with no denial, the way will be paved for a healing catharsis. The initial process of the therapeutic endeavor must be cathartic in order for subsequent healing and progression to occur. It is this spirit of honesty that must pervade efforts to look at the history of psychology. Then, perhaps the past errors of the profession may be avoided in the future.

Different Worldviews

The lack of a systematic and relevant cross-cultural psychology has its genesis in both the fundamental differences in the worldview between people of the First World and people of the Third and Fourth Worlds and policies that perpetuate the low socioeconomic status of the majority of people of color. There is an inherent problem in attempting to impose one system of cognition onto a group of people who have a different system of cognition. White Americans have a linear orientation to their thinking, but it does not follow that this is the only way to think or conceptualize the world. Primitive peoples, as they are called in the anthropological literature, have a different way of being in the world. The phenomenological essence, in terms of conceptualization of space and time, is radically different from that of "civilized" people. For instance, some Native American tribes do not conceptualize history as a temporal event but as a spatial phenomenon. This basic difference in seeing the world can become an uncrossable bridge for the practitioner who has been trained in a colonialistic institution where only the Western worldview is seen as valid (Duran, 1984).

Most of the cultures currently served by psychology originally had their own useful systems of psychotherapy until the colonialization process removed or suppressed them. The way in which a culture conceptualizes disease and healing is one of the crucial issues that needs to be addressed by psychology. Traditional treatment modalities are not relevant to a culture that sees psychopathological phenomena as having an etiological ideology that is different from that of the dominant culture. Those who impose First World theoretical constructs on Third and Fourth World populations are guilty of conspiracy to commit ethnocide (United Nations, 1949). Native Americans, for example, derive some of the most useful practices for health from their religious beliefs. Yet, prior to 1981, religious freedom was not a Native American right. In reality, for most Fourth World peoples, mental health cannot be explicated separately from holistic spiritual and religious practices.

Consciously or unconsciously, psychologists often violate the essence of culture by inappropriately treating culturally bound behavior as if it were pathological. This is a practice that must not be tolerated, because culture is not intrinsically good or bad, it just is. The essence of culture is a way or system of being in the world. Under no circumstances should people be penalized for being in the world using a different system of cognition. Equally as important in the recognition of culture as a factor in treatment or prevention of mental illness is the relationship between members of certain cultural groups and society's institutions. The relationships among people of color or any underclass individuals and business, industries, the legal and correctional institutions, social service agencies, and governmental power structures are key determinants of mental health status.

The world of relevant cross-cultural psychotherapy is not unattainable, but much work needs to be done in order to realize it. It must be acknowledged that policies of service delivery have been an integral part of a system that is searching for any means of social control in order to continue the social, political, economic, and spiritual exploitation of Third and Fourth World peoples. By being aware of the part that they have played in the colonialistic process, psychologists can begin to implement healthier strategies for all people.

In the development of a relevant and new cross-cultural psychology, it is imperative to stop psychological imperialism. Undoubtedly, this will have its genesis in the research area. Researchers who further the interests of institutions that function for a system interested in the continual oppression of people of color must be opposed. It is very easy, even for researchers from an oppressed group, to continue working toward oppressing their brothers and sisters, especially when all of the institutional rewards are given to those who are part of the status quo.

Not one SPP *overtly* specifies the oppression of people of color as part of its policy. This policy is very subtle and difficult to detect, but it does exist nonetheless. In recruiting ethnic faculty and students, for instance, criteria can be established that allow only the selection of those who fulfill certain requirements—usually that the person of color exhibit some or all of the qualities that strengthen the status quo. Yet, these policies are legal and even ethical according to the rules governing the profession. Otherwise, there would be sanctions and expulsions from psychological fraternities for these violations, and we have no knowledge of a single case being brought to light in regard to these issues.

Recommendations

It would be unscrupulous and unacademic to discuss the issues mentioned in this chapter without suggesting solutions. Self-determination is the fundamental ideology in attempting to construct relevant research and clinical psychology. Precedence has been provided by the U.S. government's passage in 1978 of the American Indian Self-Determination Act (Public Law 93-638), which gave Native Americans the right to be self-determined. (No one, however, has addressed the political narcissism of an audacious government that thinks it has the power and morality to *allow* self-determination. Self-determination is an a priori right, not one to be granted by convention.)

Community Autonomy

People of color should be encouraged and allowed by institutions to define the direction of psychological research and practice within their communities. This is the sine qua non of having a relevant psychology and would be the beginning of the process of absolution for the profession. Blauner (1969) has supported the notion of complete community autonomy, which radically opens doors and fully allows participation in mainstream institutions. For psychologists to believe that solutions can come from outside the oppressed communities is akin to professional narcissism, bordering on imperialism. Such solutions merely ensure that the problems will continue and eventually the whole society suffers from such thinking.

Critical pedagogy seeks emancipation from the "hidden curriculum" of modern-day American education that works to socialize students to conformity, obedience, passivity, and to the perpetuation of values of the predominant culture (Apple, 1971). According to the thinking of Freire (1986), it is impossible for the oppressor to liberate the oppressed. In an ideal situation, the oppressed people, in enacting their liberation, also will liberate the oppressor. Thus, the act of liberation is a process that has love as a basic guiding principle—something that is never mentioned in most Western psychology.

Freire (1986) delineated the process by which communities can be empowered to develop their own autonomy. Psychology should learn to facilitate group praxis through listening to the communities.

> *To Freire, the purpose of education should be human liberation so that learners can be subjects and actors in their own lives and in society. To promote this role, Freire proposes a dialogue approach in which everyone participates as equals and co-learners to create social knowledge. The goal of group dialogue is critical thinking by posing problems in such a way as to have participants uncover root causes of their place in society—the socioeconomic, political, cultural, and historical context of personal lives. But critical thinking continues beyond perception—towards the actions that people take to move beyond powerlessness and gain control over their lives. (Wallerstein & Bernstein, 1988, p. 382)*[1]

SPP Leadership

The Freirian approach is relatively simple and can be implemented at once by SPPs. It consists of a three-stage method to be performed with the equal partnership of the community. Decisions are not imposed as much as thought out critically by the partnership model. As described by Wallerstein and Bernstein (1988), the Freirian approach comprises the following steps:

1. Listening to and understanding the thematic content of the issues important to the community.
2. A participatory dialogue using a problem-posing method.
3. Praxis or positive changes that people have conceptualized in the dialogue.

The Freirian method, if implemented within SPPs, would be the beginning of a

---

[1]From "Empowerment Education: Freire's Ideas Adapted to Health Education" by N. Wallerstein and E. Bernstein, 1988, *Health Education Quarterly, 15*, p. 382. Copyright © 1988 by John Wiley & Sons, Inc. Reprinted by permission of John Wiley & Sons, Inc.

solution that would empower a relevant cross-cultural psychology. In order to begin the dialogue, SPPs must have people of color within their institutions. SPPs can lead the way by making it possible for faculty to be more integrated. This can be done by hiring and giving tenure to faculty of color. The hiring and tenure, however, can come about only if people of color see the institutional environment as committed to the resolution of these age-long problems. The solution does not reside in hiring people of color who will be expected to perform according to a White status quo, because this will be interpreted as perpetuation of colonialistic praxis. Once SPPs are safe places for critical analysis and praxis at the faculty and administrative levels, then it follows that students from these communities will be attracted by the cultural relevance of training programs.

Culturally Relevant Research

The fact that culture needs to be relevant at the research level as well as the clinical training level cannot be stressed too strongly. Researchers traditionally think that they are free from bias because they are practicing science. This obliviousness allows them to reinforce the status quo. Nothing is further from the truth than to believe that all science is free from bias. Researchers need to make their research and research methodology relevant to Third and Fourth World peoples. Rewarding research that maintains the status quo encourages co-conspiracy with the imperialism and White supremacy mentality within psychology's ranks.

The task ahead is a great and challenging one. Psychology has the opportunity to address some very difficult problems. By so doing, it can begin to turn itself into a force that can empower and liberate people who are disenfranchised and oppressed. By meeting the challenge in an honest and open way, psychology can set the standard for other disciplines and contribute to the well-being of all segments of society.

PART VII
EPILOGUE

24

PUERTO RICO CONFERENCE: THE MEDIUM WAS INDEED THE MESSAGE

Edward Bourg

California School of Professional Psychology
Berkeley, California

and

Kenneth Polite

Biola University
La Mirada, California

In all psychological interventions, process and content outcome are related inextricably. In most situations, psychologists lack the precision to prescribe process variables that will ensure positive outcomes. Moreover, they disagree about different intervention processes derived from alternative theoretical perspectives. Yet most psychologists would agree that process is critical, often determinative, of content outcome. This was certainly the case at the National Council of Schools of Professional Psychology (NCSPP) midwinter 1988–1989 Puerto Rico conference.

Because of its importance, the Puerto Rico conference process and its effect on content outcome are the focus of this chapter. Our purpose is threefold:

1. To present some central process issues to supplement the more content-oriented chapters and conference resolutions presented in this volume.
2. To give the reader some of the "feel" of the Puerto Rico conference in order to facilitate understanding how the participants' conflict, anxiety, and excitement shaped the resolutions and played a critical role in shaping attitudes about the conference proceedings.
3. To suggest some guidelines in dealing with multicultural issues in psychological organizations such as educational programs and professional associations.

Two important limitations of this conference process summary should be emphasized. First, this presentation inevitably is biased by the authors' experiences at the Puerto Rico conference. Our roles on the conference steering committee placed us at the structural center of the process. The steering committee, composed of three White people and five people of color, was an amalgam of the executive committee and the conference program committee. Although our roles on the steering committee gave us access to important elements of "the action," they also shaped our perceptions. Therefore, our summary of what happened cannot be construed as a summation of the individual experiences of the 59 participants.

Second, this chapter is based on our abstractions of the Puerto Rico conference, as well as the many formal planning meetings that occurred during the year preceding the conference. Because the preconference meetings were under the aegis of different planning subcommittees, participants at these meetings did not necessarily overlap. In total, thousands of words were spoken, and hundreds of thoughts and feelings were expressed. We, as members of one subcommittee, were not present at all preconference planning meetings, thereby limiting our ability to abstract the planning stages of the conference process. During the conference, critical problems arose between the responsible planning committees because of differences in expectations and problems in communication.

Critical Incidents

We have chosen to adopt the "critical incidents" methodology used in the group dynamics literature. The incidents selected to represent the group process are illustrative of three central themes: (a) mutual trust among members of NCSPP, (b) enfranchisement of people of color within the organization, and (c) personal and cultural diversity.

Designating the Editors of This Volume

Early in the conference planning, the officers of NCSPP had decided to establish a program committee, separate from the executive committee. Vehicles for interface were created (e.g., the president served as a liaison between the executive committee and the program committee). In retrospect, this separation was a mistake. It increased the likelihood that distrust and concern about enfranchisement would arise, particularly because the two committees were ethnically different and distinct (the executive committee was predominantly White; the program committee was exclusively people of color). In time, cultural differences in working style and emphasis emerged. These differences were perceived negatively by the two groups. Although both committees agreed that the conference papers would be organized into a book, there was disagreement about who would be named as editors. Some months before the conference, this debate surfaced and festered in formal and informal discussions.

On the evening preceding the conference, a caucus, composed primarily of people of color and some Whites, met to discuss this question of editorship. The caucus expressed strong sentiment for designating members of the program committee as editors of the forthcoming book. Before the conference began, a specific proposal reflecting the conviction of the caucus was brought before a joint meeting of the program committee and the executive committee. Other proposals with legitimate rationales also were put forth. The discussion was very tense. Ultimately, a decision was made to combine the program committee and the executive committee into a steering committee for the conference and to name the members of the steering committee as editors, although the order of authorship was yet to be decided. *At the time*, many people on the newly formed steering committee perceived the outcome as a "political" compromise. Although the consensus was tenuous and halting, the steering committee's first joint decision did support trust, enfranchisement, and respect for cultural differences.

Further progress in these three key areas was aided by a significant, unplanned event that occurred just prior to the official beginning of the conference. The steering committee conferred with Valerie A. Batts to discuss the experiential program that she had planned for the conference participants (see chapter 2, this volume). In order to better understand one of the exercises, we spontaneously engaged in the experience ourselves; we briefly shared some of the important aspects of our own cultural backgrounds, with emphasis on how we had all experienced being members of "target" and "nontarget" groups. This personal exchange was very valuable in moving us beyond our formal roles and the posturing inherent in any political confrontation. Furthermore, it was a very humanizing experience because we learned something personal about our respective cultural experiences. This enabled us to recognize that each of us had the dehumanizing experiences of being a member of both target and nontarget groups. When the decision regarding order of authorship eventually was made, no one on the steering committee made direct reference to Batts's exercise. We believe, however, that it played a significant part in helping the committee make a decision that supported trust, enfranchisement, and respect for cultural diversity.

Steering Committee Interchange

The resolutions issued from any conference are the product of political compromise. To some extent, this is true of the Puerto Rico resolutions. However, the Puerto Rico conference process was unusual because we had chosen to deal directly with a very complex, thorny, and volatile issue, that is, inclusion and enfranchisement of people of color in NCSPP itself, and in each of its member schools.

There was tacit agreement by the White members to do something real and substantive, well beyond the weak legal imperatives of affirmative action (made weaker by subsequent Supreme Court decisions!). There was tacit agreement by the people of color to commit their talents, energy, and support to NCSPP's initiative *if* something really substantive would emerge.

The convergence of these unspoken intentions had both positive and negative consequences. Positively, many substantive resolutions emerged. Indeed, the conferees drafted so many resolutions that the steering committee initially was not able to provide the kind of forceful leadership necessary to simplify and integrate them. Negatively, as the draft resolutions came before the plenary session and commitment to them began to be discussed as a condition of membership in NCSPP, basic issues of trust, enfranchisement, and cultural diversity arose for both White people and people of color.

Whites were culturally predisposed to emphasize structural and formal issues. They became distrustful, fearing that NCSPP would attempt to mandate changes for member schools and establish structures for NCSPP that would disenfranchise the Whites (mostly men) who had controlled the organization since its inception. Many of the people of color were culturally predisposed to emphasize maintenance of relationship rather than issues of structure and form. They doubted the integrity and commitment to change of those who failed to acknowledge the criticalness of the proposed conditions of membership.

Passage of the draft resolutions bogged down. People of color began to mistrust that they would be enfranchised. They doubted that the substantive initiative, that is, changing NCSPP and its member schools from ethnocentric to multicultural, would occur. At the end of the first day's plenary session, many participants felt disheartened, anxious, and divided.

In the conference keynote speech delivered that evening, James M. Jones introduced a simple but profound concept: "affirmative diversity" (see chapter 3, this volume). The essence of affirmative diversity is that cultural differences are significant and important and that commitment to creating a multicultural environment greatly enriches an educational program or association. Jones presented data indicating that professional programs that had made a commitment to ethnic diversity were able to achieve it and sustain it.

At the next morning's planning session, the steering committee focused on trying to reconcile differences. A critical incident occurred that drew on Jones's concept and served as a model of rapprochement for the committee. A conversation between two members of the steering committee (one person of color and one White) centered on what had been the major stumbling block the day before: the issue of mandating change for member schools. The person of color disclosed that, given her particular cultural experience (as the child of a government official), mandating change by "thou shalt" was an accepted, normal way of conducting business. The White person, in turn, shared that given his particular religious cultural experience, "thou shalt" was experienced as authoritarian, an invasion of personal autonomy, and lacking in respect for collegial, professional judgment. This recognition and appreciation of cultural difference initiated a new spirit of trust and a mutual commitment to ensure mutual enfranchisement, in terms acceptable to everyone on the steering committee. Thus, the steering committee itself was empowered to act as a model of mutual trust for the plenary sessions that followed.

Plenary Session Interventions

In the plenary sessions that followed, three critical incidents occurred that fostered this spirit of mutual trust, mutual enfranchisement, and appreciation of the mutual enrichment of Whites and people of color in the creation of multicultural environments.

Incident 1

A person of color told the following fable in his presentation to the plenary session:

> There was an old medicine woman who was well known because of her power and her overall goodness. Consequently, she had a lot of followers and students. In another part of the country was a young man who was studying the ways of becoming a shaman and acquiring power, although his motivation was not simple goodness. You

see, the young man had a lot of ego invested in his quest to become a shaman—he wanted to have followers, money, prestige, and so forth. The difference here was that the old woman was unselfish and unattached to the earthly aspect of being a shaman, and her main interest was the well-being of the earth, the people, and having a relationship with the Sacred.

The young man became upset at not having all that he wanted in his shamanic quest and devised a scheme whereby he would embarrass the old woman and take all of her followers and students and once and for all be the one and only adored shaman around. His plan was foolproof and nothing short of a classic double-bind. He planned on approaching the old woman while she was in front of her followers and embarrass her to the point that he would be seen as the master shaman. He was going to carry a live hummingbird cupped in between his hands and ask her, "Is the bird alive or is it dead?" The intent here was if she said it was alive, he would quickly kill the bird thus embarrassing her. If she said the bird was dead, he would release it and allow it to fly, thus embarrassing her.

The day came for the confrontation, and the old woman was teaching in front of her students. He came in and asked, "O' wise woman, is this bird in my hand alive or is it dead?" She was talking with her eyes closed since her physical eyes were no longer that good, and without lifting her head she kindly replied, "Well my friend, it's whatever you want it to be."

The conference participants learned from the "moral" of the fable. Perhaps more important, they had the in vivo experience of an alternative learning style that cut through formal and structural precision, characteristic of Whites, to the central place of balance, harmony, and relationship in the human ecology of an organization.

Incident 2

The two steering committee members who had shared how each experienced "thou shalt" related the occurrence to the plenary session. They recounted the essence of their mutual understanding and the possibility of mutual accommodation *if* differing cultural perspectives were taken into account in reformulating resolutions. This disclosure engendered greater trust among the conference participants, who then were able to adopt three resolutions suggested by the White steering committee member. Described as follows, these resolutions promote enfranchisement and an appreciation of cultural differences. NCSPP resolved to

1. Institute the formal commitment to take substantive actions leading to ethnic diversity as a condition of membership in NCSPP.
2. Implement substantive structural changes and allocation of resources to ensure that NCSPP will become a multicultural organization.
3. Establish guidelines for member schools to lead them toward greater minority inclusion. These should include reporting mechanisms and incentives that would bring peer pressure to bear—and, perhaps more important, produce a mutual learning curve and culture of change among member schools.

Incident 3

The third incident occurred late in the final plenary session when it seemed that a spirit of mutual cooperation would ensure the near unanimous passage of the substantive resolutions (see chapter 25, this volume). Suddenly, an issue surfaced that divided the participants. After discussion, a vote was taken and the matter was decided by a narrow margin. However, a member of the executive committee (the only person of color on the committee) called the conferees' attention to the fact that, although the resolution passed, almost all people of color had voted against it. It took great courage to raise this issue because, in structural and formal terms, it could have been interpreted as "being out of order." The protagonist focused on a critical value for people of color, that is, the importance of maintaining the centrality of relationships, of mutual concern and agreement, beyond any specific content issue.

The chair of the meeting (a White person) could have retreated to the structural and formal rules of order, which are also a value, and often a central value, among Whites. Instead, he called a brief recess of the plenary session and convened an ad hoc committee, primarily composed of those participants who had spoken on either side of the issue in question. He charged the ad hoc committee with the development of an alternative resolution that could be supported by more conference participants. In other words, the chair embraced both cultural norms: structural integrity and centrality of relationships.

In the reconvened plenary session, the new resolution passed by a near unanimous vote. The process worked, to the credit of all involved. More important, it sensitized NCSPP to the need, in a multicultural organization, to take into account the wisdom of the cognitive, emotional, and cultural perspectives of every segment of the organization. In terms of "who's got the votes," an issue can be decided solely on structural and political grounds. However, if maintaining and fostering trust, ensuring a sense of enfranchisement, and respecting cultural differences remain central, then structural formalities have to be leavened by relational realities.

Conclusion

Creating multicultural educational programs and professional associations does not mean engaging in pseudomutual processes. In the early meetings of the steering committee, lack of trust, fear of disenfranchisement, and inattention to cultural differences in cognitive and emotional perception and expression led to the avoidance of open discussion and conflict. As a consequence, inherent dissension embedded in the draft resolutions was passed on to the plenary session. Within that context, the presence of a masterful chairperson and all the good will in the world could not forestall the confusion, displacement, and discouragement that, for a time, seemed to threaten the success of the conference.

When the steering committee was able to recognize that cultural difference underlay much of the content conflict, it began to function more openly, forthrightly, and effectively. Gradually, trust was inspired. Concern about individual enfranchisement was replaced with concern about inclusion of everyone's perspective. Eventually, the steering committee evolved as a functional working group that disagreed, argued, and resolved real differences of opinion and perspective. The committee, then, was better able to facilitate the plenary session meetings and model more constructive conflict resolution.

Most large and complex organizations cannot operate on a consensus model. The lesson of the Puerto Rico conference process was that consensus is not necessary. Rather, a *felt* sense of enfranchisement that leads to mutual trust is essential in multicultural organizations. Respect for cultural difference has less to do with equity and politics than it does with the perceived impoverishment of an ethnocentric organization compared with the perceived richness and excitement of a multicultural experience.

Schools of professional psychology and professional psychological organizations that have predominantly White members and operate within the context of ethnocentric cultural norms often approach the prospect of creating multicultural environments as a process of giving something away or as doing something for people of color. This basic set immediately raises issues of trust and enfranchisement for both sides. When the opportunity to create a multicultural environment begins with the basic set that the target group (in this case, people of color) is giving new life, vitality, and a unique perspective to the nontarget group (in this case, Whites), a fundamental shift is made from a win–lose to a win–win paradigm. In Puerto Rico, we all felt we won.

25

CONFERENCE RESOLUTIONS, GUIDELINES, AND CONCLUSIONS

George Stricker
Derner Institute, Adelphi University
Garden City, New York

and

James McHolland
Illinois School of Professional Psychology
Chicago, Illinois

Understanding that the rhetoric of the midwinter 1988–1989 Puerto Rico conference would be of lasting consequence only if it were translated into action, the conferees passed a series of resolutions and guidelines phrased in terms of behavioral objectives that would allow for an assessment of accountability. A general distinction was made between resolutions and guidelines. Resolutions specified actions to be taken directly by the National Council of Schools of Professional Psychology (NCSPP). Guidelines suggested directions for member schools to follow within their own systems, using their own resources. Guideline goals are the same for all member schools, but specific outcomes will be shaped necessarily by the frameworks of individual institutions.

Before acting on specific resolutions and guidelines, the membership of NCSPP endorsed the following general philosophical position:

As an expression of their professional and social responsibility, NCSPP and its member schools commit themselves to

1. **Initiating a recruitment strategy designed to increase significantly the proportion of ethnic minority students and faculty in professional schools by developing articulated programs designed to attract and support ethnic minority students and faculty, and**
2. **Developing curriculum offerings designed to prepare all students in professional schools in relevant aspects of the delivery of human ser-**

vices and health care to ethnic minority and other underserved groups and populations.

Endorsement of this resolution and its implementation are a condition of membership in the National Council of Schools of Professional Psychology.

The unanimous approval of this resolution reflected the commitment of NCSPP and its member schools to institutional change as it relates to promoting ethnic and racial diversity.

Conference Resolutions

In addition to the overarching resolution just stated, the conferees endorsed 10 specific resolutions. Seven resolutions address institutional changes within NCSPP itself, whereas three stipulate actions to be taken by NCSPP in the service of its member schools.

NCSPP

1. **NCSPP shall work toward a goal of ethnically/racially diverse representation at least comparable to that in the general population.**
   a. **The representation of member schools should reflect ethnic/racial diversity.**
   b. **Representation can be increased to three persons in order to accomplish this goal.**
   c. **NCSPP shall set up a mechanism for partially supporting every representative who contributes to ethnic/racial diversity at the midwinter meeting.**

2. **NCSPP shall have two standing committees with representatives on the Executive Committee:**
   a. **Ethnic/Racial Diversity.**
   b. **Gender Issues (first priority to be women's issues).**

3. **All NCSPP Committees/Workgroups shall be pluralistic in composition.**

4. **The midwinter conference two years from now, following the one on Curriculum and preceding the one on Evaluation, shall be concerned with Women's Issues.**

5. **Issues of cultural diversity shall continue to be a focus of future NCSPP meetings and be integrated into every major issue.**

6. **The Executive Committee shall report annually to the membership concerning NCSPP's progress in the implementation of all Conference resolutions concerning ethnic/racial diversity.**

7. **NCSPP shall actively work with [American Psychological Association] APA in the development and implementation of policies, procedures, and standards/criteria concerning the accreditation of education and training programs in professional psychology, placing particular emphasis on ethnic/racial diversity.**

Member Schools

1. **NCSPP shall establish and maintain a resource bank of ethnically/racially diverse faculty, administrators, and graduates in order to assist member schools in accomplishing their ethnic/racial diversity goals.**
2. **NCSPP shall establish a mechanism to assist member schools in developing policies and procedures for recruiting and retaining ethnically/racially diverse faculty and students.**
3. **NCSPP should give two annual distinguished contribution awards, one to a member institution and one to an individual, for outstanding work in promoting cultural diversity.**

Conference Guidelines

Ten guidelines to assist in the implementation of the commitment to ethnic and racial diversity were approved. Three guidelines are specific to NCSPP, whereas seven relate to member schools. The three guidelines affecting NCSPP were all endorsed by mail ballot and are similar in focus to the conference resolutions. Guidelines may address more than one aspect of the target goal simultaneously.

NCSPP

1. **NCSPP should conduct training workshops in curriculum development regarding issues of ethnic/racial diversity.**
2. **NCSPP should develop a data bank that would contain resource materials, such as course description materials, that would be useful in curriculum development concerning ethnic/racial diversity.**
3. **NCSPP should initiate and develop a relationship with the American Association of State Psychology Boards in order to ensure that the National Licensing Examination contains items that reflect competence in the area of ethnic/racial diversity.**

Member Schools

1. **Member schools should articulate the value of ethnic/racial diversity within each school's mission statement.**
2. **All NCSPP member schools should develop a specific plan that delineates how institutions are addressing issues of ethnic/racial diversity. In all plans, all member schools should address the following domains:**
    a. **Ethnically/racially diverse representation, input to, and participation within the admissions process.**
    b. **Development and offering of courses that address issues of ethnic/racial diversity in clinical, theoretical, and scientific areas where**

appropriate within the core curriculum (e.g., psychological development, family systems, assessment, and intervention).

c. Development of linkages within their respective communities to assist in program development and implementation from an ethnically/racially diverse perspective.

d. Development and implementation of consciousness raising and other attitude change activities designed to increase the program's awareness, sensitivity, and responsiveness to issues of ethnic/racial diversity.

e. Development and support of ethnic/racial minority student organizations.

f. Involvement of alumni in addressing issues of ethnic/racial diversity.

g. Allocation of financial and other institutional resources for the development and support of ethnically/racially diverse administration, faculty, and student recruitment and retention programs.

For the purpose of sharing resources among members, these plans will be submitted annually to NCSPP and the Executive Committee will report annually to the organization on the implementation of these plans in meeting the goals of ethnic/racial diversity.

3. The parameters of ethnic/racial diversity should be specified in each school's catalogue and materials.

4. Retention and academic advancement efforts should be geared toward offering financial, emotional, and academic support to ethnically/racially diverse students.

5. Members should have as a goal to create an administration, faculty, and student body that is at least as ethnically/racially diverse as the general population. Each member will report its goals and outcomes to NCSPP annually.

6. Faculty activity directed toward achieving ethnic/racial diversity should be given significant consideration in regard to workload assignments as well as faculty recruitment, retention, and promotion.

7. NCSPP member schools are encouraged to provide academic, experiential, and supervised clinical and research activities that lead to competence in the provision of psychological services to culturally diverse populations.

Conclusion

The midwinter 1988–1989 Puerto Rico conference was a landmark event because it marked the first time that a national, professional organization made a clear and accountable commitment to pursue a policy of affirmative diversity within the association itself and within each of its member schools. The NCSPP executive committee was expanded to make it more diverse, resources were allocated in order to ensure ethnic representation at all future meetings, and a commitment was made to the future study of women's issues. Guidelines were offered to member schools in the pursuit of affirmative diversity, and mechanisms were set in place to assist the schools in this quest. A process of program evaluation was set in motion, enabling member schools to learn from each other and continue to grow in the chosen direction. The potential of the conference is clear; its importance will be measured by future accomplishments.

The purpose of this book is to articulate NCSPP's commitment to affirmative diversity and its strategies for implementation to programs outside its aegis. It is anticipated that NCSPP's actions will have a broad impact and ripple across the waters of professional psychology. The path to the future is clear, and NCSPP is proud to be the vanguard.

REFERENCES

Abramowitz, S., & Murray, J. (1983). Race effects in psychotherapy. In J. Murray & P. Abramson (Eds.), *Bias in psychotherapy* (pp. 215–255). New York: Praeger.

Acosta, F. X. (1980). Self-described reasons for premature termination of psychotherapy by Mexican-American, Black-American, and Anglo-American patients. *Psychological Reports, 47*, 435–443.

Adams, H. G. (1986). *Minority participation in graduate education.* Notre Dame, IN: University of Notre Dame, National Consortium for Graduate Degrees for Minorities in Engineering.

Adams, H. G. (1988). *Tomorrow's professoriate: Insuring minority participation through talent development today.* Washington, DC: American Society for Engineering Education.

Adorno, T. W., Frenkel-Brunswick, E., Levinson, D. J., & Sanford, R. N. (1950). *The authoritarian personality.* New York: Harper.

Albizu-Miranda, C., Schwartz, A. N., & Snyder, C. L. (1988). A training model for minority psychologists: The Puerto Rican experience. *Science and Behavior, 3*, 5–18.

American Council on Education. (1987). *Minorities in higher education: Sixth annual status report.* Washington, DC: Author.

American Council on Education. (1988). *One third of a nation: A report of the Commission on Minority Participation in Education and American Life.* Washington, DC: Author.

American Council on Education. (1988, February 15). *Higher education and national affairs.* Washington, DC: Author.

American Psychological Association. (1986a). *Accreditation Handbook.* Washington, DC: Author.

American Psychological Association. (1986b). The changing face of American psychology: A report from the Committee on Employment and Human Resources. *American Psychologist, 41*, 1311–1327.

American Psychological Association. (1987). Resolutions approved by the National Conference on Graduate Education in Psychology. *American Psychologist, 42*, 1070–1084.

Apple, M. W. (1971). The hidden curriculum and the nature of conflict. *Interchange, 2*, 1–70.

Astin A. (1982). *Minorities in American higher education.* San Francisco: Jossey-Bass.

Atelsek, F. J., & Gomberg, I. L. (1978). *Special programs for female and minority graduate students.* Washington, DC: American Council on Education.

Atkinson, D. R. (1983). Ethnic similarity in counseling psychology: A review of research. *Counseling Psychologist, 11*(3), 79–92.

Atkinson, D. R., Morten, G., & Sue, D. W. (1979). *Counseling American minorities: A cross-cultural perspective* (2nd ed.). Dubuque, IA: Wm. C. Brown.

Atkinson, D. R., Morten, G., & Sue, D. W. (1983). *Counseling American minorities: A cross-cultural perspective*. Dubuque, IA: Wm. C. Brown.

Baekeland, F., & Lundwall, L. (1975). Dropping out of treatment: A critical review. *Psychological Bulletin, 82,* 738–783.

Banks, J. A. (1983). Ethnicity and curriculum reform. In R. J. Samuda & S. L. Woods (Eds.), *Perspectives in immigrant and minority education*. New York: University Press of America.

Banta, T. W. and others (1983). *National Institute of Education project for pre-doctoral fellows at the University of Tennessee, Knoxville*. Knoxville: Bureau of Educational Research Service.

Batts, V. A. (1982). Modern racism: A TA perspective. *Transactional Analysis Journal, 12,* 207–209.

Batts, V. A. (Speaker). (1988). *Dialog 88* [Videotape]. Louisville, KY: Meetings Internationale.

Beale, A. (1986). A cross-cultural dyadic encounter. *Journal of Multicultural Counseling and Development, 14,* 73–76.

Bell, C., & Mehta, H. (1980). The misdiagnosis of black patients with manic-depressive illness. *Journal of the National Medical Association, 72,* 141–145.

Bell, P., & Evans, J. (1981). *Counseling the Black client: Alcohol abuse in Black America*. Minneapolis, MN: Hazelden.

Bem, S., Martyna, W., & Watson, C. (1976). Sex-typing and androgyny: Further exploration of the expressive domain. *Journal of Personality and Social Psychology, 33,* 48–54.

Benson, C. (1968). *The economics of public education*. Boston: Houghton Mifflin.

Bent, R., & Jones, N. (1987). Knowledge and skills in professional psychology programs. In E. Bourg, R. Bent, J. Callan, N. Jones, J. McHolland, & G. Stricker (Eds.), *Standards and evaluation in the education and training of professional psychologists: Knowledge, attitudes, and skills* (pp. 35–44). Norman, OK: Transcript Press.

Bernal, M. E., Barron, B. M., & Leary, C. (1983). Use of application materials for recruitment of ethnic minority students in psychology. *Professional Psychology: Research and Practice, 14,* 817–829.

Bernal, M. E., & Padilla, A. M. (1982). Status of minority curricula and training in clinical psychology. *American Psychologist, 37,* 180–787.

Blauner, R. (1969). Internal colonialism and ghetto revolt. *Social Problems, 16,* 393–408.

Block, C. B. (1984). Diagnostic and treatment issues for Black patients. *Clinical Psychologist, 37*(2), 51–54.

Bloom, A. (1987). *The closing of the American mind: How higher education has failed democracy and impoverished the souls of today's students*. New York: Simon & Schuster.

Bloustein, E. J. (1988). Community Services: A new recruitment for the educated person. Commencement address presented at Rutgers, May 1988. New Brunswick, NJ.

Blumberg, P. (1980). *Inequality in an age of decline*. New York: Oxford University Press.

Boettiger, J., Perry, W., Steiny, N., Vaughn, B. E., & Williams, R. (1988). *Task Force on the Quality of Student Life: Report and Recommendations.* San Francisco: California School of Professional Psychology, Board of Trustees.

Bogardus, E. S. (1928). *Immigration and race attitudes.* Lexington, MA: Heath.

Bourg, E. F., Bent, R. J., Callan, J. E., Jones, N. F., McHolland, J., & Stricker, G. (Eds.). (1987). *Standards and evaluation in the education and training of professional psychologists: Knowledge, attitudes, and skills.* Norman, OK: Transcript Press.

Bourg, E. F., Bent, R. J., McHolland, J., & Stricker, G. (1989). Standards and evaluation in the education and training of professional psychologists. *American Psychologist, 44,* 1–7.

Boyd-Franklin, N. (1989). *Black families in therapy: A multisystems approach.* New York: Guilford Press.

Braddock, I., Jomills, H., & McPartland, J. M. (1987). How minorities continue to be excluded from equal opportunities: Research on labor market and institutional barriers. *Journal of Social Issues, 43,* 5–40.

Brislin, R. W. (1983, August). *Cross-cultural studies in social psychology of relevance to ethnic group research: Examples and recommendations.* Paper presented at the 91st Annual Convention of the American Psychological Association, Anaheim, CA.

Brown v. Board of Education of Topeka, 347 U.S. 483 (1954).

Brown, C. R. (1984). *Building unity across ethnic, religious and class divisions.* The art of coalition building: A guide for community leaders. Arlington, MA: NCBI.

Brown, S. V. (1988a). *Increasing minority faculty: An elusive goal.* Princeton, NJ: Graduate Record Examination and Educational Testing Service.

Brown, S. V. (1988b). *Minorities in the graduate education pipeline.* Princeton, NJ: Graduate Record Examination and Educational Testing Service.

Bryde, J. F. (1971). *Indian students and guidance.* Boston: Houghton Mifflin.

Caplan, N., & Nelson, S. (1973). On being useful: The nature and consequences of psychological research on social problems. *American Psychologist, 28,* 199–211.

Carnegie Foundation for the Advancement of Teaching. (1987, May/June). Minority access: A question of equity. *Change: Trendlines,* pp. 35–39.

Casas, J. M. (1984). Policy, training and research in counseling psychology: The racial/ethnic minority perspective. In S. Brown, & R. Lent (Eds.), *Handbook of counseling psychology* (pp. 785–831). New York: Wiley.

Chunn, J., Dunston, P., & Ross-Sheriff, F. (1983). *Mental health and people of color: Curriculum development and change.* Washington, DC: Howard University Press.

Clark, L. A. (1987). Mutual relevance of mainstream and cross-cultural psychology. *Journal of Consulting and Clinical Psychology, 55,* 461–470.

Clewell, B. C. (1987). *Retention of Black and Hispanic doctoral students.* Princeton, NJ: Educational Testing Service.

Committee on Employment and Human Resources. (1985). *The changing face of American psychology.* Washington, DC: American Psychological Association.

Committee to Advance Our Common Purposes. (1988a). *Procedure for group interviews* [Memorandum]. Available from Dr. Donald Peterson, School of Professional Psychology, Rutgers University, New Brunswick, NJ, 08903.

Committee to Advance Our Common Purposes. (1988b). *Report of activities for 1987–88 and proposals for action in 1988–89.* [Memorandum]. Available from Dr. Donald Peterson, School of Professional Psychology, Rutgers University, New Brunswick, NJ, 08903.

Committee to Advance Our Common Purposes. (1988c). *Report of interviews with deans, vice presidents, and committee members* [Memorandum]. Available from Dr. Donald Peterson, School of Professional Psychology, Rutgers University, New Brunswick, NJ, 08903.

Cooperative Institutional Research Program. (1987). *The American freshman: Twenty year trends, 1966–1985*. Los Angeles, CA: Higher Education Research Institute.

Copeland, E. J. (1979). Training advanced educational opportunity program students as peer group counselors for freshman students. *Journal of Non-White Concerns*, 7, 762–766.

Copeland, E. J. (1982). Minority populations and traditional counseling programs: Some alternatives. *Counselor Education and Supervision*, 187–193.

Cox, W. E., & Jobe, C. C. (1987/1988). Recruiting wars: Can higher education compete with the military? *Educational Record*, 68(4), 69(1), 63–69.

Coyle, S. L., & Thurgood, D. H. (1989). *Summary report 1987: Doctorate recipients from United States universities*. Washington, DC: National Academy Press.

Crane, D. (1972). *Invisible colleges*. Chicago: University of Chicago Press.

Cross, W. (1971). Negro-to-Black conversion experience: Toward a psychology of black liberation. *Black World*, 20(9), 13–27.

Crossland, F. E. (1971). *Minority access to college: A Ford Foundation report*. New York: Schocken Books.

DeAngelis, T. (1988, November). Sex, race/ethnicity data in survey. *APA Monitor*, p. 40.

Duran, E. F. (1984). *Archetypal consultation: A service delivery model for Native Americans*. Bern, Switzerland: Peter Lang.

El-khawas, E. (1988). *Campus trends* (Higher Education Panel Rep. No. 77). Washington, DC: American Council on Education.

Erlich, H. J., Pincus, F. L., & Morton, C. (1987). *Ethnoviolence on campus: The UMBC study*. Baltimore, MD: National Institute Against Prejudice and Violence.

Espin, O. (1979, April). Ethno-Cultural concerns. Paper presented at the meeting of the Association for Counselor Education and Supervision, Las Vegas, NV.

Fannon, F. (1963). *The wretched of the earth*. New York: Grove Press.

Ferguson, M. (1980). *The aquarian conspiracy*. Los Angeles, CA: Tarcher.

Fernandez, C. (1979). *Ethnic group insulation, self concept, academic standards, and the failure of evaluation*. Saratoga, CA: R. & E. Research Associates, Inc.

Feshbach, S. (1978). The environment of personality. *American Psychologist*, 33, 447–455.

Fields, C. (1988, May/June). The Hispanic pipeline: Narrow, leaking and needing repair. *Change*, pp. 20–27.

Fishman, D. B., & Neigher, W. D. (1987). Technological assessment: Tapping a "third culture" for decision-focused psychological measurement. In D. R. Peterson & D. B. Fishman (Eds.), *Assessment for decision* (pp. 44–76). New Brunswick, NJ: Rutgers University Press.

Ford, D. L. (1986). *Faculty salary differentials by race: A case study of suspected treatment discrimination*. (ERIC Document Reproduction Service No. ED 265753). Unpublished manuscript.

40 years on. (1982, July 31). *Washington Post*, p. A-20.

Foster, G. (1969). *Applied anthropology*. Boston: Little, Brown.

Fowler, R. D. (1987). Assessment for decision in a correctional setting. In D. R. Peterson

& D. B. Fishman (Eds.), *Assessment for decision* (pp. 214–239). New Brunswick, NJ: Rutgers University Press.

Freire, P. (1986). *Pedagogy of the oppressed*. New York: Continuum.

Garcia, L. T., Erskine, N., Hawn, K., & Casmay, S. R. (1981). The effect of affirmative action on attributions about minority group members. *Journal of Personality, 49*, 427–437.

Garrison, H. H., & Brown, P. W. (1985). *Minority access to research careers: An evaluation of the Honors Undergraduate Research Training Program*. Washington, DC: National Academy Press.

Gilbert, G. M. (1951). Stereotype persistence and change among college students. *Journal of Abnormal and Social Psychology, 46*, 245–254.

Gillin, J. (1955). National and regional cultural values in the United States. *Social Forces, 34*, 107–113.

Giorgis T. W., & Helms, J. E. (1978). Training international students from developing nations as psychologist: A challenge for American psychology. *American Psychologist, 33*, 945–951.

Gordon, E. W. (1985). Social science knowledge production and minority experiences. *Journal of Negro Education, 54*, 117–132.

Gould, S. (1981). *The mismeasure of man*. New York: Norton.

Government–University–Industry Roundtable. (1987). *Nurturing science and engineering talent*. Washington, DC: National Academy Press.

Green, M. F. (Ed) (1989). *Minorities on campus: A handbook for enhancing diversity*. Washington, DC: American Council on Education.

Gross, H., Knatterude, G., & Donner, L. (1969). The effect of race and sex on the variation of diagnosis and disposition in the psychiatric emergency room. *Journal of Nervous and Mental Disease, 148*, 638–642.

Gunnings, I., & Simpkins, G. A. (1972). A systemic approach to counseling disadvantaged youth. *Journal of Non-White Concerns, 1*, 4–8.

Guthrie, R. (1976). *Even the rat was white: A historical view of psychology*. New York: Harper & Row.

Hackman, J. R., & Helmreich, R. L. (1987). Assessing the behavior and performance of teams in organizations: The case of air transport crews. In D. R. Peterson & D. B. Fishman (Eds.), *Assessment for decision* (pp. 283–313). New Brunswick, NJ: Rutgers University Press.

Haley, G. L. (1984). Who are Georgia's psychologists? *Georgia Psychologist, 37*, 1311–1327.

Hammond, W. R. (1987). Wright State University's successful approach to recruitment and retention of black students in clinical psychology. *Black Issues in Higher Education, 5*, 12.

Hammond, W. R. (1988). [Survey of Ohio licensed psychologists: 1987]. Unpublished raw data.

Harrison, D. K. (1975). Race as a counselor-client variable in counseling and psychotherapy: A review of the research. *Counseling Psychologist, 5*, 124–133.

Havighurst, R. J., & Neugarten, B. L. (1975). *Society and education* (4th ed.). Boston: Allyn & Bacon.

Henderson, N. D. (1979). Criterion-related validity of personality and aptitude scales: A comparison of validation results under voluntary and actual test conditions. In C. D. Spielberger (Ed.), *Police selection and evaluation* (pp. 179–195). Washington, DC: Hemisphere Press.

Hirsch, E. D. (1987). *Cultural literacy: What every American needs to know.* Boston: Houghton Mifflin.

Hodgkinson, H. L. (1985). *All one system: Demographics of education, kindergarten, through graduate school.* Washington, DC: Institute for Educational Leadership.

Howard, A., Pion, G. M., Gottfredson, G. D., Flattau, P. E., Oskamp, S., Pfafflin, S. M., Bray, D. W., & Burstein, A. G. (1986). The changing face of American psychology: A report from the Committee on Employment and Human Resources. *American Psychologist, 41,* 1311–1327.

Ivey, A. E., Ivey, M. B., & Simek-Downing, L. (1987). *Counseling and psychotherapy: Integrating skills, theory and practice.* Englewood Cliffs, NJ: Prentice-Hall.

James, R. L. (Ed.). (1980). *Black psychology.* New York: Harper & Row.

Jensen, A. (1969). How much can we boost IQ and school achievement? *Harvard Education Review, 39,* 1–123.

Jones, E. E. (1984). Some reflections on the Black patient and psychotherapy. *Clinical Psychologist, 37* (2), 62–65.

Jones, E. E., & Korchin, S. J. (1982). *Minority mental health.* New York: Praeger.

Jones, J. (in press). Piercing the veil: Bicultural strategies for coping with prejudice and racism. In H. J. Knopke (Ed.), *Opening doors: Perspectives on race relations in contemporary America.* Tuscaloosa, AL: University of Alabama Press.

Jones, J. M. (1986). Racism: A cultural analysis of the problem. In J. Dovidio & S. Gaertner (Eds.), *Prejudice, discrimination and racism* (pp. 279–314). Orlando, FL: Academic Press.

Jones, J. M. (1987). *Student recruitment and retention: A marketing and program development job for psychology.* Unpublished manuscript.

Jones, J. M. (1988a). Racism in black and white: A bicultural model of reaction and evolution. In P. A. Katz & D. A. Taylor (Eds.), *Toward the elimination of racism: Profiles in controversy* (pp. 117–135). New York: Plenum Publishing Corporation.

Jones, J. M. (1988b). Why should Black undergraduate students major in psychology? In P. J. Woods (Ed.), *Is psychology for them? A guide to undergraduate advising* (pp. 178–181). Washington, DC: American Psychological Association.

Kanter, R. M. (1977). *Men and women of the corporation.* New York: Basic Books.

Kardiner, A., & Oversey, L. (1951). *The mark of oppression: A psycho-social study of the American Negro.* New York: Norton.

Katz, D., & Braly, K. (1933). Racial stereotypes of one hundred college students. *Journal of Abnormal and Social Psychology, 28,* 280–290.

Katz, J. (1985). The sociopolitical nature of counseling. *American Psychologist, 13,* 615–624.

King, C. (Ed.). (1983). *The words of Martin Luther King, Jr.,* New York: Newmarket Press.

Korman, M. (Ed.). (1976). *Levels and patterns of professional training.* Washington, DC: American Psychological Association.

LaFromboise, T., & Rowe, W. (1983). Skills training for bicultural competence: Rationale and application. *Journal of Counseling Psychology, 30,* 589–595.

Lazarus, P. J., Bild, R., & Diaz, E. (1985). Multicultural influences on the development of the young child. In C. S. McLoughlin & D. F. Gullo (Eds.), *Young children in context: Impact of self, family and society on deveopment.* (pp. 183–217). Springfield, IL: Charles C. Thomas.

Lefley, H. & Pedersen, P. (Eds.), *Cross-cultural training for mental health professionals.* Springfield, IL: Charles C. Thomas.

Lorion, R. (1978). Research on psychotherapy and behavior change with the disadvantaged: Past, present, and future directions. In S. L. Garfield & A. E. Bergin (Eds.), *Handbook of psychotherapy and behavior change: An empirical analysis* (2nd ed., pp. 903–938). New York: Wiley.

Malgady, R. G., Rogler, L. H. & Constantino, G. (1987). Ethnolcultural and linguistic bias in mental health evaluation of Hispanics. *American Psychologist, 42*, 228–234.

Maruyama, M. (1978). Psychotopology and its applications to cross-disciplinary, cross-professional, and cross-cultural communication. In R. E. Holloman & S. A. Arutinov (Eds.), *Perspectives on ethnicity*, (pp. 23–75). The Hague, the Netherlands: Mouton.

McConahay, J. B., Hardee, B. B., & Batts, V. A. (1981). Has racism declined in America? *Journal of Conflict Resolution, 25*, 563–579.

McDougall, W. (1921). *Is American safe for democracy?* New York: Charles Scribner's Sons.

McKenna, M. A. (1988, March). Shaping change: The need for a new paradigm in higher education. *Higher Education and National Affairs, 37*, 7–8.

Menges, R. J. & Exum, W. H. (1983). Barriers to the progress of women and minority faculty. *Journal of Higher Education, 54*, 123–144.

Memmi, A. (1965). *The colonizer and the colonized.* Boston: Beacon Press.

Mercer, J. R., & Lewis, J. F. (1978). *System of multicultural pluralistic assessment (SOMPA): Student assessment manual.* New York: Psychological Corporation.

Miller, G. (1969). Psychology as a means of promoting human welfare. *American Psychologist, 24*, 1063–1075.

Miller, M. J. (1983). The invisible client. *Personnel and Guidance Journal, 62*, 30–33.

Morgan, R. F. (1985). *The iatrogenics handbook.* Toronto, Ontario, Canada: IPI Publishing Limited.

National Center for Education Statistics. (1982). *Digest of education statistics.* Washington, DC: Author.

National Center for Education Statistics, Office of Educational Research and Improvement. (1985–1986). *Digest of education statistics.* Washington, DC: U.S. Government Printing Office.

National Center for Education Statistics. (1988a). *Digest of education statistics.* Washington, DC: Author.

National Center for Education Statistics. (1988b). *Racial/ethnic data for fall enrollment and earned degree recipients.* Washington, DC: U.S. Government Printing Office.

National Council of Schools of Professional Psychology. (1987). *Survey on minority issues.* (Available from the Committee on Minority Representative and Service to Underserved Populations, California School of Professional Psychology, 1350 M Street, Fresno, California, 93721).

National Research Council. (1987). *Summary report 1986: Doctorate recipients from United States universities.* Washington, DC: National Academy Press.

National Research Council. (1987). *Doctorate recipients from United States universities: Summary reports, 1977–1987.* Washington, DC: Author.

National Science Foundation. (1987). *Early release of summary statistics on academic science and engineering resources: October, 1987.* Washington, DC: Author.

National Science Foundation. (1988a). *Doctoral scientists and engineers: A decade of change* (NSF Report No. 88-302). Washington, DC: Author.

National Science Foundation. (1988b). *Profiles—Psychology. Human resources and funding* (NSF Report No. 88-325). Washington, DC: Author.

National Science Foundation. (1988c). *Science and engineering doctorates: 1960–86* (NSF Report No. 88-309). Washington, DC: Author.

National Science Founcation. (1988d). *Women and minorities in science and engineering* (NSF 88-301). Washington, DC: Author.

Neutzler, M. (1986). *Psychologists: MO health manpower* (Report No. 2.20). Jefferson City, MO: State Center for Health Statistics.

Newman, F. (1985). *Higher education and the American resurgence*. Princton, NJ: Carnegie Foundation for the Advancement of Teaching.

Nieves, L. (1978). *College achievement through self-help: A planning guidance manual for minority students*. Princeton, NJ: Educational Testing Service.

1988 annual report of the board of trustees of the federal old-age and survivors insurance and disability insurance trust funds. (1988). Washington, DC.

Nobles, W. (1976). Extended self: Rethinking the so-called Negro self-concept. *Journal of Black Psychology, 2*, 15–24.

Office of Comprehensive Health Planning. (1989). [Florida's health manpower 1988 psychologist survey]. Unpublished raw data.

O'Neil, J. (1987). A 21st century vision-meeting unmet needs. *Visions, 1*(1), 2.

Orum, L. S. (1986). *The education of Hispanics: Status and implications*. Washington, DC: National Council of La Raza.

Ottinger, C. A. (Ed.). (1989). *Higher education today: Facts in brief*. Washington, DC: American Council on Education.

Padilla, A. M., & Olmedo, E. (1977). Empirial and construct validation of a measure of acculturation for Mexican-Americans. *Journal of Social Psychology, 105*, 179–187.

Padilla, A. M., & Ruiz, R. A. (1974). *Latino mental health: A review of the literature*. (HSM 73-9143). Washington, DC: U.S. Department of Health, Education, and Welfare.

Parham, T., & Helms, J. (1981). The influence of Black students' racial identity attitudes on preferences for counselor's race. *Journal of Counseling Psychology, 23*, 250–257.

Paul, G. L. (1987). Rational operations in residential treatment settings through ongoing assessment of client and staff functioning. In D. R. Peterson & D. B. Fishman (Eds.), *Assessment for decision* (pp. 145–203). New Brunswick, NJ: Rutgers University Press.

Pedersen, P. (1986). Developing interculturally skilled counselors: A prototype for training. In H. P. Lefley & P. B. Pedersen (Eds.), *Cross-cultural training for mental health professionals* (pp. 73–88). Springfield, IL: Charles C. Thomas.

Pedersen, P. (1988). *A handbook for developing multicultural awareness*. Arlington, VA: American Association for Counseling and Development.

Pedersen, P., Sartorious, N., & Marsella, A. (Eds.). (1984). *Mental health services: The cultural context*. Beverly Hills, CA: Sage.

Persico, C. (1974). *The student movement and institutional disruption*. Unpublished doctoral dissertation, Stanford University, Stanford, CA.

Persico, C., & McEachron, N. (1971). *Forces for societal transformation in the United States, 1950–2000*. Menlo Park, CA: Stanford Research Institute.

Peterson, D. R. (1979a). Assessing interpersonal relationships in natural settings. *New Directions for Methodology of Behavioral Science, 2*, 33–55.

Peterson, D. R. (1979b). Assessing interpersonal relationships by means of interaction records. *Behavioral Assessment, 1*, 221–236.

Peterson, D. R. (1986a). Organizational dilemmas in the education of practicing psychologists. In J. Callan, D. Peterson, & G. Stricker (Eds.), *Quality in professional psychology training: A national conference and self-study* (pp. 9–22). Norman, OK: Transcript Press.

Peterson, D. R. (1988). [The phylogeny of prejudice, or why we love our own and hate those others.] Unpublished sermon, Kirpatrick Chapel, Rutgers University, New Brunswick, NJ.

Peterson, D. R. & Fishman, D. B. (Eds.). (1987). *Assessment for decision.* New Brunswick, NJ: Rutgers University Press.

Pine, G. J. (1972). Counseling minority groups. *Counseling and Values, 17*, 35–45.

Pion, G., Kohout, J., & Wicherski, M. (1988). *Characteristics of graduate departments of psychology: 1987–88.* Washington, DC: American Psychological Association, Office of Demographics, Employment and Evaluation Research.

Pomales, J., Claiborn, C., & LaFromboise, T. (1986). Effects of Black students' racial identity on perceptions of White counselors varying in cultural sensitivity. *Journal of Counseling Psychology, 33*, 57–61.

Ponterotto, J. G. (1988). Racial/ethnic minority research in the *Journal of Counseling Psychology*: A content analysis and methodological critique. *Journal of Counseling Psychology, 35*, 175–182.

Ponterotto, J. G., & Casas, J. M. (1987). In search of multicultural competence within counselor education programs. *Journal of Counseling and Development, 65*, 430–444.

Porche-Burke, L. M., & Olmedo, E. L. (1988). *Ethnic minority mental health training: The CSPP-Los Angeles experience.* Unpublished manuscript.

President's Commission on Mental Health, Special Populations Task Force (1979). *Task panel report to the President's Commission on Mental Health* (Vol. 3). Washington, DC: U.S. Government Printing Office.

Ramirez, M. (1983). *Psychology for the Americas: Mestizo perspectives on personality and mental health.* New York: Pergamon Press.

Rendon, L. I., & Nora, A. (1987/1988). Hispanic student: Stopping the leak in the pipeline. *Educational Record, 68/69*, 79–85.

Ridley, C. R. (1984). Clinical treatment of the nondisclosing black client. *American Psychologist, 39*, 1234–1244.

Ridley, C. R. (1985). Imperatives for ethnic and cultural relevance in psychology training programs. *Professional Psychology: Research and Practice, 16*, 611–622.

Rollman, S. A. (1978). The sensitivity of Black and White Americans to nonverbal cues of prejudice. *Journal of Social Psychology, 105*, 73–77.

Russo, N. F., Olmedo, E. L., Stapp, J., & Fulcher, R. (1981). Women and minorities in psychology. *American Psychologist, 36*, 1315–1363.

Ryan, W. (1976). *Blaming the victim.* New York: Random House.

Ryan, W. (1981). *Equality.* New York: Random House.

Sampson, E. E. (1977). Psychology and the American ideal. *Journal of Personality and Social Psychology, 33*, 767–782.

Sampson, E. E. (1978). Scientific paradigms and social values: Wanted—a scientific revolution. *Journal of Personality and Social Psychology, 36*, 1332–1343.

Samuda, R. J. (1975). From ethnocentrism to a multicultural perspective in educational testing. *Journal of Afro-American Issues, 3*, 4–18.

Sarason, S. B. (1972). *The creation of settings and the future societies*. San Francisco: Jossey-Bass.

Schein, E. H. (1985). *Organizational culture*. San Francisco: Jossey-Bass.

Schuman, H., Steeh, C., & Bobo, L. (1985). *Racial attitudes in America*. Cambridge, MA: Harvard University Press.

Sherover-Marcuse, R. (1980). *Unlearning racism*. Unpublished manuscript.

Shuey, A. (1966). *The testing of Negro intelligence*. New York: Social Science Press.

Siehl, C. (1985). After the founder: An opportunity to manage culture. In P. Frost, L. Moore, M. Louis, C. Lundberg, & J. Martin (Eds.), *Organizational culture* (pp. 125–140). Beverly Hills, CA: Sage.

Smith, E. J. (1973). *Counseling the culturally different Black youth*. Columbus, OH: Charles E. Merrill.

Smith, E. J. (1985). Ethnic minorities: Life stress, social support, and mental health issues. *Counseling Psychologist, 13*, 537–579.

Spence, J. T., Helmreich, R., & Stapp, J. (1974). The Personal Attributes Questionnaire: A measure of sex-role stereotypes and masculinity and femininity. *JSAS Catalogue Selected Documents in Psychology, 4*, 43.

Spiegel, J., & Papajohn, J. (1986). Training program in ethnicity and mental health. In H. P. Lefley & P. B. Pederson (Eds.), *Cross-cultural training for mental health professionals* (pp. 49–71). Springfield, IL: Charles C. Thomas.

Stapp, J. (1979, November). Minorities and women: Caught in a revolving door? *APA Monitor*, p. 14.

Stapp, J., Tucker, A. M. & VandenBos, G. R. (1985). Census of psychological personnel: 1983. *American Psychologist, 40*, 1317–1351.

Storm, H. (1972). *Seven arrows*. New York: Ballantine Books.

Sue. D. W. (1973). Training Third World students to function as counselors. *Journal of Counseling Psychology, 20*, 73–78.

Sue, D. W. (1977). Counseling the culturally different: A conceptual analysis. *Personnel and Guidance Journal, 55*, 422–425.

Sue, D. W. (1981). *Counseling the culturally different: Theory and practice*. New York: Wiley.

Sue, D. W., Bernier, J. E., Durran, A., Feinberg, L., Pedersen, P., Smith, E. J., & Vasquez-Nuttall, E. (1982). Cross-cultural counseling competencies. *Counseling Psychologist, 10*, 45–52.

Sue, D. W., & Sue, S. (1972). Ethnic minorities: Resistance to being researched. *Professional Psychology, 2*, 11–17.

Sue, S. (1977). Community mental health services to minority groups: Some optimism, some pessimism. *American Psychologist, 32*, 616–624.

Sue, S. (1988). Psychotherapeutic services for ethnic minorities: Two decades of research findings. *American Psychologist, 43*, 301–308.

Sue S., Allen, D., & Conaway, L. (1978). The responsiveness and equality of mental health care to Chicanos and Native Americans. *American Journal of Community Psychology, 6*, 137–146.

Sue, S., & McKinney, H. (1975). Asian Americans in the community mental health care system. *American Journal of Orthopsychiatry, 45*, 111–118.

Sue, S., McKinney, H., Allen, D., & Hall, J. (1974). Delivery of community mental health services to Black and White clients. *Journal of Consulting and Clinical Psychology, 42*, 794–801.

Sue, S., & Morishima, J. K. (1985). *The mental health of Asian Americans*. San Francisco : Jossey-Bass.

Sue, S., & Zane, N. (1987). The role of culture and cultural techniques in psychotherapy: A critique and reformulation. *American Psychologist, 42*, 37–45.

Suinn, R. M., & Witt, J. C. (1982). Survey on ethnic minority faculty recruitment and retention. *American Psychologist, 37*, 1239–1244.

Terman, C. M. (1916). *The measurement of intelligence*. Boston: Houghton Mifflin.

Thomas, A., & Sillen, S. (1972). *Racism and psychiatry*. New York: Brunner/Mazel.

Thomas, G. E. (1986). *The access and success of Blacks and Hispanics in U.S. graduate and professional education*. Washington, DC: National Academy Press.

Trickett, E. J., Watts, R. J., & Birman, D. (1988, October). *Perspectives on people in contexts*. Paper presented at the Conference on Human Diversity. University of Maryland, College Park, MD.

Trimble, J. E. (1988, August). Multilinearity of acculturation: Person-situation interactions. In J. W. Berry & J. E. Trimble (Chairs), *Methodology for studying psychological acculturation*. Symposium conducted at the Ninth International Congress of the International Association for Cross-Cultural Psychology, Newcastle, New South Wales, Australia.

Turner, S. M., & Jones, R. T. (1982). *Behavior modification in Black populations: Psychosocial issues and empirical findings*. New York: Plenum Press.

Tyler, F. B., Sussewell, D. R., & Williams-McCoy, J. (1985). Ethnic validity in psychotherapy. *Psychotherapy, 22*, pp. 311–320.

United Nations. (1949). *Proceedings from the meeting on genocide and ethnocide*. Unpublished manuscript.

U.S. Bureau of the Census. (1984). *Census of the population* (Series No. PC 80-1, D1-A, Table 253). Washington, DC: U.S. Government Printing Office.

U.S. Bureau of the Census. (1986). *Statistical abstract of the United States: 1987, (107th Edition)*. Washington, DC: U.S. Government Printing Office.

U.S. Bureau of the Census. (1986/1988). *Current population reports* (Series P-25, No. 995 and 1022). Washington, DC: Author.

U.S. Bureau of the Census. (1987). *Current population reports* (Series No. P-60). Washington, DC: U.S. Government Printing Office.

U.S. Bureau of the Census (1988, March). United States population estimates by age, sex, and race: 1980 to 1987. *Current Population Report* (Series No. P-25, 1022). Washington, DC: U.S. Government Printing Office.

U.S. Bureau of the Census. (in press). School enrollment social and economic characteristics of students: October 1986. *Current Population Reports* (Series P-20). Washington, DC: U.S. Government Printing Office.

U.S. Congress, Office of Technology Assessment. (1988). *Educating scientists and engineers: Grade school to grad school* (OTA Publication No. SET-377). Washington, DC: U.S. Government Printing Office.

U.S. Congress, Office of Technology Assessment. (1989). *Higher education for science and engineering: A background paper* (OTA Publication No. BP-SET-52). Washington, DC: U.S. Government Printing Office.

U.S. Department of Commerce. (1983). *General social and economic characteristics, U.S. summary census of population, 1980*. Washington, DC: U.S. Government Printing Office.

U.S. Department of Education. (1976–1986). *Fall enrollment: Racial, ethnic and sex enrollment data from institutions of higher education*. Washington, DC: U.S. Office for Civil Rights.

U.S. Department of Education, National Center for Education Statistics. (1984). *Minority enrollment in graduate and professional schools*. Washington, DC: U.S. Office for Civil Rights.

U.S. Department of Education, Office for Civil Rights. (1988). *Data on earned degrees conferred by insitutions of higher education by race/ethnicity and sex*. Washington, DC: Author.

U.S. Department of Health and Human Services, Public Health Services, Human Resources Services Administration, Bureau of Health Professions, Division of Disadvantaged Assistance. (1988). *HCOP Digest* (U.S. GOP 1989-241-2801/05319). Washington, DC: U.S. Government Printing Office.

U.S. Department of Labor, Bureau of Labor Statistics. (1987). *Employment and earnings* (Vol. 34, No. 1). Washington, DC: U.S. Government Printing Office.

Van Maanen, J., & Barley, S. R. (1985). Cultural organization: Fragments of a theory. In P. Frost, L. Moore, M. Louis, C. Lundberg, & J. Martin (Eds.), *Organizational culture* (pp. 31–54). Beverly Hills, CA: Sage.

Vaughn, B. E. (1988, spring). Incorporating multicultural issues in professional training. *National Council of Schools of Professional Psychology Newsletter*, 2(3), 3–8.

Vaughn, J. C. (1985). Minority students in graduate education. In B. L. R. Smith (Ed.), *The state of graduate education* (pp. 151–168). Washington, DC: Brookings Institution.

Vermilye, D. W. (Ed.). (1977). *Relating work and education*. San Francisco: Jossey-Bass.

Wallerstein, N., & Bernstein, E. (1988). Empowerment education: Freire's ideas adapted to health education. *Health Education Quarterly*, *15*, 379–394.

Watts, R. J. (1987). Development of professional identity in Black clinical psychology students. *Professional Psychology: Research and Practice*, *18*, 1–8.

Webster's Ninth New Collegiate Dictionary. (1983). Springfield, MA: Merriam-Webster.

White, J. (1984). *The psychology of Blacks: An Afro-American perspective*. New York: Prentice-Hall.

White, K. (1989). *Race in psychotherapy: A case presentation*. Paper presented at the 7th Annual Conference on Ethnic Minority Issues in Psychology, New York, NY.

Wilderson, F. B. (1983). Shared problems of culturally distinct people seeking a place in the educational process. In R. J. Samuda & S. L. Woods (Eds.), *Perspectives in immigrant and minority education* (pp. 79–85). Lanham, MD: University Press of America.

Williams, R. L. (1970). Black pride, academic relevance and individual achievement. *Counseling Psychologist*, *2*, 18–22.

Wilson, R. (1987, February). Recruitment and retention of minority faculty and staff. *AAHE Bulletin*, pp. 11–14.

Wilson, R., & Carter, D. J. (1988). *Minorities in higher education: Seventh annual status report*. Washington, DC: American Council on Education, Office of Minority Concerns.

Wilson, R., & Justiz, M. J. (1987–1988). Minorities in higher education: Confronting a time bomb. *Educational Record, 68/69*, 8–14.

Wirt, S. E., & Beckstrom, K. (Eds.). (1974). *Living quotations for Christians*. New York: Harper & Row.

Woods, E. (1977). Counseling minority students: A program model. *Personnel and Guidance Journal, 55*, 416–418.

Woods, P. J., & Wilkinson, C. S. (Eds.). (1987). *Is psychology the major for you? Planning for your undergraduate years.* Washington, DC: American Psychological Association.

Wrenn, C. (1985). Afterward: The culturally encapsulated counselor revisited. In P. Pedersen (Ed.), *Handbook of cross-cultural counseling and therapy* (pp. 323–329). Westport, CT: Greenwood Press.

Wright, J., & Hutton, B. (1977). Influence of client socio-economic status on selected behaviors, attitudes, and decisions of counselors. *Journal of Counseling Psychology, 24*, 527–530.

Wyatt, G. E., & Parham, W. D. (1985). The inclusion of culturally sensitive course materials in graduate school and training programs. *Psychotherapy, 22*, 461–468.

Yamamoto, J., James, Q., & Palley, N. (1968). Cultural problems in psychiatric therapy. *Archives of General Psychiatry, 19*, 45–49.

Yamamoto, J., Lam, J., Choi, W-I., Reece, S., Lo, S., Hahn, D., & Fairbanks, L. (1982) The psychiatric status schedule for Asian Americans. *American Journal of Psychiatry, 139*, 1181–1184.

NCSPP PUERTO RICO CONFERENCE PARTICIPANTS

NCSPP MEMBER SCHOOL REPRESENTATIVES

Alan Barclay	*Wright State University*
Joseph W. Bascuas	*Antioch—New England Graduate School*
Kathi Borden	*Pepperdine University*
Edward Bourg	*California School of Professional Psychology: Berkeley/Alameda*
W. Gary Cannon	*California School of Professional Psychology: Fresno*
Richard Cox	*Forest Institute of Professional Psychology*
Elizabeth Davis-Russell	*California School of Professional Psychology: Los Angeles*
Evelyn Diaz	*Caribbean Center for Advanced Studies*
James Dobbins	*Wright State University*
Eduardo Duran	*Pacific Graduate School of Psychology*
Glenace Edwall	*Baylor University*
Keith Edwards	*Biola University*
Philip Farber	*Florida Institute of Technology*
Martin Fisher	*Adelphi University, Derner Institute*
Wesley Forbes	*California School of Professional Psychology: Fresno*
David Foy	*Fuller Theological Seminary*
Jeffrey Grip	*Chicago School of Professional Psychology*
W. Rodney Hammond	*Wright State University*
Archibald D. Hart	*Fuller Theological Seminary*
Jacqueline S. Jackson	*Pacific Graduate School of Psychology*
Nelson Jones	*University of Denver*
Mary Beth Kenkel	*California School of Professional Psychology: Fresno*

Marc Lubin	*Illinois School of Professional Psychology*
Hector Machabanski	*Chicago School of Professional Psychology*
Ethel Magidson	*Massachusetts School of Professional Psychology*
Lourdes Mattei	*Antioch—New England Graduate School*
James McHolland	*Illinois School of Professional Psychology*
Daniel McKitrick	*Oregon Graduate School of Professional Psychology*
Robert Morgan	*Pacific Graduate School of Psychology*
Robert Moriarty	*Forest Institute of Professional Psychology*
Andrea Morrison	*Wright Institute*
Don Nelson	*Indiana State University*
Nancy Newton	*Chicago School of Professional Psychology*
Esteban L. Olmedo	*California School of Professional Psychology: Los Angeles*
Nolan Penn	*Fielding Institute*
Connell F. Persico	*California School of Professional Psychology: Los Angeles*
Donald R. Peterson	*Rutgers University*
Roger Peterson	*Antioch—New England Graduate School*
Kenneth Polite	*Biola University*
Lisa Porche-Burke	*California School of Professional Psychology: Los Angeles*
Kjell Rudestam	*Fielding Institute*
Salvador Santiago-Negron	*Caribbean Center for Advanced Studies*
Saul Siegel	*Wright Institute*
David L. Singer	*Antioch-New England Graduate School*
Karen Smith	*Chicago School of Professional Psychology*
George Stricker	*Adelphi University, Derner Institute*
Siang-Yang Tan	*Fuller Theological Seminary*
Warwick G. Troy	*California School of Professional Psychology: Los Angeles*
Raymond Trybus	*California School of Professional Psychology: San Diego*
Leon VandeCreek	*Indiana University of Pennsylvania*
Billy E. Vaughn	*California School of Professional Psychology: San Diego*
Frank Webbe	*Florida Institute of Technology*
Bruce J. Weiss	*Massachusetts School of Professional Psychology*
Robin Young-Rivers	*Spalding University*

INVITED PARTICIPANTS/OBSERVERS

Valerie A. Batts	*VISIONS, Inc.*
Ira Cohen	*American Psychological Association*
Christine C. Iijima Hall	*American Psychological Association*
James M. Jones	*American Psychological Association*
Jessica Kohout	*American Psychological Association*
Paul Nelson	*American Psychological Association*